T0243840

Real Toads,
Imaginary Gardens

Real Toads, Imaginary Gardens

On Reading and Writing Poetry Forensically

PAISLEY REKDAL

W. W. NORTON & COMPANY

Independent Publishers Since 1923

For my students

CONTENTS

Real Toads,
Imaginary Gardens

On Reading and Writing Forensically

W hat does it mean to read a poem?

This is a question I get asked often, largely by friends curious about my teaching job, but also by strangers at readings interested in my work as a poet. The question is difficult to answer, in large part because it assumes that a poem is unlike anything else composed of words, whether a novel or a fortune cookie or a billboard. But why should reading a poem—let alone writing one—be treated as a different experience, reliant on different skills? And yet, why shouldn't it be? I admit that my own resistance to imagining reading poetry as a fundamentally unique skill belies how I myself think of poetry: not that it is an exceptional literary form but that it concentrates into itself many of the devices and singularities we associate with other genres. For that reason alone, poetry demands, if not a higher level of knowledge, a more conscious attention to how we think about and use language.

Part of the reason for this is that we can't even agree on what constitutes a poem, let alone a good one. Is a prose poem a poem? What about a poem written in fragmented sentences? Should we read a Shakespearean sonnet the same way we read a free-verse poem? What about a poem that's shaped like a pair of wings, or which uses photography, or becomes a graph? Must poems be rhymed? Should they be in stanzas? Should they be original work, or can they be found in government documents and on the backs of cereal boxes? Are poems revelations about a self, or are they imaginations of other people?

There are as many ways to read and write a poem as there are types of poetry. And as each poem becomes its own unique expression of form and content, poems teach us how to read them *as* we read them. This is one reason we also have to toss out any preconceptions about what constitutes a poem, since bad readings of poetry—or bad readings of any kind of literature—happen the second we predetermine what a "good" piece of writing should look like, how it should sound, who should write it, and how it should behave. But while I hesitate to state what ultimately constitutes a poem, I do think that poems represent certain aspects of reality and our feelings about them. Poems are composed of words that carry expressive weight; they are profoundly engaged with emotional and physical sensation, with the substantive facts of the world but also with our private feelings about ourselves *in* the world. This doesn't, naturally, ring true for all poems or types of poems, but it's an idea that I think we commonly have about poems, and it's a good starting point to considering what it means to read or write a poem, and how and why we generally share poems, even if these same assumptions make us bad readers of the particular poem before us.

That said, a poem can meet these requirements and not move us at all, and a poem might refuse to meet any of these requirements and delight. We don't know what we'll like unless we read widely, read against even what makes us, initially, comfortable. Of course, for many people, reading poetry at all makes us squirm, and one reason for this is that we assume that poetry requires that we read it more deeply than other forms of literature: in other words, that reading poetry abandons pleasure and becomes work. This is largely due to the implicit belief that somehow poetry is meant to make us better people, an assumption that's been historically baked into the culture we've absorbed. According to this thinking, poetry isn't merely a literary genre, it's one of the few art forms that should prove its usefulness to us as humans based on how it should—and often doesn't—expand our empathetic limits. As I said, I don't trust broad statements about what poetry is, what it must do, what feelings it should engender in me as a reader, or how it should enrich my life or pocketbook, largely because for every example or platitude I might fall back on, I can think of a dozen others that violate this same presupposition. If anything, poems offer me patterns of expectation and then disregard them in ways I find either delightful, annoying, instructive, or baffling.

And yet that doesn't stop people—particularly poets—from making grand statements. "A poem is a meteor," wrote Wallace Stevens. Or: "A poem is a well-wrought urn," revised Cleanth Brooks. "A poem might be called a pseudo-person," argued W. H. Auden. Donald Hall insisted that poems were "the unsayable said," while Ralph Waldo Emerson believed they were "what will and must be spoken." But if we can't agree on what poems are, it seems we also can't agree on what poems are meant to achieve. Poetry "is something which is done to us, not just said to us," wrote literary critic Terry Eagleton, meaning not only that language should have bodily effects but also that the meaning of any poem becomes self-referential: what a poem's words suggest is inherently bound up in our experience of the poem itself. For earlier critics, however, poetry was not only meant to be an art form we experience but a way of shaping our very souls. Plato, for instance, distrusted poetry, declaring it an irrational form and the poet "a sophist, a maker of counterfeits that look like the truth," which in turn led people to copy what they read, drawing them away from pursuing the good. Aristotle, in his *Poet-*

ics, argued the opposite. Poetry leads us to reason, he insisted, since the situations we see played out onstage in classical Greek theatre allow us to see the variety and consequence of human choice, and thus select for the good. Horace, influenced by Aristotle, believed poetry "delights and instructs;" Longinus, echoing Horace, said poetry's instructive qualities must precede its pleasurable ones. Sir Philip Sidney declared that poetry's representations could exceed and even perfect nature, while Percy Bysshe Shelley famously declared poets to be "the unacknowledged legislators of the world." Poetry, in fact, was both a divine and organic process whose very language could help advance civilization itself.

In other words, poetry is a total snooze: the spiritual equivalent of broccoli consumed solely for the nutrition of our souls. And who wants that? "I, too, dislike it," Marianne Moore famously quipped, about her (not entirely) ironic disgust with poetry's presumed self-importance. No wonder the poet and writer Ben Lerner, in his essay "The Hatred of Poetry," argues that this long-standing link we've made in the West between personhood and poetry creates expectations around poems that can't be fulfilled. We search for poems that will transform individual existence into "universal" truths about humanity itself. Poems, according to this thinking, should rehabilitate human experience, and when they don't, we turn our frustration with their failure into hatred. Lerner argues that our awareness of this gap between the real and the ideal is unresolvable, but our cultural conditioning means we won't abandon our desire for what we want poems to do, even when faced with the dismal fact of what poems are: "made things," as Aristotle reminds us.

It's a comforting thought, perhaps, that poetry should make us better humans, but even a quick tour of history's dictators uncovers a startling number of amateur poets. So perhaps it's better to define a poem and poetry, then, not by what it is meant to do for us as moral beings but by what it does to us as writers and readers. And what it can do, and often does do, is make us feel the physical effects of language in our bodies. "If I read a book [and] it makes my whole body so cold no fire can ever warm me, I know *that* is poetry," wrote Emily Dickinson. "If I feel physically as if the top of my head were taken off, I know *that* is poetry." Marianne Moore put it a different way: a poem is an "imaginary garden with real toads in them," an artificial structure, yes, but one in which something genuine can live. I think it's that combustible interaction between the arbitrary imagination and the real that produces Dickinson's physical response, a sensation I myself have had, once on a plane after reading the first pages of the Danish poet Inger Christensen's book-length poem, *Alphabet*. Reading those first few lines, I felt a fizzy, rushing heat rise from my stomach to my throat. I couldn't wait to read the next page, and the next, and the next. It also made me want to re-create this experience in words for myself.

Another way of saying it: I know I'm in the presence of poetry when I, too, want to write it.

For me, reading, teaching, and writing poetry are organically entwined. I've learned to write poems not only through my own close reading of them but through my engagement with them as a teacher. I've also become a better teacher of poetry because I'm a poet, since the creative ways I use language for myself influence how I interpret it in the classroom for others, including those with no personal investment in poetry. It's also why, when I work through specific questions of form and reading with my classes, I use exercises that work equally well in a literary or a creative classroom. Often, we learn how and why a thing works when we ourselves have to create it, even if we have no desire to continue writing creatively. And we become better creative writers ourselves when we are forced to critically engage with how *others* have made poems. I don't believe that reading or writing well occurs as an isolated act, just as I don't believe that poetry only teaches human values, even as I do believe that poetry helps us translate our most complex ideas about politics, morality, nature, and ourselves through the literary devices found everywhere in poems. I believe that to read poetry well teaches you how to think and write more carefully; in turn, it teaches you how to better observe the world.

The way I approach poems is a direct result of how I came to poetry. I discovered poetry both late and early: I was sixteen when I began reading and writing poems for pleasure, but I was probably in my thirties before I felt comfortable talking about how poems functioned, how they could be read, why I liked some poets and not others. This may sound like a large age gap, but many of the poetry-specific classes I took at school either focused on particular time periods of literary history or were loosely led writing workshops in which pedagogy was assumed to be self-directed or Socratic. Everyone talked about what they *liked*, but no one seemed much interested what a poem *did*. Specific aspects of craft were rarely discussed outside of general formal "rules" that were violated by almost every poem I admired, which meant poetry itself—the more I studied it—accrued a greater and more impenetrable air of mystery. *Why* did this poem have such an emotional effect on me? And, more important, how could I duplicate this effect on others?

The result of my education was that poetry felt like something that existed outside of reason, self-control, or even practical skill. To some extent, that's true. A good poem slips through you, eluding your conscious mind, or just working more effectively through it, its strengths shaped by the years you spent writing terrible poems as practice. Great poems flirt with convention, whether formal or perceptual. But that doesn't mean that there aren't forms within which poems function or that, by closely studying a poem's structure, we can't understand the powerful

effect that the combination of certain patterns of sound and syntax, etymology and image, and rhythm and repetition can have
on us. These elements can be understood and studied, with the
result that we become both better readers and writers of poetry
itself. I had to teach myself these things over decades as a teacher,
just as I had to learn how to explain these things to the undergraduates, high school students, and schoolteachers I came in
contact with as a state poet laureate and writer. Now as a teacher
who oversees graduate students leading their own classrooms
for the first time themselves, I see that many of the knowledge
gaps my own poetic training contained can be filled by a book
like this one.

So this book is a series of questions focused on craft: the
craft of imagery; the craft of the sentence, the word, and the
line; the craft of rhythm and sound; the craft of formal conventions and modes. By working your way through these questions
of craft, you begin to see how a poem takes shape, how it accrues
meaning through the intersection of these identifiable elements.
For budding poets, these same questions can then be applied
to your own writing, to track how these elements function in
your drafts. They can also be put to the test via the creative
exercises I include at the end of each chapter. A poem is a lad-
der of skills, each of its elements carefully selected by a poet
who employs their combination for particular effects. The way
we read these effects, of course, is also the result of how we've
read other poems from the past, thus how we remain attuned
to larger cultural associations. As we carefully move through
the elements of the poem currently in front of us, however,
we see how our understanding of each separate part shifts and
changes in relation to other elements of the poem. It is through
this layering—or collision—of components that we learn how to
read a poem. The poem's meaning is not merely its stated subject, then, but how that subject matter becomes reflected in the

poet's lineation and syntax, her diction and rhythm, her repetition of certain sounds and images.

Everything I detail in this book is, of course, a strategy, since each poem invents its own rules. Poems in general share things in common, though individual poems do not behave in the same ways. The sonnets produced in the sixteenth century, for example, look fundamentally different from the sonnets produced in the twenty-first. This is not a failure of contemporary poetry to preserve the values of the past nor a failure of the past to anticipate the desires of the present, since these were poems written in their moment of time out of the subjective desires of specific authors. To read or write a poem, then, is to be familiar enough with historically predetermined modes and structures that we understand what conversation the poem has engaged, what conventions it's accepted or denied, and how these decisions ultimately speak to the subject of the poem itself.

Likewise, reading a poem is not about reaching some preordained and unanimously understood answer. Just as there is no one "right" way to write a poem, great poems allow for and invite multiple interpretations. I often remind students that the poem does not lie buried inside a heap of words that must be chipped away until the poem's perfect form is uncovered. Every choice made in a poem causes a cascade of others, none of them inevitable, many of them based on expectations around reception and context. Instead of rules, then, what I present to you is a shared vocabulary and a wider sense of poetry's history that should allow you to name the things you see happening on the page, and which also give you critical directions in which to look when reading or writing poems on your own. Faced with work that's unfamiliar, rather than taking in the whole of it at once, start with an image, or a particular phrase, or a specifically noteworthy rhyme. From there, move outward. This book will, ideally, help you to move from the smallest building blocks of a poem to more global concerns of mode and form. I call this laddered way of reading "forensic," as I want readers to treat any poem they encounter the way a detective might treat a crime scene: with a scientific interest in gathering evidence and material, to let these details reveal the scene's narrative, rather than jumping in with an interpretation and making the details fit the preordained conclusion.

To help my own students read forensically, I provide a "Forensic Guide" with questions they should answer, ranging from the easy (what images and figurative language appear in the poem?) to the formally more difficult (what kinds of rhythms and rhymes do you hear?). These questions build upon each other, so that students reading a poem through this guide will begin to see the poem's meaning emerge through layers of analysis. Of course, the reader might not be able to address every question raised by the Forensic Guide, since certain questions may not be relevant to their poem; regardless, the guide exists as a grounding device, a way of tethering our reading to the concrete concerns that structure any piece of literature.

To show you how these questions might be answered, throughout the book, I'll examine different poems via a specific question from this guide. The poems themselves will be from a range of authors, some for more advanced readers, some for novices. That said, the same skills apply to reading both levels; in fact, I've found that many of the poems I teach to graduates and undergraduates work perfectly well for high schoolers; what changes, however, is the type and number of critical questions that you ask around them. With that in mind, each chapter also ends with some experiments to help students navigate other suggested poems, to play with the same questions of craft themselves. All suggested poems can be found on the Poetry Foundation or the Academy of American Poets websites: both excellent, free resources for a wide range of poets and poetry, and both of which include biographical information about the poets I've suggested. This will help teachers not only plan their lessons but allow readers to expand their reading list and put theoretical questions of reading and form into practical use, with helpful context. Finally, I'll finish the book with a reading of one poem to which I apply each forensic lens I've previously used as a model to examine. It's one thing to be told how to read and write critically, it's another thing to see someone doing it.

But the bulk of the book will be, as I said, questions of craft. These questions may generate a variety of responses, but readers shouldn't worry that their responses are wrong; instead, in answering these questions, readers should be as accurate as they can to their sense perceptions. Other readers will, of course, notice different things and may even have a contradictory sense of the poem's structure, rhythms, imagery, or narrative. But by sticking close to what we observe, we allow ourselves to take in all the evidence we need from which we can slowly build an interpretive reading. Without this evidence, jumping into an argument about what we think a poem means only encourages us to speculate, even to fabricate readings based on what private sense-memories a poem triggers.

If you use this forensic guide as a writing exercise, you can assign class members to write one page on a specific poem that answers as many of the guide's questions as possible. Obviously, the writer won't be able to address all or even most of the questions raised in a single page, especially if certain questions don't apply. These questions are simply to be used as prompts for drafting responses. After the students have finished writing their answers, they can write at least two questions that arise for them and which they want to discuss. These questions should resist asking about issues of basic clarification, and they shouldn't focus on praise or criticism. Instead, they should pose questions about the poem that surface organically for the student based on her forensic notes.

You can use this forensic guide in literature classrooms and also in writing workshops, where writers apply the same questions to their classmates' drafts. For me, this has become a way to help creative writing students hone their skills, bolstering the bridge between what and how they read and what they want to create. It's also helped students see more clearly where their own drafts succeed or fail with their readers. As I wrote before, we become better writers when we become more attentive readers. With that in mind, this is a book devoted to the pleasures of close reading that will, I believe, encourage any poet to be more ambitious with her work. When we take the same critical care with our own writing that we take with published poems, we are bound not only to see the patterns behind our failings but, more important, new and more adventurous paths open up in the ways we represent our worlds.

HOW TO READ FORENSICALLY: A GUIDE

1. *What are the first things you notice in the poem?*

2. *What images are in the poem?*
    Are these images concrete or abstract?
    What senses are invoked?
    What kinds and types of figurative language appear?
        Examples include allegory, allusion, symbol, metaphor, and simile.
    Are there multiple images?

What is the tenor and vehicle, and the ground and tension, of these images?

Are there images that estrange? Examples include synesthesia, metonymy, and synecdoche.

Do the images connect or are they in tension?

Is there a poetic conceit?

3. *Who speaks and to whom?*

What is the poem's form of address?

Is the speaker a persona?

Does the speaker use apostrophe?

Is the poem written in second, third, or first person?

4. *How would you characterize the poem's syntax?*

Is the syntax hypotactic or paratactic? Complex or simple?

When and where does the poem's syntax shift?

In what ways might the poem's syntax reflect the poem's subject matter?

5. *What kind of lineation does the poet employ?*

What is the relationship between the poem's sentences and its lines?

Does the poem use a lot of enjambment?

Are the lines broken for particular visual effect?

If you were to change up the poem's lineation, what information might you lose or gain?

6. *What word choice and diction does the poet use?*

Are there many Latinate or Germanic root words?

How would you characterize the poet's tone?

Are there particular passages or moments in the poem that move into one etymological register versus another?

What sounds do you hear?

Does the poem employ any nonsense words or phrases?

7. *What rhymes do you hear?*

Are there particular kinds and types of rhymes and, if so, which ones?

Are the stanzas organized by rhyme?

Do any sounds or phrases repeat?

Does the poem use parallelism?

Are there any actions or images in the poem that "rhyme"?

8. *Does the poem employ meter?*

Is the poem written in syllabic, accentual, or accentual-syllabic verse?

What kinds and types of metrical feet do you find in each line?

Does the meter of the poem ever diverge from its rhythm?

Does the poem's tone shift at all when its meter changes?

Is there a relationship for you between the poem's meter and its content?

9. *Is the poem written in a conventional form?*

Which formal conventions does the poem follow?

Which formal conventions does it alter or violate?

Does the poem's form conflict at any point with its argument?

Does the poem resist its formal resolution?

Is the poem's ending "open" or "closed"?

10. *What is the poem's mode?*

What conventions of this mode does it employ?

What conventions of this mode does it subvert?

What sense of time, place, and history does the
poem invoke?

Does the mode return to or revise other literary works in
this same mode that you recall?

11. *What further questions do your forensic notes raise?*

CHAPTER ONE

What Are the First Things You Notice?

So, understanding that we might approach reading a poem forensically, how would you read this?

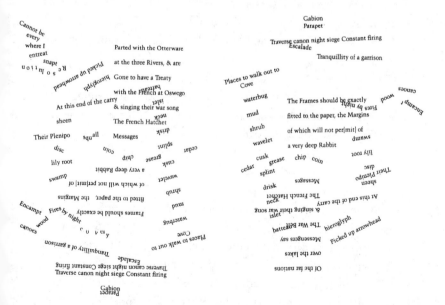

Some of you, faced with this poem, might immediately want to hurl this book against a wall. But I want to start here *because* it so obviously disorients. Maybe you're automatically turned off by what looks visually intimidating, or maybe you're excited by how it looks, intrigued by all these phrases and nouns tossed onto the page like stones and sticks thrown to the ground. And that might be an excellent first way of approaching the poem: to notice how this page resembles a collection of materials rather than—or perhaps more than—a collection of words.

So take a moment and examine the page. Treat the poem, for a moment, more as a work of visual than textual art, or at least as a poem interested in combining visual and textual strategies. Me, I know that questions of representation have long occupied Susan Howe, the writer of this passage, which comes from her long poem "Thorow." Howe is a poet and visual artist renowned for her collages. Howe wrote "Thorow" after a visit to Lake George, New York, the site of the Seven Years' War, also known as the French and Indian War and, in the introduction to her book, *Singularities* (from which this passage of "Thorow" was taken), she said she'd been struck by the ways this town had grown up alongside and over indigenous territory, reimagining itself into a vacation spot rather than a place shaped by violent conflict. Howe's poem is filled with quotes from Henry David Thoreau (whose name she playfully alludes to in the title) and James Fenimore Cooper, whose novel *The Last of the Mohicans* was set in Lake George.

No one would get that information from just looking at this page, of course. The passage is, instead, a hodgepodge of text: something that disrupts its own reading even as it invites closer examination. When someone says that they read poetry, you might imagine them reading expressive poems like the sonnets of Shakespeare or the odes of Ross Gay: poems that have a clearly imagined sense of place and time, that communicate feelings and ideas in language that's both transparent and personal. Poems, in other words, that use images and symbols and that rely upon recognizable formal devices such as rhyme or rhythm. Poems that, at the very last, stay within the margins of the page.

I love reading those poems, but I also love poems like Howe's, because I think there's something to be gained from confronting poems that challenge what I normally like and expect from reading. Reading with the goal of emotional transparency puts the poet in a position of tremendous power: the poet is meant to communicate her unique vision of the world to me though words she's chosen, which then must carry for me definable meanings. I'm a good reader, then, when I hew closely to the intention of the poet, when I'm able to see how her words communicate translatable ideas. I can ignore the field of the page entirely in favor of focusing on the connotation and denotation of words, not about how these words themselves get visually arranged. A poem like "Thorow," however, even as it's clearly assembled to reflect Howe's intention, abandons recognizable conventions about poetry and syntax and, by doing so, releases some of that authorial control back to me, the reader. The poem invites me to make a similar mess of my reading practice.

But all poems, you could argue, make such an invitation. "Thorow" is just an extreme example of how we might approach reading poetry as a whole. Because the fact is, I can enter any poem anywhere I like: through sound or syntax, through an image that enraptures, through its sense of place and time, even through its explicit (or implicit) address to the reader. By choosing a starting place in a poem and asking questions about *why* I notice that particular element of the poem, I can open the poem up and out, as well as learn something about myself in the process. Why am I drawn to *this* bit of language? What has it activated in me and what, in turn, do I activate in it while reading?

So, absent all conventional expectations for reading this poem, what do I notice about "Thorow"?

The first thing I notice is that, in order to read all the words of this poem, I have to continually rotate the page. The second thing is that this page divides into two halves of text that mirror each other, but not exactly. The words "parapet" and "gabion," for example, appear as a two-line stanza or **couplet** in the bottom-left and top-right corners of the page, but they aren't equally spaced apart. I note, too, that some passages repeat exactly, such as "Traverse canon night siege Constant firing," or these lines:

> Places to walk out to
> Cove
> waterbug
> mud
> shrub
> wavelet
> cusk

Or:

> The frames should be exactly
> Fitted to the paper,   the Margins
> Of which will not per[mit] of
> A very deep Rabbit

But some sections of text don't reappear in the same arrangement at all, such as "Cannot be/every/where I entreat."

I also notice that, though the writing of the poem suggests visual overlap, none of the phrases *actually* overlap. Instead, phrases get extremely close to each other, with some words even appearing to snake slightly, such as "covery," which wobbles down the page, or the phrase "Fires by night," which threads between the phrase "exactly" and "the Margins." These gradations of textual movement make me think that Howe either had to micro-adjust the page in order to type each syllable up exactly, or that she cut apart certain words with an X-Acto knife to achieve the effect she wanted. Either way, even as the passage suggests random fragmentation, it also reveals the poet's meticulous attention to detail: a formal precision I might assign to more conventionally fussy forms, like the sonnet.

I also notice that the poem hovers between language I might read as documentary, like lines snipped from a history book or nineteenth-century biography, such as "Parted with Otterware/ at the three rivers & are/ Gone to have a Treaty/ with the French at Oswego," and something that feels more personal to Howe: "picked up an arrowhead" or even the word "hieroglyph."

"Hieroglyph" becomes this passage's touchstone word for me, since I can't help but feel the poem's untranslatable center, even as the whole of it seems interested in language itself. There are lots of references to mark-making and writing. Howe mentions margins and messages and paper and frames, but she also references hatchets and treaties. There are, too, images of war: the phrase "singing war songs" appears twice, as do words like "garrison," "encampment," and the likely quoted phrase "canon under siege." Even "gabion" and "parapet" recall war, as they're usually attached to military structures. Scattered among all these images, however, I find single nouns like "cove" and "waterbug" and "shrub," which make me aware of a natural environment sprouting in between this military and found historical language. Putting all these elements together, I can begin to see this poem as a collision of nature and history writing, and to picture Howe's fragments as the visual remnants of violent battle itself—bits and pieces of bodies, destroyed environments and battlements, the legal protections offered by treaties themselves left in tatters.

Would Howe agree with my reading? Possibly not all of it, but I suspect she'd be pleased with the effort. I also don't believe that a completely accurate reading of this poem—that is, a reading that comprehensively anticipates all of Howe's intentions—could exist. Howe isn't writing a narrative about a particular battle or moment of history so much as trying to help me re-experience the historical and natural effects of conquest. Her work is mimetic, rather than narratively representational. While there are unique historical referents here—allusions to Oswego and the French treaty for instance—her poem doesn't attempt to be an accurate record of that particular event. Instead, the poem invites me to pick through and examine its fragments, much like an archaeologist might pick apart an ancient battle site, allowing me to assemble my own history of place.

Howe's poem is, oddly, a great exercise for reading forensically because, released from the pressure and possibility of producing a "right" reading, I'm allowed to formulate questions and connections out of what I see. I believe good reading happens when we focus not on interpretation, but on honing the questions that we ask about a poem. It's when we demand that readers tell us what a poem means, rather than ask *how* the poem means, that we shut down our reading. This is why I like to start even introductory students with "Thorow," since I can direct their attention to the particulars that attract them. I ask, for example, if there are any repetitions in shape and language that occur. I ask what visual elements they note about the poem, where their eyes move as they navigate the page, what lines seem to intersect. I ask if they sense a single speaker or multiple speakers in the fragments of language that appear in the poem. When questions about the author arise, I tell students a little about Howe's trip to Lake George, and then I give them a short piece to read about the Seven Years' War. I let students work in pairs or small groups, asking them to compare the kinds and types of language they find, to discuss what differences they sense between this language, and to locate the visual placement of these phrases on the page.

Basically, I ask my students any question *other* than what Howe's poem means. Howe wants to make us treat the page archeologically, and so I encourage readers to think like scientists. What evidence does Howe leave behind? As unromantic as that sounds, thinking in this manner frees me from the anxiety that I've missed something, that the poem has gone beyond me or talked over my head. In many ways, I accept that there's something about any poem I will never comprehend, and that perfect knowledge isn't, finally, the point. The goal is to see how the poet has playfully reinterpreted the world, and my own perception of the world, through her unique formal choices. Having been able to articulate those choices, I can then experience for myself some part of her interpretation. Maybe this is why I don't find Howe's poem all that intimidating: I'm not being asked to say anything definitive about the poem or the Seven Years' War or even about Howe herself, since Howe's collaging resists that particular legibility. Instead, Howe has invited me to become another author of "Thorow," reassembling the information she's gathered, in essence putting me more actively in the world of the poem.

Limits of Interpretation

The multiplicity of meaning in "Thorow" may be, on the surface, more extreme than, say, that in a poem like Keats's "Ode to a Nightingale," but the fear it sparks in a reader is the same. Because we associate the lyric with personal revelation, poems invite an incredibly subjective experience on the reader's part as well. Poetry is an active relationship between writer and reader, and poems activate a reader's imagination most through word choice that offers variation and amplification of the poem's subject. I often say that poems are the act of telling two or more stories at the same time while using the exact same language in order to remind myself that every word in a poem does double duty. Words have connotations and denotations, social associations and dictionary definitions, and we understand that we are in the realm of the symbolic when connotation and denotation become equally important to our reading. For instance, if I were to say, "My friend suddenly turned green," this could suggest my friend suddenly felt ill or envious, not just that her face literally turned green. "Green" has a multitude of meanings, from money to jealousy to fertility to inexperience to nature to luck. We've gathered these meanings together over time through common use but also through literature, which preserves and capitalizes upon the color's symbolic meaning. When I see the word "green" in a poem, then, I am primed to have a variety of responses based on other ways I've seen and heard that word used. I have the same complex responses to other colors and objects: everything from owls to apples, crosses to gardens, crowns to hearts come with symbolic associations that I've learned through art and literature. But you and I also have personal associations with these words outside of their cultural meanings, because these words represent sensory experiences that we've had on our own.

It's this clash between the personal and the social, our individual encounters with the world and the ways we are acculturated into representing them, that can cause readers to feel confused. *Why doesn't the poet just say what she means?* we snarl at the page. But the poet has done just that, by weaving together vivid sense details while also considering the ways in which these same details speak to other narratives. We might consider a poem as a nexus, a spoke from which we can see the immediate words on the page radiate out into richer conversations that unfold behind and through its images, through history itself as the poem engages other artworks through its use of allusion.

I think that what also confuses readers about poetry is the sense that because a poem can feel like a revelation of the poet's interior life, the images and words she uses are also ultimately private, outside of a reader's comprehension. A poem might thus mean anything a reader wants it to mean based on her intuition. Howe's poem certainly risks this response. But though we bring our own meanings to a poem because we've either experienced what the poem describes or because we have specific associations with its words, we still work within the same linguistic parameters the poet worked in. If I hold up a magic marker and ask you what it is, you could reply that it is a pen, or a writing instrument, or a marker. Only an unhinged person would insist it's a Volkswagen. Words can mean a lot of things, but their definitions and connotations aren't infinite. When Howe uses a word like "shrub," I'm pretty sure she means a bush. This is all a fancy way of saying that if you don't understand something in a poem, you can trust the dictionary to help you figure it out. Also, if you feel a particular emotion when reading a line, it's likely the poet wanted you to feel this, so you might want to scribble in the margins just what you sense. What is the phrase that's drawn your attention? What is the sound that calls to your ear? What image captivates you and what other images does it call to mind?

I think it's the fact that there are *so many* interpretive moments that a poem offers us to examine that feeds our anxiety about reading them. Poems ask us to notice lineation, rhyme, rhythm, images, even punctuation—all at the very same time. This gives us the illusion of having a vast variety of meanings that unfold, when in reality our choices are ultimately constrained by how we read these different poetic elements, not separately but together.

Thus, even though Howe's poem may be initially difficult because it looks unusual, the circle of its meaning slowly tightens around its own visual and textual repetition. But open-ended or avant-garde poems like Howe's aren't the only ones that allow for multiple interpretations. Even conventional poems can engender a variety of responses. For example, here is Carol Ann Duffy's "Warming Her Pearls":

WARMING HER PEARLS

for Judith Radstone

Next to my own skin, her pearls. My mistress
bids me wear them, warm them, until evening
when I'll brush her hair. At six, I place them
round her cool, white throat. All day I think of her,

resting in the Yellow Room, contemplating silk
or taffeta, which gown tonight? She fans herself
whilst I work willingly, my slow heat entering
each pearl. Slack on my neck, her rope.

She's beautiful. I dream about her
in my attic bed; picture her dancing
with tall men, puzzled by my faint, persistent scent
beneath her French perfume, her milky stones.

I dust her shoulders with a rabbit's foot,
watch the soft blush seep through her skin
like an indolent sigh. In her looking-glass
my red lips part as though I want to speak.

Full moon. Her carriage brings her home. I see
her every movement in my head. . . . Undressing,

taking off her jewels, her slim hand reaching
for the case, slipping naked into bed, the way

she always does. . . . And I lie here awake,
knowing the pearls are cooling even now
in the room where my mistress sleeps. All night
I feel their absence and I burn.

You can see that the poem's narrator, an unnamed lady's maid,
is attracted to her mistress, as all the work she undertakes—
particularly the "warming" of the mistress's strand of pearls
around her own neck—becomes erotically charged. That much
is clear, but depending on how you read the triangulation of
mistress-servant-objects throughout the poem, you might come
away with a very different reading of why and what the servant
really desires.

For instance, you might first characterize the maid as passive,
one who silently "dream[s] about [the mistress]/ in [her] attic bed,"
but notice that many of her fantasies suggest she thinks that the
mistress reciprocates her interest. In the third stanza, for example,
the maid pictures "dust[ing the mistress's] shoulders with a rabbit's foot," an action that causes an imaginary flush of corresponding desire in the mistress. The maid's "faint, persistent scent" on
the pearls she warms also "puzzle[s]" the mistress as she dances
with her suitors. By envisioning their scents comingling, Duffy's
maid breaks down the class and gender boundaries that would have
ordered her world: the maid "becomes" part of her mistress, just
as her unseen presence overpowers the mistress's attention to her
male suitors. Of course, this all depends on how much we trust the
maid. She could be an unreliable narrator or self-deluding mas-
ochist, as some of my students have argued: someone who likes to
tell herself that the strand of pearls her mistress "bids" her wear are
"slack on [her] neck," an image of loosened boundaries and control.

Or you could go in a different direction entirely. Does the maid, in breaking down these symbols of wealth, reimagine herself as empowered? Is her desire about love or ownership, a secret wish to manipulate her mistress's body through the objects that she cares for? Does the maid even desire the mistress at all, or just her things? For instance, notice how absent the mistress is as a person throughout the poem, how she only appears as a series of body parts attached to objects that signal status. Even the syntax of the poem's last lines refers to the maid feeling the burning absence not of the mistress's body, but the pearls. While the pearls of course symbolize the mistress, they remain objects that only the mistress owns, thus **metonyms** for her position.

You can see that there's little dispute about the situation of the poem and the fact of the maid's feelings, but there can be a lot of argument about how we characterize the maid. Duffy's own intentions about how the maid should be interpreted might be interesting to discover and debate, but texts very often work alongside of—or even counter to—their author's intent. As a writer, I'm often surprised by the connections that editors and readers make in my work, which yield interpretations I not only didn't anticipate but couldn't have controlled for. If "Thorow" invites a reader to select for herself meaningful connections of text, "Warming Her Pearls" also allows for diverging, and equally compelling, evaluations. That's exciting in a classroom when we're talking about a poem. But it also raises another question: What are the limits of interpretation? Or: When do we know our reading of a poem is a bad one?

I asked a group of students heatedly arguing over the maid's motives this question, and they responded that a bad reading would be one that's self-imposed. When a person forces her own story onto the poem, or makes the poem reflect only what she wishes were in it, then the interpretation has abandoned what's on the page. But what happens when, say, a reader insists that

"Warming Her Pearls" is an examination of a BDSM relationship, as more than a few of my students have done? Can you apply a feminist perspective to a poem written far before the social advent of feminism? Could you apply a trans reading to a medieval saint's life, or a Marxist approach to a Shakespearean sonnet? In finding some aspect of ourselves in a poem, do we risk applying anachronistic terminology and ideas merely to reflect our own biases, the hope that we can find ourselves in the texts that appeal to us?

I don't personally believe that we should or even can see aspects of ourselves in *all* the poems that we read, probably not even the bulk of them. I think it stretches our critical imagination to read outside our experience, even outside of the language we would choose to depict our experience. But I also don't believe that we should ignore whatever small slivers of ourselves and our interests that we find in the text, because that way, too, we might uncover a new way of reading. Good alternative readings of a poem don't dismiss the evidence the text itself provides; they make different interpretive connections *between* that evidence. These interpretations, ideally, are not arguing to become absolute evaluations themselves but models for how we might read a text in and against our present moment.

The Power of Alternative Readings

Alternative readings of poems are everywhere, and I encourage them, since literature can be so pliable. When it comes to poetry, I have to admit that definitive readings don't exist, just as poetic rules themselves don't finally exist. We work within patterns and limitations that we also defy. That's what interests me about literature: the fact that a poem, even as it has a circumscribed set of meanings based on the poet's selections, has a far more expansive interpretation once readers engage with it. Sylvia Plath's "Daddy," for example, is a poem that's undergone so many interpretations over time that it's practically a poetry anthology unto itself. Read this poem and consider how you would imagine, or characterize, its speaker.

DADDY

You do not do, you do not do
Any more, black shoe
In which I have lived like a foot
For thirty years, poor and white,
Barely daring to breathe or Achoo.

Daddy, I have had to kill you.
You died before I had time——
Marble-heavy, a bag full of God,
Ghastly statue with one gray toe
Big as a Frisco seal

And a head in the freakish Atlantic
Where it pours bean green over blue
In the waters off beautiful Nauset.
I used to pray to recover you.
Ach, du.

In the German tongue, in the Polish town
Scraped flat by the roller
Of wars, wars, wars.
But the name of the town is common.
My Polack friend

Says there are a dozen or two.
So I never could tell where you

Put your foot, your root,
I never could talk to you.
The tongue stuck in my jaw.

It stuck in a barb wire snare.
Ich, ich, ich, ich,
I could hardly speak.
I thought every German was you.
And the language obscene

An engine, an engine
Chuffing me off like a Jew.
A Jew to Dachau, Auschwitz, Belsen.
I began to talk like a Jew.
I think I may well be a Jew.

The snows of the Tyrol, the clear beer of Vienna
Are not very pure or true.
With my gipsy ancestress and my weird luck
And my Taroc pack and my Taroc pack
I may be a bit of a Jew.

I have always been scared of *you,*
With your Luftwaffe, your gobbledygoo.
And your neat mustache
And your Aryan eye, bright blue.
Panzer-man, panzer-man, O You——

Not God but a swastika
So black no sky could squeak through.
Every woman adores a Fascist,
The boot in the face, the brute
Brute heart of a brute like you.

You stand at the blackboard, daddy,
In the picture I have of you,
A cleft in your chin instead of your foot
But no less a devil for that, no not
Any less the black man who

Bit my pretty red heart in two.
I was ten when they buried you.
At twenty I tried to die
And get back, back, back to you.
I thought even the bones would do.

But they pulled me out of the sack,
And they stuck me together with glue.
And then I knew what to do.
I made a model of you,
A man in black with a Meinkampf look

And a love of the rack and the screw.
And I said I do, I do.
So daddy, I'm finally through.
The black telephone's off at the root,
The voices just can't worm through.

If I've killed one man, I've killed two——
The vampire who said he was you
And drank my blood for a year,
Seven years, if you want to know.
Daddy, you can lie back now.

There's a stake in your fat black heart
And the villagers never liked you.
They are dancing and stamping on you.

They always *knew* it was you.
Daddy, daddy, you bastard, I'm through.

"Daddy" has generated so many different critical responses in part because critics have tended to focus on how much we should assume the poem's speaker is "actually" Plath. But though Plath has been labeled a "confessional" poet, I find that label insufficient for what Plath has achieved in this poem, since the term suggests an admission of guilty reality, not projection. But readers coming to "Daddy" have to take into consideration how many fantasies and myths exist in the poem. There is the social fantasy of the vampire and Frankenstein figures, there is the private myth of the father and the husband, and there is the biographical reality of Plath's suicide attempts. These of course run up against historical facts—not only facts about Plath's actual husband and father but of the Holocaust. "Daddy" performs that clash of real with fantasy through its simple diction and rhythms, its rhymes that reiterate the same "you" sound throughout, reinforcing the poem's sense of childish accusation which becomes, over the poem, amusing and absurd.

Some readings of "Daddy" have focused solely on its Holocaust imagery, as critics have argued that Plath appropriates the Holocaust when she compares her husband and father to Nazis, her strained relationships with these men to being a Jew in Nazi Germany. For these critics, Plath's comparison is overblown, even obscene. Other critics, however, have suggested that Plath's histrionic tone is the point: the poem isn't autobiography but self-parody. But beyond Plath's own personal history, there's also the historical context in which Plath wrote "Daddy" to consider. "Daddy" is filled with tropes from popular early twentieth-century horror movies, and Plath's generation was among the first to encounter images from the Holocaust in the media. What if Plath understood that the real horrors of Hitler and the Holocaust—images repeated on film and shared, too, via the increasingly popular medium of TV—would eventually become just as thrilling and as illusory to us as Frankenstein and Dracula have to previous generations? That is, would they, through repeated sharing, become less real and more spectacular? I don't know if Plath believed that, but it's an argument I could make through reading the ways that "Daddy" employs its movie images. If Plath's own personal history becomes a monster story that she tells and retells, do we do something like this with history itself?

One of the things that makes "Daddy" generate so many responses, of course, is that we all have access to the facts of the Holocaust, but we don't all have access to the facts of Otto Plath, Plath's father, or Ted Hughes, Plath's husband. The Holocaust is public in ways these two men might not be, thus while we recognize that her use of the Holocaust is meant to be playful, we can't be sure what she says about Otto and Hughes is. The problem with the poem might not just be its use of the Holocaust but real people's lives.

But again, are they "really" meant to be themselves? Is Plath, in "Daddy," "really" Plath? Here is where my own experience as a poet matters to my reading. I understand that poems relying on life are, often, fabrications. I myself change facts and narrative elements to suit the trajectory of the poem at hand, not to track diaristic fact. It's how I distinguish poetry from autobiography or history writing; just as the language I choose to relay my life in poetry "sounds" different from the language I would use to write my biography, so, too, does my sense of fidelity to time and fact and audience change. The "I" is always a construction in poetry, the speaker always flirting with persona, the person I address a fantasy of my design. Plath's poem, I believe, takes this fact one step further to create a performance of the *idea* of a female self, rather than an actual one. Perhaps because of this, I feel comfortable with the ambiguity a poem like "Daddy" raises; I understand this is a poem as much about overblown projection as it is any expression of Plath's true, if temporary, feelings. I think it's fine to admit what I can't know or finally prove about the Plath behind "Daddy," even as I carefully build the scaffolding for reading her poem as a whole. None of us can ever know what produced a poem, and as a writer, I'm happy consigning some level of creativity to mystery.

Alternative Readings Versus Misreadings

My reading of Plath, of course, won't be shared by all readers. And my alternative reading of "Daddy" is categorically different from a misreading of the poem, which is wrong based on issues of fact or definition. One reader of "Warming Her Pearls," for example, wondered whether the word "carriage" referred to a literal carriage or to the woman's body. A second look at the line, of course, and she understood Duffy meant a horse-drawn carriage. But why had she thought it meant the woman's body? It's because "carriage" can also refer to one's demeanor and physical movements, and Duffy's poem is filled with descriptions of the mistress's body—her shoulders, her hair, her slim arms, her throat. As the maid objectifies her mistress, we, too, are primed to attach her body to these same objects that adorn and contain her. My student's misreading was wrong, which I pointed out, but it also reminds us how Duffy employs projection and objectification throughout the poem.

We might want to correct people for their misreadings and move on, but there might be something gained by following—if briefly—a reader's mistaken logic and addressing why it's wrong. As a teacher, I've even found it useful to anticipate misreadings as a starting place for discussion, so as to help students navigate these problems. Likewise, I use these anticipated misreadings to figure out what contextual knowledge students will need as they encounter the poem. People who are not well versed in the Bible or with Christian theology, for example, may miss some of the bite to Gerard Manley Hopkins's odes. If you don't understand that "freckled" or "dappled" refers equally to moral stains as to actual mottles, you might think that "Pied Beauty" is a poem about how much Hopkins likes spotted things, not a more radical statement that, without original sin, we would have no need for Christ's salvation, thus sin itself might be beautiful.

Misreadings and context-gathering are a natural part of reading poetry. And sometimes poems deliberately flirt with misreadings through suggestive line breaks. As readers of poetry, we have to be patient with ourselves and the poem, since poetry requires our careful attention to all the poem's working components. Some readers may be frustrated by the fact that a good poem will provoke a plethora of responses. At heart, these readers will want to know if their reading is the "right" one, or to believe the poem could have *only* been written one way for it to work. Once a poem is taught in a classroom or praised in workshop, the assumption is that its aesthetic or social values are, if not laudable, at least inevitable, because they were the poet's singular and correct options.

But writing poetry has taught me that there is nothing inevitable to a poem; there are merely choices. Some are more interesting or provocative choices than others, and a good poet learns to recognize which ones produce more exciting results. But once the poem is finished? Anything can happen to it. We read differently across communities and time, and the poem changes its meaning to us in part because of these evolving readings. We have been talking about Plath's poem over generations because at first her choices looked bold and original, then ethically dubious, then cartoonish or overwrought. One fantasy about reading is that the poem should stay frozen in time, that it resonate the same way and mean the same thing over successive time. But as one student reminded me—the same one who, interestingly, misread the word "carriage"—a poem survives *because* we reread it. When we adapt Shakespeare to suit our present moment, or question whether the medieval saint and writer Christina of Markyate was trans, we aren't just teasing out an alternative reading within the text that the writer herself may not have been conscious of, we are, in our reinvestigations, making their work a *living* document.

For that reason, perhaps it's better to think of a poem not as an unstable but an organic art. It's why the relationship I develop with a poem doesn't occur in a single moment but over the course of a life. I'm not the same person who read Plath at sixteen and fell in love; my understanding of her poetry has deepened and changed as I've grown older. And I have to say that I like having those other readings of Plath in mind, to feel her poems change and change again when I return to them. If we can all agree on the exact meaning of a poem, doesn't that suggest the poem itself may be too narrow, even lifeless? Maybe "Daddy" ceases to move me as a poem about Plath's relationship with the men in her life and becomes more interesting to me as an example of how Plath's generation tried to reckon with the Holocaust. It's not that "Daddy" ceases to be a personal poem: it just becomes something *other* than biography to me.

All this is to say that when we read or write a poem, we read and write ourselves as much as the poem. We remember moments of our own wonder, pain, and joy, our past shames and delight, to see if they align with the experiences being related to or by us; we recall past works of literature that we've read, to see if the poet's or our own allusions are drawn from a shared wellspring. And we read, too, the limitations of our knowledge: we sense, when we come across an image or reference a poet makes that we cannot identify, where we and the poet finally divide. And when we edit our own work as poets, we let the conscious mind take over when the subconscious one has finished playing. When it comes to reading or writing poetry, we have to balance between the forensic and the creative, between staying within the bounds of definition and fact and moving into the realm of the interpretive. Poetry helps us to articulate ideas we didn't know that we knew, to come to conclusions we couldn't have reached on our own. In that, we read the world through images, and we read and make a poem with every aspect of ourselves.

EXPERIMENTS

- Select one work from the list of **shaped** or visual poems below and write down all the things you notice about it. Where does your eye go first? How does your eye move around the page? What differences in typeface or font do you notice? What is legible to you and what isn't? How does the title influence what you see? Are there different kinds and types of language in the poem? Is the poem composed of different kinds of physical material? Is there any relationship you can discover between the shape of the poem and what is being said?

- Cut out a series of interesting phrases or words from some newspapers, books, or magazines. Now collage these different phrases together. Start with the line that most interests you, then find words or phrases that appear to contextualize, embroider upon, or disagree with this statement. Play with visual arrangement so that these other bits of text become part of a conversation with your starting phrase. Pay attention to size and shape of font, as well as spacing of the text. What kind of narrative emerges from your collaging?

SUGGESTED WORKS TO CONSIDER

George Herbert, "Easter Wings" and "The Altar"
Douglas Kearney, "Falling Dark at the Quarters"

Anthony Cody, "Cada día más cerca del fin del mundo"
mIEKAL aND, "mi'kmaq book of the dead"
Eugene Gomringer, "Silencio" and "o"
Scott Helmes, "haiku #62"
Augusto de Campos, "hearthead"

All poems can be found at either the Poetry Foundation website, the Academy of American Poets website, or on UbuWeb.

CHAPTER TWO

What Images Are in the Poem?

O nce you've spent time making notes about what you notice about a poem, you can focus on the senses and scenes the poem evokes. Our senses are the building blocks of poetry, the primary way we translate our physical experience of the world into language. This translation, of course, occurs through **imagery**, which is the figurative language that approximates what we can smell, hear, see, taste, and touch. It's the image that helps us describe and make comprehensible the world, and it's our ability to read images that helps us understand poems.

Here's a short poem from Korea that does just that. It's from *Asian Figures*, a collection of translations by W. S. Merwin of Asian and Southeast Asian aphorisms.

> Quiet
> Like a house where the witch
> Just stopped dancing.

The first thing to notice is that this poem relies on **simile**, which uses "like" or "as" to compare different things or states of being. It's an arresting poem that I first found in a book called *Best Words, Best Order* by poet and novelist Stephen Dobyns, who points out that the power of this simile isn't just in its originality but in the way it makes us aware of the passage of time. Reading this image, he argues, we don't just sense the house's silence, we understand the essential impermanence of this quiet, because we're simultaneously asked to imagine both the wild sound of a witch dancing and the brief pause she's taken in her romp. It's a poem that extends the simile beyond a simple juxtaposition between something noisy and something quiet because it makes us aware that the dancing could start up again at any minute. Silence here isn't just the absence of sound, it's a feeling of both relief and dread.

We tend to treat images as concrete descriptions of people or objects that engage one or more of our physical senses. In that, we might imagine the image itself is temporal since it's linked to sensation. But this poem reminds me that the image can do more than describe a single moment in time: it also anticipates change or connects to other states of being and moments of time. At its best, it radiates out from perception to emotion, thus to a larger narrative than the immediate situation the image describes, as you can see in this two-line poem (also called a **distich**) by the American poet Louise Bogan:

> At midnight tears
> run in your ears.

As with the Korean poem, an issue of time is at stake, since Bogan's poem compresses an entire unspoken drama into a single image of a person in bed, weeping. Why is this person weeping? Bogan's poem is titled "Solitary Observation Brought Back from a Sojourn in Hell," a title that anyone who's lived through the pandemic might have some thoughts about, though I myself read the poem as referring to a collapsed love affair. Though the poem's use of the second person declares its situation may be experienced by anyone, the title suggests a specific event that the speaker herself once experienced, and the image of tears pooling in one's ears gives me proof of her own past feelings. But I'm also invited to imagine other details about the speaker from this image, including her reluctance to admit her grief, since she only gives way to sorrow at night when alone.

Extremely short poems like Bogan's are rare in English: there are few notable one- or two-line poems, and we tend to classify these as **epigrams** or **aphorisms**. One of the most famous one-line poems is W. S. Merwin's **monostich** "Elegy":

> who would I show it to

But there is also Alexander Pope's biting epigram from 1730, which he had engraved on the collar of a puppy he then gifted to Frederick, Prince of Wales:

> I am my master's dog at Kew;
> Pray tell me, sir, whose dog are you?

Epigrams are witty, often satiric statements commenting on human behavior; aphorisms are concise, generally revealing declarations about human truths. In their brevity and compression, they share something with the **haiku**, as their power resides in an image that speaks both to the moment of time in which the poet stands and to a larger experience of time and human change the image gestures to.

Likely you're familiar with the haiku: a short poem totaling seventeen syllables, broken down into three single-line units of five, seven, and five syllables each. Haiku are some of the first poetic forms we're taught to write, in large part because their gentle formal constraints and reliance on single, concrete images make these poems feel less intimidating. But haiku are anything but simple. At their best, haiku speak to the way our minds work: as we remember and dream in fragments, so we experience the world in powerful explosions of sense and emotion we later work into language. Matsuo Bashō, one of the Japanese masters of the haiku, even believed haiku to be more a mode of seeing than a form of poetry. As the haiku connects sense with personal reflection, and so much seasonal change and activity happens over the course of three lines, the form suggests impermanence but also interdependence: we are not just among the things we observe, we, too, are what we observe.

Time and place play an outsize role in haiku, as these poems evoke a specific season, either by name or by some physical association with it. These references usually occur in either the first or third unit of this three-phrase poem, and are widely recognizable to readers, containing references to autumn or the springtime appearance of plum blossoms, giving the poem a sense of the world's cyclical changes while also suggesting the porous boundary between the self and the natural world. But while in Japan haiku would begin with a nod to a classical poetry, in the West, the haiku has been absorbed by writers as a moment of fresh, spontaneous and direct observation. Both Western and Japanese haiku privilege plain speech, and even as these poems rely upon poetic conventions, they feel original in part because their immediacy highlights the writer's personal engagement with the world. Images aren't just repeated for conventional effect, they are written as if just seen or discovered, as you can see in this haiku by Bashō:

> Year after year,
> The monkey's face
> Wears a monkey's mask.

Written on New Year's Day, 1693, this haiku delights because it's a sly self-portrait as well as social commentary. Who isn't trapped by how we're seen in society, how we have to perform for others? Underneath the self is just more persona, so where does the true self finally reside? Here natural duplicity reflects human duplicity; thus, monkey and human and mask collapse into the same image. In that, Bashō's poem recalls for me this other short poem by an anonymous Japanese poet:

> The traitor
> Has the best
> Patriot costume.

Again, this poem compresses in a single gesture a larger argument about the world that the reader has to articulate for herself. How is this comparison true? That, of course, is the question behind all figurative language—are the two related things here accurately described *and* accurately compared? If so, in what ways? I find this Japanese poem biting because it forces me to consider what actual patriots and traitors share in common, which is an attachment to rhetoric that can be twisted to different ends. This poem was written centuries ago in Japan. And yet it speaks to me as truthfully and powerfully in twenty-first century America as when, and where, it was first written.

Imagism and Modern American Poetry

While haiku may be originally Japanese, it's had and continues to have a strong impact on American poetry, as you can see from this three-line poem, "Calling," by A. R. Ammons:

> Wind rocks
> the porch chair
>
> somebody home

What I love about "Calling" is the surprise that unfolds over the two stanzas and how the movement of the poem itself changes how I understand the title. I know from the poem's first two lines that wind causes the porch chair to rock, and yet that split between the first and second stanza—disrupting the haiku form that the poem's shape suggests—implies that "somebody home" could refer both to the presence of the wind and possibly also the question called into the house by the speaker, asking if anyone is present. That stanza break also forces me to pause to take in the eerie, disembodied rocking of the chair. Suddenly the image and its deliberately unclear syntax feels uncanny, ghostly. Somebody is home, but it is not human. Are we calling to it? Is it calling to us? Personally, I can't help but read "Calling" as Ammons's ars poetica, to imagine that the wind here might also be like writing poetry itself—an unseen force familiar to readers of Percy Bysshe Shelley's "Aeolian Harp," which compares wind blowing through the harp to the inspiration that moves through the poet. Poetry, too, is a calling: something inanimate that still enlivens the physical world. We are inhabited by spirits, and in describing their movements, the movement of our minds, we write poems.

Even the form of "Calling," for me, is ghostly: the poem is *like* a haiku, but it's not a strict translation of the haiku's form. It has the spirit of the haiku without trying for exact duplication. The poem is a series of hauntings, then, a call and response between a revered Japanese poetic form and an American idiom.

You might also think of Ammons's poem as a nod to the Modernist movement called Imagism: a pre–World War I, free-verse school of European and American poets that wanted to do away with what one of its founders, the American poet Ezra Pound, derisively called "Victorian slither." Imagism focused on pared-back, direct language written with an attention to the natural rhythms of speech rather than conventional rhythms of formal verse. Like haiku, images weren't meant to be decorative but "direct treatment[s] of a thing," as the critic F. S. Flint wrote in his 1913 essay "Imagism" for *Poetry*. Imagism was wildly, if briefly, popular in American poetry, inspiring poets like H.D. and Amy Lowell, and perhaps best characterized by Pound's famous poem "In a Station of the Metro":

> The apparition of these faces in the crowd:
> Petals on a wet, black bough.

As you can see, Pound here collapses the human and natural worlds but, as with haiku, there's a complex sense of movement and even time in his comparison. It's not the faces themselves being compared to the petals, but *the apparition* of these faces.

"Apparition" means a ghostly figure, something just coming into view. By choosing this word, Pound lets me see petals, human faces, and also these faces settling into place in my mind. I have to sense not just location and season then but a sense of movement and disembodiment. People flicker in and out of my perception, much in the same way they might in an actual station in the metro. And just as each of these faces shimmers into view, I see that they are all part of an anonymous crowd. There's something beautiful yet interchangeable about them, and because they are petals on a wet black bough, I also see them in rain, I see them being blown off branches. I see them falling; I imagine them dying. They are human and thus transitory because mortal, part of and subject to a natural cycle of springtime and death, but here described in a situation that shouldn't at all recall the natural: an underground metro station. In this, Pound has understood something about traditional haiku's collapse of self and non-self, human and natural, and translated it all into his own contemporary context.

Pound has captured all of this in just two lines. I've had to unpack this poem's thinking for myself over the course of a paragraph, and I could easily write another two on the poem's use of the colon, that slant rhyme of "crowd" with "bough," the way it snaps shut the poem's closure. I could talk about the poem's four- and five-beat rhythms, which give the poem its sense of finality, or I could talk about when the poem was written, after the First World War, just when British and American writers were becoming unsettled by the effects of technology on modern life. I could do all that, but my point is that the power of a good image is how it makes the reader acutely aware of its many connections and all the attending cultural, psychic, and artistic consequences of those connections. A strong image doesn't alert us just to something true in the moment of observation but also how this moment speaks to larger, perhaps even cyclical, movements of time.

What Kinds and Types of Figurative Language Appear? On Symbol, Allusion, and Allegory

As images are the building blocks of poetry, it's helpful to distinguish between the general kinds and types of figurative language that comprise images, since these different figures of speech ask us to perceive and feel their meanings differently. For instance, when Gerard Manley Hopkins writes in his poem "Spring and Fall," "Márgarét, áre you gríeving/ Over Goldengrove unleaving?," he's using **symbolism** to suggest that the young child, Margaret, is experiencing for the first time an awareness of her own aging and mortality.

SPRING AND FALL

Márgarét, áre you gríeving
Over Goldengrove unleaving?
Leáves like the things of man, you
With your fresh thoughts care for, can you?

Ah! ás the heart grows older
It will come to such sights colder
By and by, nor spare a sigh
Though worlds of wanwood leafmeal lie;
And yet you wíll weep and know why.
Now no matter, child, the name:
Sórrow's spríngs áre the same.
Nor mouth had, no nor mind, expressed
What heart heard of, ghost guessed:
It ís the blight man was born for,
It is Margaret you mourn for.

Here the natural world gives voice to what Margaret can only articulate for herself in bodily and spiritual awareness ("[w]hat heart heard of, ghost guessed"). Spring and fall then aren't simply seasons, they're **archetypal symbols** of youth and late middle age, likely familiar because you've seen these figures repeated before in painting and literature. Archetypal symbols are, as the poet Stanley Plumly said, "experience tied to time" because they represent common stages or events we recognize as emblematic of natural or human cycles. They are also culturally received images we recognize from other works of art: images of gardens in the West may recall the Garden of Eden, for example, while cherry blossoms in Japan signal spring. We learn, both through experience and through reading or research, how to interpret these symbols. Archetypal symbols are related to but different from **conventional symbols**, whose meanings are specific to communities, such as national flags, religious signs, or military insignia. We can have both personal and communal feelings attached to these symbols, and sometimes conventional symbols become archetypal ones in poetry, as with the Christian cross. Archetypal and conventional symbols assume a broadly shared use and meaning. But with **private symbols**, which are unique to individual authors, we have to construct their meanings by how they appear over the course of a specific text, such as Melville's white whale in *Moby-Dick* or Kafka's insect in *The Metamorphosis*.

The use of archetypal or conventional symbols in particular is an example of **allusion**, a word whose etymology comes from the Latin *alludere*, which means "to joke" or "to jest." Allusion is when one work of art briefly makes either direct or indirect reference to another, whether through symbolism or outright name-dropping. Allusions don't, of course, need to be amusing in and of themselves, though there's something playful about the way a poem uses other artworks to expand its immediate range. Allusions occur everywhere in poetry, from references to characters in the Bible or Greek mythology to mentions of historical and pop-culture figures, even to a specific line or phrase lifted from another song or poem—an allusion made, of course, recognizable to us as a brief reference in order to distinguish it from plagiarism. Allusions assume a well-read reader, or at least a patient one since some allusions may pass us by without the aid of Google. But allusions are the lifeblood of poetry, and all poets to some extent rely on them: they're the poetic equivalent of musical sampling, a way of amplifying your own lyrics while speaking back to and colluding with other artists.

Allusions stand apart from **allegory** in poetry, even as allegory depends entirely upon a poet's use of allusion. Allegory has two definitions: the first being when an entire work of art takes second place to its meaning, the second being when abstract concepts in an artwork are themselves personified. In the first case, allegory requires that the events and characters of the poem's immediate narrative function as a cover-up for the real story the poem wishes to tell, usually a moral, political, or historical lesson readers can intuit through the poem's use of symbolism. Picasso's painting *Guernica*, for example, is a famous allegory for the Span-

ish Civil War, just as June Jordan's "Letter to the Local Police"
is an allegory for how Black people get surveilled by their white
neighbors. Jordan's persona poem, written from the point of
view of an older white man, is a letter purportedly complaining
to the police about "a regular profusion of certain unidentified
roses" growing in his neighborhood, but as the poem continues,
you can tell from the Jordan's descriptions that the poem is less
about flowers than the "unruly" and "indecent" lives of Black and
mixed-race people these roses represent.

LETTER TO THE LOCAL POLICE

Dear Sirs:

I have been enjoying the law and order of our
community throughout the past three months since
my wife and I, our two cats, and miscellaneous
photographs of the six grandchildren belonging to
our previous neighbors (with whom we were very
close) arrived in Saratoga Springs which is clearly
prospering under your custody

Indeed, until yesterday afternoon and despite my
vigilant casting about, I have been unable to discover
a single instance of reasons for public-spirited concern,
much less complaint

You may easily appreciate, then, how it is that
I write to your office, at this date, with utmost
regret for the lamentable circumstances that force
my hand

Speaking directly to the issue of the moment:

I have encountered a regular profusion of certain
unidentified roses, growing to no discernible purpose,
and according to no perceptible control, approximately
one quarter mile west of the Northway, on the southern
side

To be specific, there are practically thousands of
the aforementioned abiding in perpetual near riot
of wild behavior, indiscriminate coloring, and only
the Good Lord Himself can say what diverse soliciting
of promiscuous cross-fertilization

As I say, these roses, no matter what the apparent
background, training, tropistic tendencies, age,
or color, do not demonstrate the least inclination
toward categorization, specified allegiance, resolute
preference, consideration of the needs of others, or
any other minimal traits of decency

May I point out that I did not assiduously seek out
this colony, as it were, and that these certain
unidentified roses remain open to viewing even by
children, with or without suitable supervision

(My wife asks me to append a note as regards the
seasonal but nevertheless seriously licentious
phenomenon of honeysuckle under the moon that one may
apprehend at the corner of Nelson and Main

However, I have recommended that she undertake direct
correspondence with you, as regards this: yet
another civic disturbance in our midst)

I am confident that you will devise and pursue
appropriate legal response to the roses in question
If I may aid your efforts in this respect, please
do not hesitate to call me into consultation

Respectfully yours,

You'll note that, while Jordan makes these roses possess ste-
reotypically racialized characteristics, they aren't *actually* characters. In that, her allegorical poem differs from the second category
of allegory I noted, which is poetry that makes abstract concepts
like truth, disdain, or chastity themselves into human characters. This second type of allegory is rare in contemporary literature, but you'll see it in earlier works like Edmund Spenser's *The
Faerie Queene* or John Bunyan's *The Pilgrim's Progress*. Sometimes
authors are assumed to have written allegories, even though they
themselves deny writing them. When I say I read A. R. Ammon's
"Calling" as an ars poetica, for example, I'm calling the poem
an allegory for the art and act of writing poetry. Ammons could
reasonably refute my reading and insist it's just a poem about
wind and a rocking chair. Certainly, both readings are possible,
and one doesn't automatically negate the possibility of the other.
Thus while some poems, like *The Pilgrim's Progress* make their
allegorical objectives clear, other poems allow us to make allegorical interpretations based on how we respond to their images.

Making Language Figurative: Metaphor and Simile

These interpretations, of course, must still be based on reason-
able reactions to the poem's language. As I wrote before, I can't
make a poem mean anything I like without ignoring the words
on the page. Interpretations of the same poem can be conflict-
ing and, in that sense, exciting to debate, but critics generally

agree to the same details surrounding place, event, character, and plot that the poet has laid out. My personal interpretation, then, is based on judging the relationship that develops in the poem between the literal events and objects being described and their figurative effects on me as a reader. Again, images are constructed through comparative language: something *is like* or *is the same as* something else. That's the basic difference between simile and metaphor. But while both are closely related forms of comparative figuration, this distinction means that simile allows for the possibility of difference, while **metaphor** insists upon equivalence in its most profound parts. Of course, if I said to a friend, "My father is a bear," no pure equivalence really exists between them in her mind: she understands I'm speaking about some fundamental bearishness inherent to my father's nature, not that my father is in reality a bear. But if I were to say, "My father is like a bear," that might cause her to ask, "When and in what way?" She wouldn't immediately understand that I'm speaking about his character, but about some personality trait he displays according to circumstance. In this case, simile requires that I explain more about my father, while metaphor gets to the heart of how I believe my father might fundamentally be perceived.

That's a subtle difference, but it's important to understand because we use figurative language all the time, not just in poems but daily speech: "We are waging a war on drugs," we say, or "Their marriage is a cancer." Similes might require more explanatory writing on the part of the poet, but metaphors require more active interpretation on the part of the reader.

Are There Multiple Images?

Short poems may be composed of a single image, but most poems contain a series of images, and it's through mining the layers of these images—their variety and even contradiction—that we begin to make sense of the poem's thinking. For instance, here is the first stanza of Sylvia Plath's poem "The Moon and the Yew Tree":

> This is the light of the mind, cold and planetary.
> The trees of the mind are black. The light is blue.
> The grasses unload their griefs at my feet as if I were God,
> Prickling my ankles and murmuring of their humility.
> Fumy spiritous mists inhabit this place
> Separated from my house by a row of headstones.
> I simply cannot see where there is to get to.

This is a poem that stopped my breath the first time I read it. The opening line is a metaphor, since consciousness ("the light of the mind") acts as another moon illuminating the landscape of the poem. From the start, then, Plath yokes human consciousness to the moon she describes, just as she later turns the moon itself into a face, a fist, a criminal, even the place in which she now lives:

> The moon is no door. It is a face in its own right,
> White as a knuckle and terribly upset.
> It drags the sea after it like a dark crime; it is quiet
> With the O-gape of complete despair. I live here.
> Twice on Sunday, the bells startle the sky—
> Eight great tongues affirming the Resurrection.
> At the end, they soberly bong out their names.

> The yew tree points up. It has a Gothic shape.
> The eyes lift after it and find the moon.
> The moon is my mother. She is not sweet like Mary.
> Her blue garments unloose small bats and owls.
> How I would like to believe in tenderness—

The face of the effigy, gentled by candles,
Bending, on me in particular, its mild eyes.

I have fallen a long way. Clouds are flowering
Blue and mystical over the face of the stars.
Inside the church, the saints will be all blue,
Floating on their delicate feet over cold pews,
Their hands and faces stiff with holiness.
The moon sees nothing of this. She is bald and wild.
And the message of the yew tree is blackness—blackness
    and silence.

The moon keeps changing figurative shape throughout the poem, becoming at last the speaker's own mother, but not a "sweet" one, Plath writes, not like Mary, the mother of Christ. The moon instead "is bald and wild": it sees nothing of the speaker's psychic struggles, her desire for tenderness, for a kind of faith the church itself, with its "cold pews," cannot offer. Instead, the moon's "garments unloose small bats and owls" as it shines grimly down on the speaker and the yew tree, too, which itself registers nothing.

What is the poem "about"? From reading Plath's ever-shifting images, I sense a speaker stripped of hope, faith, comfort, even maternal tenderness. Her two poles of sense—the moon and the yew tree—offer little in terms of physical direction, let alone emotional or moral consolation. The yew tree points straight up, perhaps like hands raised in prayer or a church spire, but they bear only a message of "blackness and silence." If the light of the moon reveals to the speaker the world's essential indifference and even cruelty, the yew tree, too, denies me solace. Plath herself is caught between blazing, intellectual clarity about this fact, and numb acquiescence to its consequences. It's a bleak poem, whose direct syntax and gothic images make me feel slightly scoured after reading it.

Compare this poem to Elizabeth Bishop's "The Fish," however, and you see a very different way in which contradictory or
changing imagery works. Bishop starts her poem with the claim "I
caught a tremendous fish," which she then describes as "a grunt-
ing weight,/ battered and venerable/ and homely." Battered, ven-
erable, and homely, interestingly, become effective structuring
ideas for the rest of the images that follow in the poem, which
toggle back and forth as the speaker tries to describe her catch.

THE FISH

> I caught a tremendous fish
> and held him beside the boat
> half out of water, with my hook
> fast in a corner of his mouth.
> He didn't fight.
> He hadn't fought at all.
> He hung a grunting weight,
> battered and venerable
> and homely. Here and there
> his brown skin hung in strips
> like ancient wallpaper,
> and its pattern of darker brown
> was like wallpaper:
> shapes like full-blown roses
> stained and lost through age.
> He was speckled with barnacles,
> fine rosettes of lime,
> and infested
> with tiny white sea-lice,
> and underneath two or three
> rags of green weed hung down.
> While his gills were breathing in

the terrible oxygen
—the frightening gills,
fresh and crisp with blood,
that can cut so badly—
I thought of the coarse white flesh
packed in like feathers,
the big bones and the little bones,
the dramatic reds and blacks
of his shiny entrails,
and the pink swim-bladder
like a big peony.
I looked into his eyes
which were far larger than mine
but shallower, and yellowed,
the irises backed and packed
with tarnished tinfoil
seen through the lenses
of old scratched isinglass.
They shifted a little, but not
to return my stare.
—It was more like the tipping
of an object toward the light.
I admired his sullen face,
the mechanism of his jaw,
and then I saw
that from his lower lip
—if you could call it a lip—
grim, wet, and weaponlike,
hung five old pieces of fish-line,
or four and a wire leader
with the swivel still attached,
with all their five big hooks
grown firmly in his mouth.

A green line, frayed at the end
where he broke it, two heavier lines,
and a fine black thread
still crimped from the strain and snap
when it broke and he got away.
Like medals with their ribbons
frayed and wavering,
a five-haired beard of wisdom
trailing from his aching jaw.
I stared and stared
and victory filled up
the little rented boat,
from the pool of bilge
where oil had spread a rainbow
around the rusted engine
to the bailer rusted orange,
the sun-cracked thwarts,
the oarlocks on their strings,
the gunnels—until everything
was rainbow, rainbow, rainbow!
And I let the fish go.

The fish's skin is described as "homely" and "like wallpaper," then it is described as "speckled with barnacles ... infested/ with tiny white sea-lice." Is the fish like wallpaper or a ship; is it ancient and beautiful, or something rotting with vermin?

Later, the fish changes again, becoming something dangerous and faintly militaristic to Bishop, with gills "that can cut so badly" and a lip that's "grim, wet, and weaponlike," the very hooks in its mouth "like medals with their ribbons/ frayed and wavering." These same hooks then get imagined as being like "a five-haired beard of wisdom," while the fish's flesh is described in tender, almost feminine terms: the "coarse white flesh/ packed in like feathers" and the pink swim-bladder "like a big peony."

Bishop has literally caught the fish but not figuratively, as the similes and metaphors she uses pile up, change, and change again. What is this fish? Dangerous or helpless, fish or fowl, domestic or military relic? Even as Bishop continues to examine the fish, the fish looks up but not quite back at her, its own eyes "far larger" than Bishop's, "but shallower... the irises... packed/ with tarnished tinfoil." As Bishop writes, "They shifted a little, but not/ to return my stare."

No wonder Bishop releases the fish by the poem's end: she never really saw it to begin with. In essence, the variety of contradictory images Bishop uses to describe this fish speak to the real subject of the poem: not the fish itself but her inability to represent the ambiguity of nature and reality. "The Fish" reveals an essential disconnect between the speaker and the fish she wishes to present us; language strains but ceases to capture the world right in front of us. Even the poem's images—so consistently precise in Bishop's hands—dissolve at the end, collapsing into a brilliant but shapeless mass of color and light. "Everything/ was rainbow, rainbow, rainbow!" Bishop declares, then lets the fish slip from her grasp.

Parts of a Metaphor: Tenor and Vehicle

Bishop's use of metaphor reminds me that we often do our most complex thinking not in declarative statements but through images. When William Carlos Williams said, referring to poetry, "No ideas but in things," he meant that describing the things of this world is one of the first ways we communicate ideas that exist outside their material realities, such as love and desire, anger and jealousy. But Williams's phrase also suggests we might comprehend abstract ideas through, potentially, *other* relationships they have to parallel or even wholly different narratives and images. It's through the small detail then that we move to a larger awareness of ourselves and our sense of the world: the image allows us fragments of pure attention. This may be one reason why we've historically seen poetry in moral terms; when we so closely study others, how can we not see this attention as a form of attachment or reverence?

Understanding, then, that metaphors are not just a way of describing but thinking about the world, we might then benefit from studying how metaphors themselves work. In particular, we want to distinguish between **tenor** and **vehicle** in comparative language, to see how these two things together can make an image either succeed or fall apart. Simply put, the tenor of a metaphor is the object, person, or idea being described, while the vehicle is the image that describes it. Here is a poem by Lucille Clifton that I think deftly uses tenor and vehicle to its advantage, with both erotic and disturbing results.

CUTTING GREENS

curling them around
i hold their bodies in obscene embrace
thinking of everything but kinship.
collards and kale
strain against each strange other
away from my kissmaking hand and
the iron bedpot.
the pot is black,
the cutting board is black,
my hand,
and just for a minute
the greens roll black under the knife,
and the kitchen twists dark on its spine
and I taste in my natural appetite
the bond of live things everywhere.

Reading this poem, I might boil Clifton's poem un-usefully down to the following statement: cutting greens recalls for the speaker her "bond [with] live things everywhere." In that, she compares her physical act of and appetite for cooking with the natural and perhaps "obscene" kinship she has with other bodies. Breaking this comparison down further, I could say that this kinship is the tenor of Clifton's poem, while the act of cutting greens becomes the vehicle for her understanding of this bond. That's the global tenor and vehicle of the poem. In reality, Clifton's poem relies on a complex cascade of other tenors and vehicles to make this larger comparison work, since cutting collards and kale probably won't make anyone automatically aware of how we are all intimately connected with one another.

The poem's first tenor—that is, the first object described—is the greens, but notice how Clifton's vehicle makes them appear like people: they have "bodies in obscene embrace" that "strain against each strange other." Notice, too, how the poem's syntax makes these greens appear to resist the speaker's "kissmaking hand," as well as the bedpot and cutting board she places them on, all of which are described as black. The speaker's hand, too, is black in this poem, since her hand appears immediately after this list of other objects, all of them eliding together in blackness, much in the way that the greens, too, "roll black under the knife."

Clifton's images morph suggestively together, turning the greens into Black bodies, the food itself becoming not just culturally but racially symbolic through this interplay of tenor and vehicle. But notice, too, that even the briefest images in Clifton's poem—"kissmaking hand" for example—rely on this same interplay. Clifton's tenor is the hand, but "kissmaking" suggests tenderness, intimacy, but also courtly or even royal address through this invented adjective. Clifton's vehicle, then, is the embrace implied by this word, and it speaks back to the larger subject of this poem, which is "the bond of live things everywhere." It might also resonate with the phrase "natural appetite," if we think of human intimacy itself as an appetite, much like erotic hunger or desire.

But does that appetite stem only from hunger? What strikes me about the poem is that, though the act of cooking greens is meant to nourish the speaker, the sense of resistance, the reimagination of all these objects as bodies, makes this kitchen also the site of suggested violence. Almost all the non-human tenors— kitchen, collards, bedpot—take on human vehicles. Thus the kitchen suddenly has a spine, collards writhe and twist, and the pot and cutting board recall Clifton's own skin. Clifton starts the poem with the phrase "obscene embrace" to describe how the speaker grips these vegetables, and the "kissmaking hand" appears to deliver as much pain as pleasure, since she, too, holds the knife under which these greens "roll black."

Exactly how "natural" are the appetites being fed in this kitchen? Is the bond only one of shared humanity, or also the shared pain that Black people might particularly experience, even at their own hands? Is this the reason why Clifton's speaker, while cutting these greens, is at first "thinking of everything *but* kinship" (emphasis mine), since she perhaps also wants to resist linking the act of dismembering these bodies with her own hunger for them? "cutting greens" is an unsettling, richly suggestive poem whose diverse readings are enabled by Clifton's shifting metaphors.

Ground and Tension in Images

I wrote before that a reader looking at the global comparison Clifton makes in "cutting greens" might not automatically link the act of cooking with one's awareness of a larger cultural and human connection. That's because the **ground** and **tension** of the comparison need to be more fully established, which Clifton does over the course of her poem. Ground is what allows tenor and vehicle to work in tandem; it's what the compared things share in common, thus what allows the comparison itself to make sense. Tension, in contrast, refers to all the aspects and items that are *dissimilar* between tenor and vehicle.

As I said before, no pure equivalence exists in a metaphor—my father is not literally a bear, so when I metaphorically compare the two, I'm also inviting readers to imagine the tension—the differences—that exist in that comparison. Obviously, my father is human and a bear is a wild animal; my father's bad humor is certainly less threatening than a bear's, even though emotionally it may be frightening to me. But the ground remains suggestive enough to be possible for a reader to imagine, since it invites her to see both the bear and my father as large, imposing, physically impressive.

All comparisons require a balance between ground and tension to create surprise. Too much tension, and the image falls apart. If I write, "The moon is a refrigerator," this image won't make sense to anyone but me, since the moon shares nothing obviously in common with a refrigerator. My metaphor has too much tension, not enough recognizable ground. Too much ground, however, and my comparison will bore. If I were to write instead, "The moon is like a rock in the sky," the comparison is dull or accidentally humorous because, well, the moon really *is* a rock in the sky. There's too much ground being shared by "moon" and "rock." But if I were to write, as Plath did, "The moon is a white face," I have to see the ways in which the moon is and is *not* like a face, which I can do, since both are round, both can be pale, both can seem to look at you directly, even as one is human and the other a planet.

This is what Clifton has done in "cutting greens": through the repetition of black imagery, the ways in which she consistently describes the greens and kitchen in human terms, she establishes more ground and lessens the tension of her metaphors, while still keeping the images themselves strange enough that we can feel the uncanniness of vegetable bodies becoming human ones. By doing this, Clifton makes us reevaluate our own appetites, as our nourishment, too, might not arise just from human intimacy but also violent hungers.

Are There Images That Estrange? On Synesthesia, Metonymy, and Synecdoche

Clifton's poem reminds me that one delight of imagery is how it makes the mundane fresh and wild; it defamiliarizes what we might, in our daily lives, grow numb to, even cease to perceive. At the heart of metaphor lies uncertainty, even though the description itself may be clear. We cannot see every part of the poet's mind or meaning, though the image lets us come close. At its best, this uncertainty—the tension that we recognize as existing between the two things being compared—allows for multifaceted responses. Rather than lock a poem down into one interpretation, we might find ourselves experiencing what John Keats called "negative capability" or, as he put it, "when a man is capable of being in uncertainties, Mysteries, doubts, without any irritable reaching after fact & reason." Negative capability gives the poem its fractal quality, in which multiple and alternate interpretations can coexist and coincide. In essence, poems can ask as many questions as they answer. This is, I believe, part of what the Polish poet and Nobel laureate Wisława Szymborska was suggesting in her Nobel lecture. "[A]ny knowledge that doesn't lead to new questions quickly dies out," she wrote. "[I]t fails to maintain the temperature required for sustaining life." Poems, she declared, raise endless questions; in effect, they tell the reader, "I don't know." The tension inherent in metaphors that delight us also allows for difference to be felt, for mystery to deepen, and for ambiguity to be explored.

Strangeness, then, is not something to be avoided in poetry

but cultivated. And there are many ways to cultivate strangeness. Here are some lines from Arthur Rimbaud's "The Drunken Boat":

The bitter redness of love ferments!

I have dreamed of the green night with dazzled snows

A kiss slowly rising to the eyes of the sea,

The circulation of unknown saps,

And the yellow and blue awakening of singing phosphorous!

What startles me about these images is how they blend or blur different senses and concepts together. I might easily see phosphorous as yellow or even blue in my mind, but I have never imagined it as singing. I can imagine lips kissing, but seeing a kiss suddenly rise to the eyes of the sea forces me to imagine the sea possessing human features. This blending of different senses, or of describing one sense in terms of another, is called **synesthesia**. Arthur Rimbaud, Charles Baudelaire, and André Breton, all French Surrealists, were famous for employing this device, and it also characterizes the work of Dadaist and Futurist writers. For them, synesthesia was not merely an aesthetic affectation, even as all these artists were profoundly influenced by visual art. Instead, poetry had to be experienced through *all* the senses. As Rimbaud himself wrote, "The poet makes himself into a seer by a long, tremendous and reasoned derangement of all the senses." Baudelaire, in his poem "Correspondences," even argued that "the sounds, the scents, the colors correspond."

The Surrealists had a strong influence on American poetry, including on Frank O'Hara, one of the leading lights of the New York School of poets, which took its name from the school of Abstract Expressionist painters working in New York at the same time. But while O'Hara was influenced by art, his images aren't constrained to painting: they were found on the streets he walked which gives his poems a casual and urbane air of spontaneity and individualism, which you can see in the following poem.

A STEP AWAY FROM THEM

It's my lunch hour, so I go
for a walk among the hum-colored
cabs. First, down the sidewalk
where laborers feed their dirty
glistening torsos sandwiches
and Coca-Cola, with yellow helmets
on. They protect them from falling
bricks, I guess. Then onto the
avenue where skirts are flipping
above heels and blow up over
grates. The sun is hot, but the
cabs stir up the air. I look
at bargains in wristwatches. There
are cats playing in sawdust.
                              On
to Times Square, where the sign
blows smoke over my head, and higher
the waterfall pours lightly. A
Negro stands in a doorway with a
toothpick, languorously agitating.
A blonde chorus girl clicks: he
smiles and rubs his chin. Everything
suddenly honks: it is 12:40 of
a Thursday.
                    Neon in daylight is a
great pleasure, as Edwin Denby would
write, as are light bulbs in daylight.

I stop for a cheeseburger at JULIET'S
CORNER. Giulietta Masina, wife of
Federico Fellini, *è bell' attrice.*
And chocolate malted. A lady in
foxes on such a day puts her poodle
in a cab.
        There are several Puerto
Ricans on the avenue today, which
makes it beautiful and warm. First
Bunny died, then John Latouche,
then Jackson Pollock. But is the
earth as full as life was full, of them?
And one has eaten and one walks,
past the magazines with nudes
and the posters for BULLFIGHT and
the Manhattan Storage Warehouse,
which they'll soon tear down. I
used to think they had the Armory
Show there.
        A glass of papaya juice
and back to work. My heart is in my
pocket, it is Poems by Pierre Reverdy.

Though O'Hara's images are far more direct than those of the
French Surrealists he admired, you can still see their influence
in lines like "laborers feed their dirty/ glistening torsos sandwiches," or in descriptions of women who become "skirts flip-
ping/ above heels." At one point, O'Hara's syntax blurs enough
to make it unclear whether it's the laborers or their Coca-Cola
bottles who wear yellow helmets, just as it's unclear at the end
whether it's O'Hara's heart or a volume of poems in his pocket;
whether, in fact, his heart is the volume of poems itself.

"A Step Away from Them" feels at first like an overload of sensory information, until we get to the penultimate stanza:

> First
> Bunny died, then John Latouche,
> then Jackson Pollock. But is the
> earth as full as life was full, of them?

It's at this point I understand that the poem is an **elegy**, and having acknowledged this, as well as his own mortality, the speaker switches from using "I" to "one" when referring to himself:

> And one has eaten and one walks,
> past the magazines with nudes
> and the posters for BULLFIGHT and
> the Manhattan Storage Warehouse,
> which they'll soon tear down.

You might notice that O'Hara characterizes people via the objects attached to them or the things that they do. There is the "Negro" who "stands in a doorway/ with a toothpick, languorously agitating," for example, while a "blonde chorus girl . . . clicks" down the walk. There are also "several Puerto/ Ricans on the avenue today," O'Hara writes, "which makes it beautiful and warm": a moment in the poem I love, while I also flinch slightly at O'Hara's exoticization. But if O'Hara reduces Puerto Ricans to the warmth of a sunny avenue, I see, too, that he turns everyone in this poem into bits and pieces, depersonalizing them in a manner reminiscent of those Abstract Expressionist paintings he admired. The speaker never mentions his own race, but it's obvious from the way he focuses on identities that he sees himself as somehow apart from the people he notices, and that depending on who the "them" refers to—his dead friends or living strangers on the street?—this difference also includes race. But racial difference, for O'Hara, here seems to be attached to attraction, erotic as well as aesthetic: the Black man and the

Puerto Ricans are vibrant and enticing, different from the memory of his friends, whose deaths pierce the pleasures the speaker experiences on the street. Loss, in fact, tangles O'Hara's syntax: "But is the/ earth as full as life was full, of them?" he asks in a line that practically chokes on its own grief.

O'Hara's tortured syntax, the consistent ways he blurs and elides people with objects, for me makes all his observations feel not specifically dehumanizing but instead part of a seamless whole. In the end, as he's done with everyone else in the poem, the speaker objectifies and depersonalizes himself, becoming "one" instead of an "I," or perhaps becoming all "eye"—something that takes everything in, without hierarchies or restrictions.

O'Hara's depersonalizations are achieved through his use of **metonymy** and **synecdoche**, figures of speech that—like metaphor—also rely on ground and tension. Metonymy is an expression of speech that substitutes one thing for another based on a close material, conceptual, or causal relationship. Metonymy comes from the Greek, *metynomia*, which means "a change of name," and we see it when we refer to the British royalty as "the Crown," or when we talk about soldiers as "boots on the ground." When O'Hara refers to women as "skirts . . . flipping over heels," this is an example of metonymy.

Synecdoche is a specific form of metonymy, as it is a figure of speech that uses a part of a thing to refer to the whole, oftentimes parts of the body that suggest states of feeling or consciousness that we associate with them, such as the heart for romantic feeling, or physical materials that the objects themselves are composed of, such as referring to playing the piano as "tickling the ivories." In effect, synecdoche is symbolism itself. Synecdoche comes from the Greek *synekdoche*, meaning "simultaneous meaning." If a person asks for another's "hand" in marriage, that's synecdoche. When Pound referred to the crowded mass of humanity in the subway as "faces in the crowd" or O'Hara writes, "My heart is in my/ pocket it is Poems by Pierre Reverdy," these, too, are examples of synecdoche.

What's important to note is that, though these are figures of speech related to metaphor, they function differently from conventional metaphor. As I've said before, metaphor suggests a profound similarity between two different things; metonymy and synecdoche, by contrast, are based on contiguity. When we refer to police or military officers as "the brass," we are pointing out that such personnel commonly wear brass-colored insignia and medals. That said, sometimes metonymy and metaphor can be at work at the same time, as in the common phrase "lend me your ears." The metaphor occurs in the verb "lend," which causes the reader to see the relationship between paying attention for a short period of time, and lending someone an object. Metonymy, however, occurs in the noun "ears," which stands in for a person's attention itself.

Likely, you find the slight differences between these terms confusing. I once got into a text war with a half dozen poets about the exact difference between metonymy, metaphor, and synecdoche, an argument that served less to clarify definitions over the course of a day than to make us all privately hate one another, so if you muddy these terms yourself, know this: literary critics and luminaries alike have died on this hill, and no one finally cares. If you want to refer to moments of synecdoche in a poem by the term metonymy, that's fine—technically you'll even be right. The important thing to remember is that poets use aspects of people, objects, and even events to refer to the whole of these things, and that these forms of figurative language work to present, if not a clearer image of the thing itself in its present moment, a shorthand for how we conceptually relate them to other ideas and objects.

On Private Symbolism

Based on some of my examples here, you can see that we use metonymy and metaphor all the time, both in poetry and daily speech. Overused metaphors we understand to be cliché, even as we unthinkingly revert to them. But poems, in order to make language new, rely upon images we *haven't* heard before, and by doing so move us away from conventional symbols we can catalogue to private ones we must interpret as the poem unfolds. Here's an example of a poem that uses private symbolism by the Nobel Prize–winning poet Octavio Paz.

MOTION

If you are the amber mare
I am the road of blood
If you are the first snow
I am he who lights the hearth of dawn
If you are the tower of night
I am the spike burning in your mind
If you are the morning tide
I am the first bird's cry
If you are the basket of oranges
I am the knife of the sun
If you are the stone altar
I am the sacrilegious hand
If you are the sleeping land
I am the green cane
If you are the wind's leap
I am the buried fire
If you are the water's mouth
I am the mouth of moss

If you are the forest of the clouds
I am the axe that parts it
If you are the profaned city
I am the rain of consecration
If you are the yellow mountain
I am the red arms of lichen
If you are the rising sun
I am the road of blood

Reading these images, I can't say that I grasp them as easily as I do Bishop's "The Fish," largely because the images feel specific to Paz's interior landscape but also because they don't resolve themselves into one single way to understand the connection between "I" and "you" in the poem. In fact, if I were to ask a reader how she might characterize the relationship between "you" and "I," she might answer that the speaker sometimes feels passionately, sometimes rageful, sometimes peaceful, sometimes spiritually connected to the "you." The two figures in this poem appear sometimes in concert, sometimes at odds. This is because the speaker alternately figures himself as something violent (he is "the axe that parts" the you's "forest of the clouds," for instance) and as something gentle, as we see in the lines "If you are the morning tide/ I am the first bird's cry." At times, the speaker's purpose seems to contradict, even profane the "you," as you can see in this couplet: "If you are the stone altar/ I am the sacrilegious hand." At times, "I" and "you" appear to function in concert, the two nourishing and even protecting each other, as when Paz writes, "If you are the water's mouth/ I am the mouth of moss."

This is, of course, if I believe I should treat these lines solely as couplets. But the poem is **stichic**, meaning it's written as a single long stanza, and though the poem repeats its "If you are/ I am" conditionals, there is no reason to stop after the completion of each statement. Notice that Paz doesn't include any punctuation; thus I could see the poem also as a cascade of consequences based on an ultimately circular logic: if you behave this way, I behave that way, which then causes you to behave another way, which causes me to behave in kind. The poem's title, "Motion," reminds me that, just as the images change dramatically over the course of this poem, intimacy between two people is never static. Relationships, too, are full of movement, and our feelings for the people we love shift for profound and often unstated reasons, which is another reason these images feel to me so intimate and, in many ways, inexpressible.

Paz's images—fluid, changeable, surreal, at times erotic and deeply spiritual—create a sense of constant restlessness. As the poem is set in no one moment of time, the images function as discrete moments that finally flow together—I begin to see a lifetime between two people through the evolution of these images, not merely a snapshot of a single speaker's lyric crisis.

I also have to notice that Paz's images aren't similes but metaphors, which is a way of suggesting to the reader that the images he presents aren't approximate but profoundly true about the two characters. I have to see the reaction each person has to the other not just as a momentary response, then, but a psychic one that encompasses their entire beings. I think that's why I feel a continuous flow of time as I read this poem, not simply because the poem cycles through so many different types of images but because, as metaphors, the images each suggest a comprehensive rethinking of the self in its relationship to others.

That, to me, is the resulting force of figurative language, whether it be conventional or private symbols, similes or metaphors. Figurative language not only helps me describe the world, it suggests my relationship to the things and people in the world. Poetry reminds me to look and look again. Through imagery and metaphor, I don't just see what is being described, I know, in the end, where I stand in relation to what I see.

Do the Images Work Together, or Are They in Tension? The Risks of Layering Imagery

Not all figurative language is automatically effective, however, and poems are rarely composed of nothing but images. And while poems may think and move through figurative language, if they layer image on top of image, they may also risk spinning out sensory details for the sake of language alone, creating what the poet Tony Hoagland, in a 2006 essay, called "the skittery poem of our moment." Hoagland argued that "the skittery poem" privileges "obliquity, fracture and discontinuity," and that poems that rely on such devices threaten to so externalize their images that they finally become divorced from experience. In effect, Hoagland warned, too many disparate images piled together tell us nothing, whether about the poet's thinking or about the narrative that inspired the poem.

I was thinking about Hoagland's essay when reading this poem by Topaz Winters:

ARS POETICA IV: STILL LIFE AS LOVER
UNARMED

Poetry, you said, is a room full of mirrors,
none of them glass.

I can go with that story. I can undress as well
as any crime scene. I'm good at softness, the noun.
At ruin, the verb that enables it.

Here I am & here I am again.
I'm a tremor of trees whipped into sun.

I'm so in love with you I want to live.
I'm so in love with you it forms the beginning
of every circle.

So maybe that's the only truth.
Voltage hissing in the air, all warm.
Even the quiet has teeth.

Of course I changed my mind,
came back to haunt you. Of course
you could teach me any dirty word
& I'd call it praying.

Poetry, you said, is the monstrosity
of being wanted.

I can go with that story. Find me
like sucking poison out of a wound.

I am better than I was & still I disappeared. & still
you didn't die in that hospital.

Reading the images in Winters's poem, I notice that my emotions are tugged this way and that; in fact, I'm unsure what to focus on or take seriously. The lines reference everything from mirrors to crime scenes to trees to electricity to praying to sucking poison out of wounds, with almost no repetition or pattern to help guide me. The title, "Ars Poetica," suggests I should take the poem as a personal aesthetic declaration, though many of the ideas about poetry itself aren't expressed by the speaker but a mysterious "you" with whom the speaker is in love. Part of the reason I struggle to understand the poem as a whole has to do with the narrative of this relationship that the poem suggests but doesn't explore. Clearly, something terrible happened to the "you" at some time, as they ended up in a hospital, but what was that event? The title refers to a "Lover Unarmed," but is that "unarmed" state literal or figurative or both? The speaker, too, was once struggling and "disappeared" but now declares she is "better": why? The poem cycles through past, present, and conditional tenses: "Here I am & here I am again," the speaker declares. "Of course I changed my mind," she adds, "Of course/ you could teach me any dirty word/ & still I'd call it praying." Somehow, what occurs in the present bears some relationship to the speaker's memory of the past and her hopes for the future. But without any clear pattern to the images themselves, what is that relationship based on?

The temporal narrative conditions of the relationship also conflict with the perpetual lyric time of the images: "Voltage hissing in the air, all warm" suggests an enduring event, just as "I'm a tremor of trees, whipped by sun" implies a fundamental identity for the speaker, while "I am better than I was & still I disappeared & still/ you did not die in that hospital" requires I have specific knowledge of the couple's personal experiences. Though each image itself is arresting, without seeing more clearly how the past intersects with the present, I am lost as to which time signature in the poem matters more. Even as the images leap and move, the poem feels curiously static; its images spin before me, but the poem overall goes nowhere.

Winters's poem again reminds me that there is, in the image, an inherent sense of time—one that may or may not be attached to the narrative of the poem as a whole. As I wrote before, in a haiku, time is made explicit by the image itself, since we experience the object *because* we are in a particular season and place. But even in longer, more narrative works, a single image can take us out of the immediate time signature of the poem to suggest that the thing being perceived has an enduring quality that survives outside the poet's current experience. "The moon is a white face," Plath writes, and I see her recognizing this fact at the moment of her looking up at the night sky while also acknowledging it as something enduringly true of how anyone might see the moon.

Because time and experience are both internalized in the image, then, when we spin out a wide and unconnected string of similes and metaphors, we slowly strip the poem of location and moment, making any specific crisis or argument more difficult to track. Each image instead becomes a discrete moment of crystallized sense rather than a process of thought. The poem offers up its images much like a warehouse offers up its array of goods.

In writing and reading poetry, it helps to remember that any image contains a high concentration of connection and meaning already packed inside it, seedlike, waiting to burst into life. The image is meant to move a reader from close observation to larger self-awareness. In that, images allow us moments of transcendence, even as they might occur in service to discursive arguments. Our sensual experience of the world privileges subjectivity, immediacy, and surprise, while our desire to narrativize our experience privileges time, causal relationships, and consequence. Basically, poems toggle continually between immediate sensation and story, between concrete and abstract realities. Poems that pursue only one direction might threaten to collapse under their own weight: they either lose the ability to ground and connect to the reader or lose the ability to surprise.

You could argue that Paz's poem "Motion" risks just this, as his images change so often, and are so privately—even mysteriously—encoded. But the architecture that frames these images—the conditional "If you are/ I am" statements—makes my complete understanding of these images' specific meanings less important. Likewise, each "if you are" statement has a clear referent and image: the "you" is an amber mare, a stone altar, the morning sun, a basket of oranges. In comparison, the "I am" statements are wilder, more private, harder to parse. Because I'm able to move from concrete images to more abstract ones and then back again, I feel less anxious moving between what I can't understand and what I can. The play between ground and tension is globally enacted throughout the poem between the differences in its coupled images. By doing this, Paz lets me feel for myself the instability of this relationship, even if I can never exactly articulate its mechanics. The variety of images in "Motion" doesn't shut me out; instead, it helps me to better experience emotional change itself.

Do the Images Connect?
On Metaphoric Conceit

If Winters's imagery has me running in a lot of different directions at once, that doesn't mean that imagistic variation and even contradiction are bad. Returning to Bishop and Plath for a moment, figurative variation might perfectly reflect a speaker's internal conflict. But lots of poems also have metaphors that work in tandem with each other, becoming elaborations upon a single theme or idea, as you can see in Clifton's "cutting greens." In that, as Sir Philip Sidney wrote in *Defense of Poesie*, these combined metaphors become the "idea" that informs and shapes the poem. When such images cohere, we call that a **conceit**—an elaborate metaphor or simile that spins out over the course of a stanza or an entire poem, as in this sonnet by John Donne, which compares the author's spiritual faith to a town under siege:

HOLY SONNETS: BATTER MY HEART,
THREE-PERSON'D GOD

Batter my heart, three-person'd God, for you
As yet but knock, breathe, shine, and seek to mend;

That I may rise and stand, o'erthrow me, and bend
Your force to break, blow, burn, and make me new.
I, like an usurp'd town to another due,
Labor to admit you, but oh, to no end;
Reason, your viceroy in me, me should defend,
But is captiv'd, and proves weak or untrue.
Yet dearly I love you, and would be lov'd fain,
But am betroth'd unto your enemy;
Divorce me, untie or break that knot again,
Take me to you, imprison me, for I,
Except you enthrall me, never shall be free,
Nor ever chaste, except you ravish me.

Here the speaker begs God not only to "break, blow, burn, and make [him] new," but to "o'ethrow [him]," since Satan, God's "enemy," has effectively "captiv'd" him, making him the devil's unwilling "betroth'd." Reason can't protect him, nor can his own good intentions: only God's grace and force—imagined here as both martial invasion and rape—can free the speaker to be "married" to his truly desired spouse. You can see that the besieged-town metaphor that predominates the first eight lines of the sonnet—its **octet**—changes to one of betrothal and divorce, then to erotic enthrallment and finally sexual violation through the **sestet**, the last six lines of the sonnet. The poem turns and turns again as Donne's conceits evolve. Donne's sonnet is structured around a trope common to medieval and Renaissance poetry, which is the comparison of a besieged town to the sexual conquest of a woman. Thus his poem, with its elaborate metaphors of subjugation, mines the medieval courtly love tradition, turning it strange to his readers because its secular metaphors are now used in service of spiritual crisis. By doing this, Donne relies upon both allusion and conceit—allusion in his courtly love tropes, and conceit in the structure of the poem's own argument according to these tropes.

A **trope** is a figure of speech so commonly used it becomes

cliché. While contemporary readers might find Donne's para-
doxical imagery unusual, even profoundly unsettling, for Renaissance readers it would have been familiar, albeit oddly used.
Donne's poem avoids being cliché in part because the trope he
uses has been applied to a very different subject. Playing with
literary tropes can become a game unto itself, and sometimes
upending them becomes the very point of a poem, as in Shakespeare's famous Sonnet 130:

> My mistress' eyes are nothing like the sun;
> Coral is far more red than her lips' red;
> If snow be white, why then her breasts are dun;
> If hairs be wires, black wires grow on her head.
> I have seen roses damasked, red and white,
> But no such roses see I in her cheeks;
> And in some perfumes is there more delight
> Than in the breath that from my mistress reeks.
> I love to hear her speak, yet well I know
> That music hath a far more pleasing sound;
> I grant I never saw a goddess go;
> My mistress, when she walks, treads on the ground.
>   And yet, by heaven, I think my love as rare
>   As any she belied with false compare.

Shakespeare's sonnet is a **blason**, a descriptive poem in praise
or blame of a person or object, which generally relies upon
hyperbole. Here, Shakespeare uses hyperbole to parody conventional Elizabethan images of feminine beauty. Though we may
not share these same ideals ourselves now, you and I can still
find the poem funny because we understand that every age produces its stock forms of flattery, and that who and what we love
does not in the end depend on meeting the banal ideal but rather
on confronting the individual reality of another. Shakespeare's

poetic conceit in effect parodies conceit itself: it suggests that metaphors, no matter how elaborate, really *can't* capture what makes another person beautiful, and it does so by also satirizing the extravagant lengths we'll go to in order to surprise and delight in language.

What Patterns Teach Us

Like a highly crafted piece of music, a poetic conceit builds and builds upon itself: it's showy, and, as Shakespeare revealed, as much about the ways we structure language as about how we represent the world. Not coincidentally, the two poems I chose to demonstrate how conceit functions are sonnets, which also tend to be rhetorical forms; it makes sense, then, for these forms to employ literary devices that aim for similar effects. But beyond understanding how elaborately connected images enhance rhetorical arguments, images themselves reveal (or perhaps betray) a poet's buried subject matter; in effect, the repetition of certain types of images tells us more about the poet's thinking than the poet might consciously admit.

The author Lance Olsen once told me that narrative arises out of repetition, and that perhaps the disruption of repetition is one way we recognize experiment. Another way of saying this is that narrative arises out of attachment: what is the image the poet *must* return to? Even if not as consciously used as a metaphoric conceit, the repetition of a particular image becomes the scaffolding from which a poet begins to build her way through a subject, to reimagine herself through her own attachments to private symbols. In many ways, repetition helps make even conventional or archetypal symbols *feel* personal, because as the poet returns to them over the course of stanzas or an entire poem, they become increasingly part of her own mythology.

In that sense, repetition becomes the most important thing to notice in a poem: if the poet keeps coming back to the same image or sound, I might recognize this not as an incidental part of the work but its wellspring. As a poet, I've certainly used the study of repetition as the first approach to revising my own work, looking for where one image calls to another, suggesting a direction the poem might take that I did not first consciously imagine. In writing workshops, I ask students to chart every repeating pattern that they find—whether of image, phrase, syntax, or sound—in their own and others' poems. Both poetry and memory move associatively, but these associations build upon each other, calling out nuances of meaning and tone as we return to them, and as narratives and motifs of memory itself return in our writing. Our obsessions best reveal the unconscious desires and anxieties to the conscious mind. That's the "deep reading" of the world that poetry inspires in us, and it's found first in the image: the seed from which the rest of the poem blooms.

EXPERIMENTS

- Find a poem from the list below and examine its imagery, specifically its similes and metaphors. Pay particular attention to the poet's use of tenor and vehicle. What are all the vehicles the poet uses? How do tenor and vehicle work together to create meaning for you?
- Write a list of abstract nouns (such as "confusion," "hunger," "joy," "despair," "delight," "jealousy," and so on) on a series of notecards or slips of paper. Do as many as you can.

Write out the five senses, one each on a notecard or slip of paper: Smell, sight, hearing, touch, taste.

Shuffle the abstract-noun cards in one basket and shuffle the sense cards in another. Randomly choose one noun and one sense card from each basket.

Now create a sentence like this: "The _____ of _____ is: _____ "

Fill in the first blank with the sense card you've drawn, fill in the second with the noun card. Then write a concrete image that metaphorically illustrates the connection between your randomly chosen words.

- With a gathering of friends, write a group poem composed of "If you are, I am" conditional statements. Have everyone in the room write a single line: "If you are _____, I am _____," in which the blanks are completed with a surprising metaphor. Then go around the room, having everyone read their line aloud.

- Write a poem in which you imagine yourself in a favorite painting come to life. What images from this painting transform when made real? What conflicts emerge for you in this new world of the painting?

SUGGESTED WORKS TO CONSIDER

William Shakespeare, "Sonnet 73: That time of year thou mayst in me behold"

Rigoberto González, "Music Man"

Emily Dickinson, "Because I could not stop for Death—" (479)

William Wordsworth, "I Wandered Lonely as a Cloud"

Malachi Black, "This Gentle Surgery"

Lorine Niedecker, "Wilderness"

Lucille Clifton, "the lost baby poem"

Ada Limón, "The Leash"
Rick Barot, "The Wooden Overcoat"
José García Villa, "Lyrics: II (17)"
Larry Eigner, "#292"

All poems can be found online, either at the Poetry Foundation
or the Academy of American Poets websites.

CHAPTER THREE

Who Speaks and to Whom?

Imagine walking up to an office door and finding this sign taped to it:

JUST STEPPED OUT

You might feel a bit confused. Exactly *when* did this person step out? Is it a specific person who has left, or everyone in the office? The sign suggests the possibility of return, but doesn't specify when, and even if, anyone will come back. Perhaps this is the writer's polite way of saying she's skipped town for good. Perhaps this sign has been forgotten about and left taped on the door from a previous break. The note's address itself is casual enough that it seems specifically addressed to someone, but who? Someone with an appointment? A passerby? You? But how could it have been written to you when the writer has no idea who *you* are?

How you choose to interpret this sign is based on your assumptions about its **deixis**, a term that refers to any words that give us a sense of speaker, addressee, time, and location. Deixis is a concept we rely upon in conversation all the time, since all communication is the resulting relationship between triangulated meaning— between the person speaking, the context in which the person speaks, and the person (or persons) to whom the person speaks. Deixis refers to that specific triangulation, and deictic language is any part of speech that helps clarify that relationship. Pronouns such as "I," "you," "he," "she," and "we"; adverbs such as "here" and "there"; and time words such as "now" or "then" are all deictic elements of speech because they clarify our understanding of what is being said, when it's said, and by whom. If we stand flummoxed before the door, unsure whether to wait, it's because the sign's sense of deixis is vague. Practical context and prior experience with other such signs may fill in some of the blanks, but that's all information that you, the reader, must provide. Deixis is a linguistic term whose ancient Greek origin means "pointing" or "reference," and a good way to remember its meaning and function is to focus on these questions when reading: Who speaks, where and why do they speak, and to whom do they speak?

These may sound like simple things to ask, but spend time looking at any poem through the lens of these questions and you'll see how quickly meaning is made or lost through deictic language. You'll also start to make out the complex relationship that exists between deixis, diction, form, and mode. Whom we speak to and on what occasion we speak determines tone and subject matter. For instance, if I speak at someone's wedding, I'll write a love poem, not an elegy. Likewise, I don't tell my mother the same things I'd admit to my best friend, and I certainly won't speak to my boss the way I speak to a child. Lyric poetry has often been defined as verse in which the self speaks to the self, but it might be better to consider lyric poetry as a thousand types and kinds of selves speaking to a thousand kinds of listeners. But while poetry allows you to speak to a lot of people at once, any single poem is almost always written from one specific perspective to another. In fact, I'd argue that a lot of bad writing has a general if unconsciously weak sense of deixis, though there are of course literary masterpieces that deliberately undercut our understanding of who speaks and who listens. If you trust the writer, or you gain trust for the writer's strategies as the piece unfolds, that weak sense of speaker and addressee may well be the point. Basically, lyric poetry, as it moves through time and across discrete narratives, activates a reader's deictic anxieties through pronouns and place indicators. It's these very elements of speech that allow for the rapid movement of a poem through time and location, that give the reader a greater sense of the poem's focus.

You can see this in Arthur Sze's poem "First Snow," which leaps across different memories and locations, each of which a reader can track by following Sze's careful use of verb tenses and well-placed deictic clues.

FIRST SNOW

A rabbit has stopped on the gravel driveway:

>   imbibing the silence,
>   you stare at spruce needles:

>>   there's no sound of a leaf blower,
>>   no sign of a black bear;

a few weeks ago, a buck scraped his rack
>   against an aspen trunk;
>   a carpenter scribed a plank along a curved stone wall.

>   You only spot the rabbit's ears and tail:

when it moves, you locate it against speckled gravel,
but when it stops, it blends in again;

>   the world of being is like this gravel:

you think you own a car, a house,
this blue-zigzagged shirt, but you just borrow
these things.

Yesterday, you constructed an aqueduct of dreams
and stood at Gibraltar,
but you possess nothing.

Snow melts into a pool of clear water;
and, in this stillness,

starlight behind daylight wherever you gaze.

By parsing out Sze's descriptions in this poem, I see that I am, in a single moment of observing this rabbit on a gravel drive, simultaneously experiencing at least two other distinct place-based memories—the first being "a few weeks ago," when a buck rubbed its antlers on a tree, which also recalls a carpenter "scrib[ing] a plank along a curved stone wall"; the second being "yesterday," when the "you" "stood at Gibraltar," dreaming of possibly greater things. Sze's poem is a collision of recollection and sensory experience then, and it's meant to enact something a lot of us are familiar with: How, when confronted with a single, startling scene, our minds flood with other related (or even unrelated) images.

The question is what all these different scenes have in common. For Sze, it's in the way this rabbit can be sighted only when it moves, since otherwise it blends perfectly into the snow-sprinkled gravel drive. The rabbit is the living creature our attention wants to track, but the "world of being," Sze writes, "is like this gravel," with all its physical possessions, activities, and desires. We are so absorbed in the quotidian details of our lives that we believe we own something, when really, Sze notes, we "possess nothing." The rabbit's flickering in and out of sight is the very recognition of that truth—we see the world before we perceive its essential transience, and our own inability to finally claim or inscribe ourselves on it.

That's a big truth to encapsulate in such a short poem, and Sze accomplishes it because he leaps across time and place to create parallel narratives that support his central metaphor. In order to keep these narratives distinct, however, he uses deictic speech and phrases—"you" as well as "yesterday," "a few weeks ago," "in this stillness," "when it stops" and "when it moves"— to help us locate where we are and what we are looking at scene by scene. Though the poem features very little overt action, it's filled with movement and change. Even tracking the verb tenses, I move from the imperfect to the present to the past to the conditional present, back to the past, and then finally the present (or is it the future?) again. By doing this, I think the poem mimetically reproduces its own argument. The reader, by tracking various memories, flits in and out of different scenes, moving so rapidly through each image that she can hold on to no sense of the world completely.

Here's another text where deixis profoundly shapes our response, including, perhaps, whether we'd even classify the work as a poem. It's called "Letter," by Langston Hughes:

LETTER

Dear Mama,
  Time I pay rent and get my food
and laundry I don't have much left
but here is five dollars for you
to show you I still appreciates you.
My girl-friend send her love and say
she hopes to lay eyes on you sometime in life.

> *Mama, it has been raining cats and dogs up*
> *here. Well, that is all so I will close.*
>   *Your son baby*
>   *Respectably as ever,*
>   *Joe*

If I didn't know Hughes was a prominent Black poet of the Harlem Renaissance, I might not first classify this note as a poem at all, treating it instead as some dashed-off note excavated from a desk drawer or library. Spend some time with it, however, and you can see the artfulness to Hughes's framing, how he creates character and narrative from a smattering of both personal and deictic details. "Joe" is writing to his mother, whom he hasn't seen in quite a while, and has little expectation to see her anytime soon, since even Joe's girlfriend says "she hopes to lay eyes on [her] sometime in life." Joe is somewhere up north, since he notes "it has been raining cats and dogs *up/ here*" (emphasis mine) and clearly he's struggling to save money in this new, expensive city. But even with his bills, Joe manages to scrape together some money for his mother, for whom he is still the "baby" of the family, even as he wants to prove himself a man, since he signs off finally with the more formal phrase, "Respectably as ever." Joe's dialect suggests either that he might lack an advanced education, or that he simply doesn't choose to write in conventionally prescribed syntax to his mother, and these facts, too, might suggest a reason for his absence from home, as he's up north looking for work that might not be available to him in his hometown.

While the letter itself isn't dated, I can tell from Joe's reference to money that five dollars means a lot to him and is likely not an insignificant amount of money to his mother, either, probably due to both their financially precarious positions. Joe's money is a sign of respect, family connection, and support, just as his letter is a brief but telling documentary portrait of a young Black man during the Great Migration, a movement of Black Americans out of the South up to the cities scattered around the North, West, and Midwest.

Reading Hughes's poem, I know who speaks, and to whom he speaks, and—to a certain extent—the occasion on which he speaks. But the larger sense of *why* he speaks is answered by the poem overall. In a single character—an "average Joe"—I start to see a portrait of a movement take shape. I start to see the economic conditions and stresses, but more important the emotional strains and also bonds of loyalty this migration tested and sustained. The letter implies, through the girlfriend's words, that Joe, too, might never see his mother again, which makes me wonder why Joe would be reluctant to travel back home. Is it lack of money that keeps him from returning? The fact that the South holds so few opportunities, and so little safety for Black men? The answer doesn't give only one definitive reason, but by reading carefully between the lines, I start to imagine all of them and, by doing so, to see the cost of this migration—both literal and figurative—on this family. I understand the "why" of Joe's leaving has affected not only his fortunes but the lives of generations of Black Americans.

In Hughes's poem, there's also a greater or shared sense of deixis here that the poem's situation implies. Though only one character speaks, I sense that Joe is a stand-in **persona**—a character or mask—that Hughes has imagined, in part to create a communal portrait, in part to push against ideas of what a poem itself should sound like. With its plainspoken language, its deliberately clichéd imagery ("it's raining cats and dogs"), even its inconsistent use of diction, Hughes's poem may refuse to be "poetic" in many of the ways his readers were trained to see or classify as poetry. But the same careful attention we bring to a historical document or a personal letter we bring to reading a poem;

Hughes's decision to make his poem as "like" a letter as possible might reveal some of the prejudices hidden in our reading. If we treat the poem only as a found document, we risk downplaying the consciously artistic use of language by Black migrants, treating it as less sophisticated. But "Letter" is highly poetic, since it is an allegory for the experience of a larger group of people than the immediate speaker. By telling one person's story, Hughes has told us another historical one. That's what poetry does when it uses specific figures and language to work outward, to get to larger, more abstract truths and realities that we could otherwise only express via facts and graphs. The Great Migration wasn't simply a historical fact, Hughes's poem reminds us: it was a personal reality that millions of families experienced.

What Is the Form of Address? Epistles and Monologues

When addressing a particular, if imagined, other, poems may remind us of other forms of intimate writing, such as private messages, letters, or texts. "Letter," for example, while it is an example of a **persona poem**, is also an example of an **epistle**, a form of poetry written as a letter, addressed either to a public or private person but never sent. "Epistle" comes from the Latin, *epistula*, meaning "letter," and as you might guess from its etymology, the epistolary poem is one of our oldest forms of poetry. Famous classical epistles include letters from Horace on morals and philosophy, but also the *Heroides* by Ovid, a collection of fictional letters from famous (and famously aggrieved) women from mythology, such as Penelope, Dido, and Ariadne, to their wayward husbands and lovers.

Epistles can be colloquial or formal, intimate or philosophical. As you can see with "Letter," the trick is understanding that it is both a very public and private form of address, thus tone becomes important for the writer to manage. In that, it shares some features of the **dramatic monologue**, a poem spoken by an imagined speaker specifically addressing someone else. But is the epistle actually meant for the person the speaker writes to, or for a wider audience? Is the epistle a self-portrait of the author or a portrait of the addressee? Is the epistle fabricated or real? The answer to all these questions is both, but that doesn't mean we always feel comfortable with the answer. Robert Lowell, for instance, once took his ex-wife Elizabeth Hardwick's personal letters to him and turned them into sonnets, which he published as *The Dolphin*. The book caused an uproar, not just because the sonnets were appropriations but because these letters were meant to be read only by Lowell.

Lowell's adaptation—or violation—of Hardwick's letters remind me that epistolary poems, even as they blur the imagined with the real, also collapse (sometimes uncomfortably) the idea of audience with addressee. With any poem, it's important to remember that the addressee is *not* the same thing as audience, because the addressee is specifically imagined, whereas the audience can be anyone. In epistolary poems, however, a natural conflation occurs between the two in our mind, even as we know the writer has manipulated details to give the appearance of familiarity with the addressee. Anyone who has eavesdropped on a conversation between friends knows that the references shared between intimates are nearly incomprehensible to strangers. Epistolary poems craft details to provide the wider audience the illusion of overhearing one person speaking or writing to another. In that sense, epistolary poems must provide *more* deictic context so that their readers can track the relationship between speaker and addressee. But understanding that this practical and imaginative constraint exists, epistolary poems still charm with the impression of private revelation, the performance of emotional urgency. In that, *desire*—whether it be erotic, or the longing to be understood—is the true subject of the epistolary poem, whether or not the "I" or the "you" is ever autobiographically true.

Desire certainly is the subject of one of my own favorite epistolary poems, "Epistle to Miss Blount, On Her Leaving the Town, After the Coronation," by Alexander Pope.

> As some fond virgin, whom her mother's care
> Drags from the town to wholesome country air,
> Just when she learns to roll a melting eye,
> And hear a spark, yet think no danger nigh;
> From the dear man unwillingly she must sever,
> Yet takes one kiss before she parts for ever:
> Thus from the world fair Zephalinda flew,
> Saw others happy, and with sighs withdrew;
> Not that their pleasures caused her discontent,
> She sighed not that They stayed, but that She went.
> She went, to plain-work, and to purling brooks,
> Old-fashioned halls, dull aunts, and croaking rooks,
> She went from Opera, park, assembly, play,
> To morning walks, and prayers three hours a day;
> To pass her time 'twixt reading and Bohea,
> To muse, and spill her solitary tea,
> Or o'er cold coffee trifle with the spoon,
> Count the slow clock, and dine exact at noon;
> Divert her eyes with pictures in the fire,
> Hum half a tune, tell stories to the squire;
> Up to her godly garret after seven,
> There starve and pray, for that's the way to heaven.
> Some Squire, perhaps, you take a delight to rack;
> Whose game is Whisk, whose treat a toast in sack,
> Who visits with a gun, presents you birds,
> Then gives a smacking buss, and cries—No words!

Or with his hound comes hollowing from the stable,
Makes love with nods, and knees beneath a table;
Whose laughs are hearty, tho' his jests are coarse,
And loves you best of all things—but his horse.
In some fair evening, on your elbow laid,
Your dream of triumphs in the rural shade;
In pensive thought recall the fancied scene,
See Coronations rise on every green;
Before you pass th' imaginary sights
Of Lords, and Earls, and Dukes, and gartered Knights;
While the spread fan o'ershades your closing eyes;
Then give one flirt, and all the vision flies.
Thus vanish scepters, coronets, and balls,
And leave you in lone woods, or empty walls.
So when your slave, at some dear, idle time,
(Not plagued with headaches, or the want of rhyme)
Stands in the streets, abstracted from the crew,
And while he seems to study, thinks of you:
Just when his fancy points your sprightly eyes,
Or sees the blush of soft Parthenia rise,
Gay pats my shoulder, and you vanish quite;
Streets, chairs, and coxcombs rush upon my sight;
Vexed to be still in town, I knit my brow,
Look sour, and hum a tune—as you may now.

While not a love poem per se, Pope's epistolary poem is still full of longing, shaped by a deep, empathetic attachment Pope has to Miss Blount (pronounced "Blunt") that feels both playful and personal, in large part because of the full rhymes of Pope's heroic couplets and because Pope so intimately imagines all the little indignities and vexations that shape Miss Blount's day. Pope, more famous perhaps for "The Rape of the Lock" and his didactic "Essay on Man," delights here with his wit and facility with rhyme, and his compassion for the real young woman at the heart of this poem.

Miss Theresa Blount—called here alternately "Zephalinda," a pet nickname Pope had given her as a child, and "Parthenia"—is, at the height of her popularity, being dragged from London's social Bohemia ("Bohea") by her mother to the countryside to be morally improved and wooed by the local mouth-breathers. What's remarkable is the sympathy Pope displays for the boredoms and indignities Miss Blount suffers: the endless "dull aunts" and "solitary tea(s)," the soul-grinding hours spent at church and prayer, even the coarse attempts at lovemaking by the local squire, who appears dubiously enamored of his pets.

Pope's imagination of these events becomes the backdrop for his portrait of Miss Blount as a real young woman with ambitions of her own: a woman who is just beginning to understand her own sexual power and may herself be a touch too enamored of the superficial charms of London life. Still, the poem doesn't lecture her on her youthful choice of amusements, since clearly Miss Blount gets enough of that at home. Though she "dream(s) of triumphs" that Pope knows would be romantic, and though these dozing visions of court life threaten to vanish in "one flirt" of her waking, Pope remains her champion. He satirizes her situation, but gently.

Notice how the poem begins by referring to Miss Blount in the third person but, by the middle of the poem, becomes explicitly addressed to her in the second. As Pope imagines Miss Blount's life through his capacities as a poet, it appears he grows closer to her as a friend as well, until by the end both Pope and Miss Blount—though separated by situation and distance—make the same frustrated gesture at their separation.

Just as the personal address in "Epistle to Miss Blount" changes, its tone also changes, moving from light-hearted comedy to social satire to something melancholy as, by poem's end, Miss Blount becomes a vision for Pope, similar to the fantasies Miss

Blount has of court life in London. She, too, changes from the fanciful "Zephalinda" to something more mysterious, abstract, even divine: "Parthenia," the Greek word for "maiden," and an explicit reference to the goddess Athena. "Parthenia," interestingly, is also the pet name Pope used for Theresa Blount's sister, Martha, with whom he had a lifelong intimate friendship—one that exceeded his with Theresa, with whom he reportedly quarreled later in life. By the time Pope's friend and fellow poet John Gay claps Pope on the back to awaken him from his reverie, the young woman he imagines or mistakes for his friend (or her sister) has vanished, as the real Miss Blount—through her inevitable maturation and marriage in the world outside this poem–will likely disappear from his life as well.

We might be tempted to classify this epistle as a conventional love poem but, though romantic in its feeling for Miss Blount, I don't read it as such. As you can tell, Pope and Miss Blount were of different ages when the poem was written. And while this fact wouldn't have precluded a relationship, the fact that "Zephalinda" becomes "Parthenia" suggests that Pope is truly romanticizing the moments *any* "Miss Blount" comes of age.

I think I sense this most strongly from the framing of the poem, in which Miss Blount is physically removed from London to the countryside, which parallels her change from young adolescence to womanhood. That's the story Pope seems really attracted to, and if we might be concerned that he fetishizes her youth, I think the romantic tone may also be complicated by Pope's biography. Sickly as a child, height dramatically stunted by illness, Pope was raised in a strict Roman Catholic family in Binfield, Berkshire, kept from school due to his family's religion. He was able to satirize so precisely the zealotry that comprised country life because he'd lived it; in fact, Theresa and Martha Blount were his neighbors.

In the end, perhaps his own physical and social differences helped Pope better imagine Miss Blount's frustrations. In his poem, Miss Blount is subject to the whims of all sorts of people and institutions: mother, aunts, the church, the squire. His understanding of the limitations of her agency might stem from his own experience of living in a body that, for some, socially limited him as a man. Perhaps that's another reason why he refers to Miss Blount's status as a maiden twice in the poem: it not only emphasizes the fact she's coming of age but that her body itself is still (in a patriarchal sense) being surveilled.

Finally, what moves me about the poem is its intensely dream-like quality. Notice how many daydreams and visions are referenced within "Epistle": there's Pope's speculative musings on Miss Blount, Miss Blount's own daydreams of court and London, then Pope's reverie of himself envisioning her back in London that, by the end of the poem, I'm lost inside a spell. These daydreams become **rhyming actions** in the poem, pairing Pope and Miss Blount together much in the same way that the rhymes in couplets create a sense of both parallelism and completion. Like Pope, I'm regretfully startled awake from this enchanting picture of Miss Blount and want to return immediately to the poem's beginning: to relive once more the few, evanescent moments in which Miss Blount is again young, vibrant, and alive, a creation both of Pope's admiration and mine.

Is the Speaker a Persona?

As you can see, Pope transformed a lot of actual, biographical details about the Misses Blount and himself into an imaginative letter that speaks to Pope's sense of their relationship as a whole, not just one season in Miss Blount's life. The fact that Pope links Theresa and Martha Blount in his epistolary poem by switching between their nicknames also reminds me that, though the poem purports to be a verse portrait, in reality it is a collage. Of course, any poem becomes such a mix: rarely does a poem's speaker stick to strict biographical details and facts, and rarely does any lyric poem comprehensively encapsulate the writer's self. All poems alchemize bits and pieces of truth to produce a larger Truth that the reader assembles ("Tell all the truth," Emily Dickinson wrote, "but tell it slant"). Thus all poems, whether epistolary or not, share something with persona poems in that the figures speaking and being spoken to are, at heart, masks.

That said, traditionally, persona poems are poems spoken by a character other than the author. They offer us the possibility of imaginatively and momentarily experiencing the thoughts and feelings of another, or of expressing ideas we ourselves may not share. Charles Baudelaire saw persona poetry as natural, claiming that the poet "[l]ike a wandering soul seeking a body . . . can enter, whenever he wishes, into anyone's personality." We may currently balk at the thought of writing in and through the body of another, dismissing this work as appropriative and inauthentic. In that, we might agree with the romantic poet Samuel Taylor Coleridge, who wrote in one 1796 notebook, "Poetry—excites us to artificial feelings—makes us callous to real ones." Certainly persona poetry's theatricality, its plasticity of perspective reveals its ancient roots with drama itself. We may prefer the declared virtues of authenticity, but this can make us terrible readers of poems if we refuse to imagine or even see where the poet and the speaker diverge. Persona poems make this split explicit, of course, often by declaring in the title who the speaker of the poem actually is.

Like the epistolary poem, persona poems question the relationship of a poem's author with its audience and, because of this, may divide into subtypes of persona poems. For example, if the persona is meant to stand apart finally from the author's identity, as with Robert Browning's Duke of Ferrara in "My Last Duchess" or Ai's Joseph McCarthy, then these poems suggest the poet has an ironic relationship to her character and encourage the reader to critically reevaluate the poem's suggestion of sincerity and "transparent" language. Some persona poems, such as John

Ashbery's "Daffy Duck in Hollywood," might even ask the reader to investigate what it means to be a self at all, parodying the idea that a poem is meant to be self-expression, and capitalizing on the rift readers feel between the "sincere" poem of personal expression and the artificial construction of poems themselves.

Other persona poems, however, suggest the revelation (or deconstruction) of the poet's truest self. In that, certain persona poems give their authors an opportunity to express attitudes that elevate their own beliefs, or feelings that they might want otherwise to repress. You can see this in John Berryman's *Dream Songs*, in which Henry, Berryman's alter ego, has yet another alter ego, Mr. Bones, with whom Henry bats about ideas about social propriety, self-control, and his own suicidal ideation. You see this, too, in the *Inferno*, where Virgil acts both as a literal guide to Dante through hell, as well as his figurative counterpart in poetry itself.

But if persona poems offer us the ability to express ideas we might privately hold or publicly disagree with, they also offer us the space to examine larger institutions or moments of history. Hughes's "Letter," for example, does this for the Great Migration, but I'm also thinking of the persona poems that Randall Jarrell wrote about World War II, in particular his famous "The Death of the Ball Turret Gunner," in which he compresses the life and death of a single airman into a mere five lines:

> From my mother's sleep I fell into the State,
> And I hunched in its belly till my wet fur froze.
> Six miles from earth, loosed from its dream of life,
> I woke to black flak and the nightmare fighters.
> When I died they washed me out of the turret with a hose.

Jarrell's poem opens on two images of physical passivity: the first, the sleeping body of the gunner's mother; the second, the body of the gunner himself who "falls" into the State. Throughout the poem, the gunner seems largely asleep; only in the fourth line does he wake to "black flak and the nightmare fighters": an image that extends the speaker's unconscious state and picks up on the previous image of the earth itself as a noose-like web of dreams. Waking is the speaker's most active moment in the poem, since otherwise he merely falls, hunches, or is sprayed out of his turret—all activities that reinforce his numbness. The airman's sleeping mother, too, is replaced by the icy, maternal image of the State, inside of which the speaker "hunch[es]," like a seal fetus, the collar of his leather bomber jacket become a symbol for the gunner's body, as if he were covered not by human clothing but fur. The subhuman condition the speaker imagines for himself is of course reinforced by the flatness of that end line, the unsentimental ways in which his remains are blithely "washed" out of the turret with a hose.

For such a short lyric, Jarrell's poem contains a remarkable compression of time and event. In five lines, the gunner is given birth to twice: first by his human mother, then by the state, which "loose[s]" him from the earth's "dream of life." This birth is also distantly recalled in that gory last line, suggestive of the cleaning of an operating table. In Jarrell's poem, the gunner is born merely to die, a bitter political analysis captured by the poem's rhyming of "froze" with "hose," which lends the poem the air of a moral epigram.

But if the gunner is figured as a feral child, passive in his resistance to the state that has both bred him for war and led him to his slaughter, in one important sense his immaturity also protects him from our critique. Jarrell's poem suggests that, because he's just born and barely conscious, the gunner is absent from any realm of political agency. It is the gunner's passivity, his very *lack* of being seen as fully adult or human, that makes him so innocent to us. We might have any number of feelings about the justice of war, but about the gunner's death we can have only pity.

Does the Speaker Use Apostrophe?

As I wrote before, all poems are addressed to someone, even if the addressee is only imagined by the poet. Sometimes this address is simply the self-conscious cry of delight, praise, or even woe in the poem that we call **apostrophe**, which you can see in Walt Whitman's poem "Apostroph":

> O mater! O fils!
> O brood continental!
> O flowers of the prairies!
> O space boundless! O hum of mighty products!
> O you teeming cities! O so invincible, turbulent, proud!
> O race of the future! O women!
> O fathers! O you men of passion and the storm!
> O native power only! O beauty!
> O yourself! O God! O divine average!

Sometimes, poems are explicitly addressed to their readers, as in John Keats's "This living hand, now warm and capable":

> This living hand, now warm and capable
> Of earnest grasping, would, if it were cold
> And in the icy silence of the tomb,
> So haunt thy days and chill thy dreaming nights
> That thou would wish thine own heart dry of blood
> So in my veins red life might stream again,
> And thou be conscience-calm'd—see here it is—
> I hold it towards you.

Or to a very specific "you," as in Will Alexander's "Based on the Bush of Ghosts," written to friend and Nigerian author Amos Tutuola:

you
Tutuola
compatible with cosmic infra-forces
with wheat that blazes
rife with its own combustible plane

Sometimes poems blur the line between addressing another and addressing the self. This occurs when the poem uses the second-person perspective entirely or, as you can see in Meghan O'Rourke's instruction-poem, when it weaves between the second- and third-person perspectives.

INVENTING A HORSE

Inventing a horse is not easy. One must not only think of
    the horse.
One must dig fence posts around him.
One must include a place where horses like to live;

or do when they live with humans like you.
Slowly, you must walk him in the cold;
feed him bran mash, apples;
accustom him to the harness;

holding in mind even when you are tired
harnesses and tack cloths and saddle oil
to keep the saddle clean as a face in the sun;
one must imagine teaching him to run

among the knuckles of tree roots,
not to be skittish at first sight of timber wolves,
and not to grow thin in the city,
where at some point you will have to live;

and one must imagine the absence of money.
Most of all, though: the living weight,
the sound of his feet on the needles,
and, since he is heavy, and real,

and sometimes tired after a run
down the river with a light whip at his side,
one must imagine love
in the mind that does not know love,

an animal mind, a love that does not depend
on your image of it,
your understanding of it;
indifferent to all that it lacks:

a muzzle and two black eyes
looking the day away, a field empty
of everything but witchgrass, fluent trees,
and some piles of hay.

O'Rourke's poem doesn't just walk its reader step-by-step through imagining a horse, it reveals where imagination finally ends when trying to encompass the reality of another being. For me, the poem's central argument resides in the sixth and seventh stanzas, when she writes:

one must imagine love
in the mind that does not know love,

an animal mind, a love that does not depend
on your image of it,
your understanding of it . . .

It's here that I realize how O'Rourke's use of the second person enhances the poem's argument. By being addressed to and framed from the perspective of "you," the poem tries to narrow the gap between O'Rourke the author and me the reader. In reality, this gap can never be bridged, because O'Rourke doesn't know me or how I would imagine a horse. She can't really be speaking to or for me at all, just as I can't invent a horse completely in my mind. Even as her images allow me to take in so much of the horse's physical embodiment, what I can't penetrate is its psyche: what it feels, or doesn't, what it actually sees and knows. Some part of the horse must always remain outside my imaginative grasp, just as I remain outside of O'Rourke's. To O'Rourke, I am, in that sense, a little like the horse itself: a being "that does not depend/ on your image of it."

Lyric Apostrophe

You could call what O'Rourke and Keats do a form of **lyric apostrophe**, a commonly used form of address in poetry, which makes the poet's voice seem widely available to all. Adrienne Rich uses it as the framing device of her poem "XIII (Dedications)":

> I know you are reading this poem
> late, before leaving your office
> of the one intense yellow lamp-spot and the
>   darkening window
> in the lassitude of a building faded to quiet
> long after rush-hour.   I know you are reading this poem
> standing up in a bookstore far from the ocean
> on a gray day of early spring, faint flakes driven
> across the plains' enormous spaces around you.
> I know you are reading this poem

in a room where too much has happened for you to bear
where the bedclothes lie in stagnant coils on the bed
and the open valise speaks of flight
but you cannot leave yet.   I know you are reading this poem
As the underground train loses momentum and before
                    running up the stairs
toward a new kind of love
your life has never allowed.
I know you are reading this poem by the light
of the television screen where soundless images
        jerk and slide
while you wait for the newscast from the intifada.
I know you are reading this poem in a waiting-room
of eyes met and unmeeting, of identity with strangers.
I know you are reading this poem by fluorescent light
in the boredom and fatigue of the young who are
        counted out,
count themselves out, at too early an age.   I know
you are reading this poem through your failing
        sight, the thick
lens enlarging these letters beyond all meaning yet
        you read on
because even the alphabet is precious.
I know you are reading this poem as you pace
        beside the stove
warming milk, a crying child on your shoulder, a book
        in your hand
because life is short and you too are thirsty.
I know you are reading this poem which is not in
        your language
guessing at some words while others keep you reading
and I want to know which words they are.
I know you are reading this poem listening for something,

> torn between bitterness and hope
> turning back once again to the task you cannot refuse.
> I know you are reading this poem because there is nothing
>   else left to read
> there where you have landed, stripped as you are.

Here, much in the same way that O'Rourke has imagined a horse for her readers, I know that Rich has imagined each of the people she is "dedicating" her poem to, even as these people are all made-up characters. In that, her use of apostrophe capitalizes on something I believe is inherent to the lyric poem in general. If the lyric collapses the distance between the moment of time and space in which a poem is written and the place in which the reader currently stands, then apostrophe in particular takes advantage of this compression, making the poem feel to the reader as if it is spontaneously unfolding before her and bringing her into an imagined and immediate fellowship with the author. This fellowship is false, of course, but lyric apostrophe suggests both immediacy *and* intimacy.

When Rich uses lyric apostrophe in "XIII (Dedication)," she does it explicitly to bring reader and writer into intimate communion. At the same time, by switching between a variety of different yous whom she addresses, she changes from intimate dedication to larger public address, widening the scope of community and showing the complex interconnectedness of our global relationship. Because each person she imagines is so distinctly rendered from the others, I understand she wants me to imagine her speaking to a wide array of individuals, not just one idealized "you," even as all these may be imaginative projections of herself. But by my imagining each different "you," I also become the "you" whom Rich addresses. I become part of a wider network, too, even as Rich's network imagines each addressee as singular and local, and privileges each "you" on account of her individuality.

Walt Whitman famously achieves something similar in "Song of Myself" when he writes these lines:

> Stop this day and night with me and you shall possess the
>   origin of all poems,
> You shall possess the good of the earth and sun, (there are
>   millions of suns left,)
> You shall no longer take things at second or third hand,
>   nor look through the eyes of the dead, nor feed on the
>   spectres in books,
> You shall not look through my eyes either, nor take
>   things from me,
> You shall listen to all sides and filter them from your self.

As you can see, both poems are wide-ranging, democratic in their address. I recognize their use of apostrophe to be not just a lyric connection between writer and reader, then, but a desire to achieve a more profound political connection.

This, of course, is a very different kind of apostrophe from the one in O'Rourke's poem, or Arthur Sze's "First Snow." Returning to Sze's poem a moment, notice that, because Sze writes the poem in second-person perspective, there is no division *at all* between speaker and addressee. Using the second person is similar to apostrophe in that the writer attempts to bridge the distance between author and reader, but it's different because the reader is asked to inhabit the experience of the author; in that, the second-person position creates an uncanny collapse between self and other. But why would Sze do that? Again, tracking Sze's central metaphor as it moves across the poem, I can't help but notice that if we possess nothing about the world that we inhabit, and if every moment of perceived time dissolves into the recollection of another, there is no reason for the self alone to be stable. Sze's awareness of the instability of the world really isn't just specific to his own experience, then: it is, like it or not, a universal truth. In that case, "you" or "I" makes no difference of perspective. There is no purpose to privileging individuation, whether of self or memory, because in the end we own nothing, perhaps not even a singular consciousness.

The Second Person and the Limits of Empathy

Looking at Rich, Whitman, and Sze, I see how apostrophe and the second person in poetry can have expansive lyric, as well as democratic, effects. But can the use of a generalized "you" also signal the *limits* of affiliation? I'm struck, for instance, by the way that the second-person perspective functions in Claudia Rankine's book *Citizen*. A book-length poem that includes lyric essays and images, *Citizen* examines the microaggressions that African Americans in particular face in public life, and the ways their race has been both artistically and socially imagined to preserve racist hierarchies. By using the second-person perspective to detail microaggressions Rankine herself may have witnessed or experienced, we might assume that Rankine is inviting us to share in her private encounters as a Black woman among white people. Certainly the second-person perspective helps ease a reader into a kind of sympathetic awareness of what it means to be Black in America while also reminding the reader of an essential difference that still exists between Rankine and her audience. Not everyone reading *Citizen* is Black; thus not everyone will have experienced the same encounters that Rankine endured. The second person perspective is not just a moment of intimate collapse between author and reader, then, so much as a directive for that reader to exist, if even momentarily, in a space she may never before have inhabited. It's a way of forcing people to experience the subjectivity of racism; a way, too, perhaps, of speaking directly to those who might discount other people's experiences of racism with the dismissive statement "Maybe it just seemed racist to *you*." At the same time, the second-person perspective may not necessarily be situated in a singular idea of "you" at all, since the microaggressions that Rankine details are so various that we could imagine them endured by an array of people over time. In that, the "you" who frames this book may be part of an ever-expanding web of yous—as each racist anecdote might be endured by a different subject, so the community of "you" grows and enlarges, across time and across the nation.

What strikes me about *Citizen* is how I read its use of the second-person perspective as both the desire for the Black individual to become one among others, one equal to others, as well as the persistent realization that the Black self is always imagined as particular; simultaneously monitored and invisible. In other words, even as the second-person perspective works to bring Rankine and the reader into closer connection, that "you" gets located back into a distinctly African American experience. Thus, the use of the second person, even as it gestures toward a universal humanity, also speaks to me of a social reality that Rankine's "you" suspects may never be overcome:

> Even now your voice entangled this mouth
> whose words are here as pulse, strumming
> shout out, shut in, shut up—
>
> You cannot say—
>
> a body translates its you—
>
> you there, hey you
>
> even as it loses the location of its mouth.

In contrast, while Tracy K. Smith's poem "Declaration" doesn't use apostrophe itself, something similar happens in her erasure poem that unearths the African American history buried within the Declaration of Independence's implied apostrophic address to American subjects and British rulers.

DECLARATION

He has

sent hither swarms of Officers to harass

He has plundered our—

                    Ravaged our—

Taking away our—

                    Abolishing our most valuable

and altering fundamentally the Forms of our—

In every stage of these Oppressions We have Petitioned for

Redress in the most humble terms:

                              Our repeated

Petitions have been answered only by repeated injury.

We have reminded them of the circumstances of
    our emigration
and settlement here.

—taken Captive
on the high Seas

to bear—

If the intended audience for the Declaration of Independence was the British monarchy and white male landowners in the American colonies, Smith's poem brings to light a different group of speakers, and with it a different historical and cultural audience. The "we" that comprises the original Declaration has here been changed to a communal and transhistorical African American voice, speaking not just to a past but present audience of living white Americans. Smith's erasure reminds us that within the Declaration lives another narrative the framers always wanted to erase but which can be easily uncovered. Her erasure also reveals the original document's fractal narrative possibilities: "taken Captive//on the high seas// to bear" is language that, in its original context, referred to the arrival of the Puritans and first colonists. In Smith's poem, of course, it refers to the Middle Passage and the slave trade. Images of British brutality against the colonists can now equally speak to white colonial abuse of African or Indigenous people, just as the legitimate demand for representation and reparations by white colonists can now express the frustration experienced by African Americans to have their own history acknowledged. The brilliance of the erasure form here allows me to see how two documents always existed within one, as the language of each community intertwines in one shared complaint: the basic desire to be recognized as human and placed as equal participants in history, even as the erasure itself highlights, too, how one group of Americans was always rendered invisible.

As you can see, apostrophe and the use of the direct or—in Smith's case—implied second person is tricky precisely because their call to the reader is both public and private, both for the self and for the other. In many cases, "you" and "I" may be false distinctions as they become, in the reader's mind, inherently elided: Who is the poet speaking to except for the self? In reality, no poet knows who will read her poem in the future, thus "you" becomes a deliberate construction that asks us to determine in what ways we, too, choose—or don't choose—to be included in that pronoun. Perhaps we sense that we cannot finally be part of the poet's address, that a place exists where the poet's vision of the world and our own must split apart, as both O'Rourke and Rankine remind us. In either way, address is one way that poets claim a community, and maybe, if we decide to see ourselves as the poem's audience, for that community to be expanded through our own perspective, our own reading, even our own bodies in time.

EXPERIMENTS

- Choose a poem from the following list and discuss who speaks, why, and for what reason. How would you characterize the speaker? Who is being addressed? If the speaker is a persona, do you agree with the way the speaker sees the events unfold around him or her? How does the speaker see him or herself? If the speaker is from another literary work you recognize, or from a historical event, how does this speaker reframe how we see either the original work or event?
- Choose a notable figure or type of person you strongly disagree with. Now write a monologue from that person's perspective, detailing that person's point of view about a moment of crisis that s/he experienced.

- Choose a relatively unknown or even imagined person—
  the spouse or child of a famous politician, artist, or actor,
  for example, or a servant or tradesperson. Write from his/
  her perspective about an important event that defined his/
  her life during a time we might recognize from history.
- Write a poem composed of a list of instructions or commands to someone.

SUGGESTED WORKS TO CONSIDER

Kevin Young, "Reward"
Deborah Greger, "Miranda's Drowned Book"
Jane Kenyon, "Gettysburg: July 1, 1863"
Ai, "Interview with a Policeman"
Thomas James, "Mummy of a Lady
    Named Jemutesonekh"
Louise Erdrich, "Captivity"
Patricia Smith, "Katrina"
Philip Levine, "What Work Is"
Matthew Olzmann, "Letter Beginning with Two Lines
    by Czesław Miłosz"
Czesław Miłosz, "Dedication"
Phillip B. Williams, "Do-Rag"
Mark Wunderlich, "Coyote, with Mange"

All poems can be found at the Poetry Foundation or the Academy of American Poets websites.

CHAPTER FOUR

How Would You Characterize the Poem's Syntax?

Years ago, in graduate school, a poet friend slipped a folded piece of paper into my notebook. *You won't believe it*, she wrote at the top of the fold. *But I just spent all afternoon arguing with my workshop about whether this was a poem.* When I unfolded the paper, I found this:

A STORY ABOUT THE BODY

Robert Hass

The young composer, working that summer at an artist's colony, had watched her for a week. She was Japanese, a painter, almost sixty, and he thought he was in love with her. He loved her work, and her work was like the way she moved her body, used her hands, looked at him directly when she mused and considered answers to his questions. One night, walking back from a concert, they came to her door and she turned to him and said, "I think you would like to have me. I would like that too, but I must tell you that I have had a double mastectomy," and when he didn't understand, "I've lost both my breasts." The radiance that he had carried around in his belly and chest cavity—like music—withered quickly, and he made himself look at her when he said, "I'm sorry. I don't think I could." He walked back to his own cabin through the pines, and in the morning, he found a small blue bowl on the porch outside his door. It looked to be full of rose petals, but he found when he picked it up that the rose petals were on top; the rest of the bowl—she must have swept the corners of her studio—was full of dead bees.

I read the paragraph twice, baffled. Wasn't it obviously a poem? I certainly didn't see any issue with poems composed of prose at the time, and I'm still not bothered by seeing the genres mixed together now, since I understand some sense of any prose paragraph "works" along similar lines to poetry, if we imagine each paragraph as a unit of sense, time, sound, and—unlike the poetic stanza—completion and unity. Having taught for years, I now know that prose poetry has been in Western literature since the nineteenth century, written by poets like Arthur Rimbaud and Pierre Reverdy, and even earlier in Japan, where Heian court poets like Sei Shōnagon wrote **zuihitsu**, fragmentary personal observations that combined poetry with prose. Hass's prose poem is just one of a long line of poems influenced by European and Latin American poets like Tomas Tranströmer and Julio Cortázar, as well as American poets Edgar Allan Poe and Russell Edson. For these poets, as for poets now, genre is always being invented.

Of course, I didn't know that information at the time. Still, I instinctively shared my friend's bafflement. Perhaps any consternation over a prose poem published over twenty years ago seems quaint to the current reader, though I still know a critic or two who believes that no true poem abandons lineation. For these critics, the very definition of a poem resides in its fidelity to the line, especially when free verse largely eschews metrical effects, and all other literary devices can be found in prose. As James Longenbach wrote in *The Art of the Poetic Line*, "Poetry is the sound of language organized *in lines*" (emphasis mine). So what happens when the line itself disappears? Does the poem subsequently vanish? Or is there a way a sentence might signal its affiliation to the line, even if it has dispensed with lineation?

Hass's prose poem for me contains a sense of line because in it I hear a clear and building rhythm, one that feels profoundly attached to the poem's use of characterization and narrative design. This rhythm doesn't come from regular prosody, of course; it has to do with the structure of Hass's sentences. If you read the poem out loud, you can hear how complex his syntax is. Hass's verse paragraph—also called a **strophe**—may be only seven sentences long, but each sentence grows increasingly byzantine, packing in clause after clause, even whole swathes of dialogue into single sentences. That's because Hass employs **hypotaxis**: a grammatical device that relies on a pileup of subordinating clauses, distinguished by subordinating conjunctions such as "although," "since," "before," "once," "while," or "because." Hypotaxis is complex syntax that suggests hierarchies of information; in effect, the reader is asked to determine *which* description or action is more important than another as she tracks a sentence's main thought, as you can see in this example:

> This morning, while walking my dog, I went to the store to buy bread, milk, cheese, which my cousin, who had eaten all these things yesterday by himself, wanted.

Closely tracking the information in this sentence, you find that its primary point is that I went to get some things from the store for my cousin, the secondary point is that I did this while walking my dog, and the third point is that my cousin wanted these things because he's greedy.

If I wanted, I could rewrite the sentence the following way:

> This morning I walked my dog and then I went to the store. I bought bread and milk and cheese for my cousin. He ate everything yesterday by himself and wanted them again today.

These sentences are an example of **parataxis**, which refers to simple, declarative sentences that combine actions through the use of coordinating conjunctions like "and," "for," "but," "or," or "nor." Parataxis literally means "placing side by side," and we can also see it at work when we put two sentences together that have no clear logical relationship between them, such as this:

It's raining. My sister flew into town yesterday.

Hypotaxis suggests hierarchies of meaning and relationship; parataxis suggests equivalence. Often, parataxis also invites reader interpretation based on this equivalence—there may be no logical relationship between my sister's arrival and the fact that it's raining, but a reader might intuit that her sudden appearance in town isn't—at least according to the Weather Channel—a cheerful event.

As you can see, Hass uses both techniques in his prose poem, which is natural, since we all move between hypotaxis and parataxis in writing and speech. But it's that movement between the two that generates the poem's building rhythm and also makes for its powerful ending. Hass's use of hypotaxis most closely tracks the young composer's internal musings, since at these moments Hass's sentences build and unfurl much like a piece of music might, or the composer's own desire for the painter. Notice how, as the composer gets emotionally closer to the painter, Hass's syntax grows hurried:

He loved her work, and her work was like the way she moved her body, used her hands, looked at him directly when she mused and considered answers to his questions.

This sentence uses a lot of paratactic coordinating conjunctions, which arrive in a pileup of detail, a catalogue of the painter's attractions that make me feel the composer's own mounting lust. Then we get this sentence:

> One night, walking back from a concert, they came to her door and she turned to him and said, "I think you would like to have me. I would like that too, but I must tell you that I have had a double mastectomy," and when he didn't understand, "I've lost both my breasts."

Notice how this one sentence carries within it three sentences of the painter's dialogue. What happens afterward is—syntactically and emotionally speaking—deflating. After the painter tells the young composer about her mastectomy, his desire clearly fades. While the next sentence also contains within it several clauses and also two lines of dialogue spoken by the composer, those two lines are flat, clipped, extremely simple: "I'm sorry. I don't think I could." At this point, Hass's syntax has wound down and become more direct. But then the poem's syntax ramps up again in those startling last two sentences:

> He walked back to his own cabin through the pines, and in the morning, he found a small blue bowl on the porch outside his door. It looked to be full of rose petals, but he found when he picked it up that the rose petals were on top; the rest of the bowl—she must have swept the corners of her studio—was full of dead bees.

Rewrite that last sentence so that the semicolon and parenthetical disappears, and the result might sound like this:

> It looked to be full of rose petals, but he found when he picked it up that the rose petals were on top. The rest of the bowl was full of dead bees she'd swept from her studio.

What a crappy ending! As you can see, it's Hass's parenthetical addition—the "she must have swept the corners of her studio" inserted into that last sentence—that creates both anticipation and psychological drama. It also allows the poem to end on a direct image that the composer and reader must immediately confront, rather than an action that we must imagine has taken place in the past. We see both how deliberate and artful the painter's response was to the young composer's sexual rejection, and we also feel the same shock of surprise with that image of the bees. Hass's poem is about artists negotiating attraction and rejection, thus his poem is also a piece of art; it is, after all "A *Story* About the Body" (emphasis mine). When I read this prose poem, I can feel three different arts at play: music (here approximated through Hass's syntax), visual art (here in the image of the bee-filled bowl), and poetry (here, again, in Hass's narrative). Hass's syntactic choices are deliberately suspenseful in order to respect each type of art, as well as to reveal some part of his characters' psychology.

Hass's poem requires that I track his punctuation in ways I might normally overlook, since absent any visual line breaks, it's the punctuation that both creates and accentuates the accelerating—and decelerating—rhythms of his clauses. In that, Hass reminds me that the first form any poem undertakes is the sentence, which may be one reason I have no problem treating prose poems *as* poems. Syntax is a container; it shapes meaning and creates anticipation in much the same ways that repeated line endings, rhymes, and metrical feet might do in formal verse. Hass's poem also reveals that sentences are revelations of character and, as such, are the foundation of poetic **voice**, heightening the poet's specific choice of diction, imagery, repetition, and tone. In that, syntactical style serves either as one of the first invitations or deterrents to the poem. For me, I notice that no matter how complex the syntax in "A Story About the Body" becomes, Hass makes subject, object, and verb clear through precise punctuation. I suspect this is because the story he wants to tell is so psychologically multilayered, residing not in action but interior revelation that, as a piece of narrative realism, it requires its syntax, punctuation, and language be transparent. That is, Hass's sentences don't call attention to themselves so that I can focus instead on the *ideas* these sentences transmit. But a lot of poems do call attention to their syntactic choices, even consciously disrupting the flow of the sentence itself, as you can see in the following poem by the poet Russell Atkins. In "Trainyard at Night," bursts of onomatopoeic language, as well as assonance and consonance (more on these in Chapter 7), erupt between Atkins's more conventional syntax, the poem dissolving into repeated sounds meant to evoke the noise of a train itself.

TRAINYARD AT NIGHT

TH UN DER·TH UN DER
the huge bold blasts black
hiss insists upon hissing insists
on insisting on hissing hiss
hiss s sss ss sss ssss s
ss sssss ssss
when whoosh!
the sharp scrap making its fourth lap
with a lot of rattletrap
and slap rap and crap—
I listen in time to hear coming on
the great Limited
it rolls scrolls of fold of fold
like one traditionally old
coldly, meanwhile hiss hiss

hiss insists upon hissing insists
on insisting on hissing hiss
hiss s ss ss sss sss s

sss s s

s

When we first learn to write, we're taught that clarity is of utmost importance, but in poetry, syntax is also an opportunity to disrupt, to find alternative ways to explore and even elevate aspects of character, mood, sound, and meaning. It's one reason I find Paul Celan's "Death Fugue" so effective, as it's through syntax that he manages to convey not only some part of the Holocaust's horror but also its enduring psychological effects on survivors. Celan, a Romanian Jew, was forced to work in a labor camp during World War II while his parents were sent to a Nazi concentration camp, where they died. Celan himself barely survived, and he lived to become one of the first postwar poets struggling to represent the Holocaust in poetry. Though fluent in French and influenced by the French surrealists, Celan chose to write in German, and his famous poem "Death Fugue"—which Celan came to dislike, preferring his later, more oblique poetic-language experiments—became one of the most celebrated poems about the Holocaust's atrocities. As you might intuit from Michael Hamburger's English translation here, the poem's original German is disorienting, its syntax difficult, if not impossible, to approximate exactly in English.

DEATH FUGUE

Black milk of daybreak we drink it at sundown
we drink it at noon in the morning we drink it at night
we drink and we drink it
we dig a grave in the breezes there one lies unconfined
A man lives in the house he plays with the serpents he writes

he writes when dusk falls to Germany your golden
    hair Margarete
he writes it and steps out of doors and the stars are flashing he
     whistles his pack out
he whistles his Jews out in earth has them dig for a grave
he commands us strike up for the dance

Black milk of daybreak we drink you at night
we drink in the morning at noon we drink you at sundown
we drink and we drink you
A man lives in the house he plays with the serpents he writes
he writes when dusk falls to Germany your golden
    hair Margarete
your ashen hair Shulamith we dig a grave in the breezes there
one lies unconfined.

He calls out jab deeper into the earth you lot you others sing
     now and play
he grabs at the iron in his belt he waves it his eyes are blue
jab deeper you lot with your spades you others play on
    for the dance

Black milk of daybreak we drink you at night
we drink you at noon in the morning we drink you at sundown
we drink you and we drink you
a man lives in the house your golden hair Margarete
your ashen hair Shulamith he plays with the serpents

He calls out more sweetly play death death is a master
    from Germany
he calls out more darkly now stroke your strings then as smoke
    you will rise into air
then a grave you will have in the clouds there one
    lies unconfined

Black milk of daybreak we drink you at night
we drink you at noon death is a master from Germany
we drink you at sundown and in the morning we drink and
    we drink you
death is a master from Germany his eyes are blue
he strikes you with leaden bullets his aim is true
a man lives in the house your golden hair Margarete
he sets his pack on to us he grants us a grave in the air
he plays with the serpents and daydreams death is a master
    from Germany

your golden hair Margarete
your ashen hair Shulamith

I like Hamburger's translation largely because he preserves, or
perhaps reinforces, Celan's syntactic awkwardness that gives the
entire poem its nightmarish quality, something I feel particularly in
the line "he whistles his Jews out in earth has them dig for a grave."
At first reading, I mentally edit the line to read "he whistles for his
Jews and has them dig a grave," a far more precise rendering of
what likely happened, though it ignores the terror of Celan's scene.
In Celan's line, the Jews are both dead and alive, if the man who
"whistles" the Jews essentially calls them out of the earth, which
the syntax suggests. Likewise, the line carries within it a tremendous amount of activity, as the Jews first respond to the man's call
then immediately begin digging graves, presumably for themselves,
which Celan's phrase "dig for a grave" suggests. However, this digging also suggests an attempted reclamation of the dead, since the
strange insertion of that preposition "for" makes me see the Jews
both digging graves for themselves *while also* unearthing others that
they have lost. In this way, death and memorialization become gro-
tesquely intertwined and repetitive acts. Celan's syntactical subversions here suggest that the Jews can simultaneously never stop being
murdered *or* remembering those who have been murdered.

Something similar happens in the line "he writes when dusk falls to Germany your golden hair Margarete." Is the "he" writing the line "your golden hair Margarete," or is the dusk falling on Germany "like" this golden hair, or are these two completely different thoughts and moments of time simply placed, paratactically, together? Likewise, in the line "your ashen hair Shulamith he plays with the serpents," are we meant to see this man teasing serpents with this "ashen hair," or is he comparing the hair to serpents or, again, are they meant to be completely separate images and phrases? I'd argue that Celan wants all these readings to be possible: the point of the poem is to turn time, event, and identity into one senseless blur. Celan's lack of clear modification all become a way of disrupting time and subject, event and consequence, thus making me feel how fundamentally irrational and arbitrary this violence was. At the same time, Celan's poem uses alliteration, repetition, and, at times, a waltzing beat, to give the poem its fugue-like qualities and hark back to the poem's historical context, which is that Jewish musicians were ordered to play music during marches, grave-digging, and executions. Certainly, the poem uses these musical elements to highlight its hallucinatory effects. But for me, it's Celan's syntax that becomes most central to the poem's fuguelike state, in which victim cannot be easily demarcated from executioner, death from life, German from Jew.

A similar disorientation happens in the American poet Tarfia Faizullah's poem "100 Bells," based on oral histories Faizullah undertook with rape victims from the 1971 Bangladesh War of Independence. Like Celan's poem, Faizullah's "100 Bells" blurs together narratives as it uses these women's oral testimonies as the frame for a fragmented account of rape's memory, a painful legacy shared across the Bangladeshi diaspora, here told by a series of unnamed speakers.

100 BELLS

for Vievee Francis

My sister died. He raped me. They beat me. I fell
to the floor. I didn't. I knew children,
their smallness. Her corpse. My fingernails.
The softness of my belly, how it could
double over. It was puckered, like children,
ugly when they cry. My sister died
and was revived. Her brain burst
into blood. Father was driving. He fell
asleep. They beat me. I didn't flinch. I did.
It was the only dance I knew.
It was the kathak. My ankles sang
with 100 bells. The stranger
raped me on the fitted sheet.
I didn't scream. I did not know
better. I knew better. I did not
live. My father said, I will go to jail
tonight because I will kill you. I said,
She died. It was the kathakali. Only men
were allowed to dance it. I threw
a chair at my mother. I ran from her.
The kitchen. The flyswatter was
a whip. The flyswatter was a flyswatter.
I was thrown into a fire ant bed. I wanted to be
a man. It was summer in Texas and dry.
I burned. It was a snake dance.
He said, Now I've seen a Muslim girl
naked. I held him to my chest. I held her
because I didn't know it would be
the last time. I threw no
punches. I threw a glass box into a wall.
Somebody is always singing. Songs

were not allowed. Mother said,
Dance and the bells will sing with you.
I slithered. Glass beneath my feet. I
locked the door. I did not
die. I shaved my head. Until the horns
I knew were there were visible.
Until the doorknob went silent.

Throughout "100 Bells," I can see that time, story, and voice are constantly disrupted; one woman's testimony splices another, just as the postwar past in Bangladesh erupts into present-day Texas. These narratives of violence are not chronological or causal but fragmented, even as each sentence is simple in its syntax. Sentences are not linked to each other here according to narrator but by their relationship to violence and traumatic memory itself. An image of dancing recalls a rape or a girl falling to the floor, "[g]lass beneath [her] feet," while a woman's post-pregnancy belly recalls the "ugly" face of a crying child. This image, too, echoes a later image of the folds of a brain "burst[ing]" with blood. Fragments call and respond as the poem unfolds, one image of singing in the poem later answered by an image of doorknobs falling silent, a celebration in the first half of the poem becoming, in the second half, the frenzied writhing of a body in pain. Faizullah's personal biography suggests that the mention of West Texas may refer to Faizullah's own childhood, thus some part of her narrative may here be interwoven with the unnamed rape survivors' testimony, complicating both the poem's sense of place and its number of narrators.

Faizullah's poem clearly relies upon parataxis, both in terms of the short sentences' lack of subordinating clauses and their dis-junctive pairing. Parataxis allows her to create a community out of a disparate group of survivors while also mimetically repro-ducing certain traumatic realities, since memories arise without narrative coherence, to be reimagined and revised by the speakers, such as when one woman says, "I did not know better. I did," or another remembers the flyswatter alternately as a whip and as a flyswatter. Thus the poem's clipped, disconnected sentences increase my anxiety as a reader while also elevating the poem's overall sense of disordered memory.

I wrote before that poets naturally move between hypotaxis and parataxis: what makes Faizullah's poem distinct is how consistently it stays in one mode. In that, her sentence structure makes me highly aware not just of what is being said but *how* it's being said. Considering her subject matter, it's not surprising that she would choose parataxis as her syntactical frame, just as Celan—when confronted by the problem of representing the Holocaust—might favor unclear modification. Both poets I think are trying to enact, not merely depict, trauma, while also remaining skeptical of the limits of what they can represent in language. For me, Celan and Faizullah recognize that syntax can do what representational imagery itself cannot, perhaps because the image itself would be too grotesque to encapsulate, or because representing only what happened without questioning *how* it continues to reverberate in a witness's language and consciousness would turn the subjects solely into spectacle.

When and Where Does the Syntax Shift? Moving Between Hypotaxis and Parataxis

If, as I wrote before, the first form of any poem is the sentence, then the first sense readers have of a poem comes through the rhythms a particular syntax can create. For poets who move between hypotaxis and parataxis, like Hass, this pattern might feel at first more natural, even more invisible than in Faizullah's poem, but that doesn't mean these patterns don't profoundly shape my reading. One of the best studies of syntax in poetry I know is Helen Vendler's *Seamus Heaney*, in which she diagrams some of Heaney's sentences and the effects these structures have on his imagery. We see this connection strongly in "St Kevin and the Blackbird," in which Vendler argues that it is through hypotactic syntax that Heaney is best able to convey Saint Kevin's physical sacrifice. When I read the poem, however, I notice that Heaney moves fluidly between hypotactic and paratactic syntax, to make very different distinctions between the kinds of pain and self-transcendence Saint Kevin undergoes. Read the poem below, but start by counting up all the times Heaney uses the conjunction "and."

ST KEVIN AND THE BLACKBIRD

Seamus Heaney

And then there was St Kevin and the blackbird.
The saint is kneeling, arms stretched out, inside
His cell, but the cell is narrow, so

One turned-up palm is out the window, stiff
As a crossbeam, when a blackbird lands
And lays in it and settles down to nest.

Kevin feels the warm eggs, the small breast, the tucked
Neat head and claws and, finding himself linked
Into the network of eternal life,

Is moved to pity: now he must hold his hand
Like a branch out in the sun and rain for weeks
Until the young are hatched and fledged and flown.

*

And since the whole thing's imagined anyhow,
Imagine being Kevin. Which is he?
Self-forgetful or in agony all the time

From the neck on out down through his hurting forearms?
Are his fingers sleeping? Does he still feel his knees?
Or has the shut-eyed blank of underearth

Crept up through him? Is there distance in his head?
Alone and mirrored clear in love's deep river,
'To labor and not to seek reward,' he prays

A prayer his body makes entirely
For he has forgotten self, forgotten bird
And on the riverbank forgotten the river's name.

I count fourteen uses of the word "and" in Heaney's poem, including one that appears in the title. But when I count up the number of sentences in the first half of the poem, I notice only three that flow over four stanzas. The first line is the first sentence, and the shortest: "And then there was St Kevin and the blackbird." But notice how, by starting with that conjunction "and," Heaney suggests that both poem and sentence starts *in media res,* as if Heaney were just overheard rattling off one among a series of saints' lives. If I spend some time looking at the syntax of the following two lines in that first section of the poem, I see that, even as Heaney describes what Saint Kevin looked like in his cell, that description is full of backpedaling and clarifications, all triggered by the adverbs and conjunctions I've put in bold:

The saint is kneeling, arms stretched out, **inside**
His cell, **but** the cell is narrow, **so**

One turned-up palm is out the window, stiff
As a crossbeam, **when** a blackbird lands
And lays in it and settles down to nest.

Here Heaney moves between hypotaxis and parataxis, since the first part of the sentence is full of subordinating information. Where is the saint kneeling? Inside his cell. And what does the cell look like? It's narrow, thus he has to stick one of his hands outside the window while he kneels to pray. And what happens once he does this? A blackbird lands in his palm and makes a nest.

Each of these descriptions and activities could be its own sentence, but Heaney stacks them together in a series of subordinating clauses that move this way and that as I trace the sentence's main idea. As Vendler notes, when we read these lines, we're asked to mentally duplicate Saint Kevin's physical situation. I'm not only encouraged to see the cell as torturously small but to see Saint Kevin's kneeling body forced to accommodate the boundaries of that cell in a series of subordinated clauses that become more cramped and descriptively particular. But notice that Heaney's hypotactic syntax changes in the last lines: "when a blackbird lands/ [a]nd lays in it **and** settles down to nest." Suddenly Heaney's syntax becomes paratactic, as these become equivalent, not subordinate actions. That pattern continues on to the next two stanzas:

> Kevin feels the warm eggs, the small breast, the tucked
> Neat head **and** claws **and**, finding himself linked
> Into the network of eternal life,
>
> Is moved to pity: now he must hold his hand
> Like a branch out in the sun **and** rain for weeks
> Until the young are hatched **and** fledged **and** flown.

Here Heaney uses a number of "ands" to link his descriptions together, which creates an extension of the scene he's depicted. Of course, what he's describing is the change of time and seasons, as well as the maturation process of the birds themselves: Saint Kevin has to hold his pose "for weeks," Heaney writes, in both sun and rain, "until the young are hatched and fledged and flown." Strip that last line of its conjunctions, and you'd have something that feels quicker, more perfunctory: "until the young are hatched, fledged, flown." The long unfurling of time would be hastened, and we wouldn't feel the full and agonizing cost of Saint Kevin's sacrifice.

Heaney's use of parataxis extends Saint Kevin's physical pain by showing that deliberate and slow unfolding of time. But I also think it underscores the reason for Saint Kevin's sacrifice to begin with. As Heaney writes, Saint Kevin "find[s] himself linked/ [i]nto the network of eternal life," meaning that the saint recognizes that he's connected to the bird and has become, as another living being, essentially equivalent to it. Kevin is one more "and" in life's network, and his recognition of this means that he loses his own sense of individuation. This loss of self suggests that he may cease to feel pain as well, which Heaney wonders about in his series of questions that comprise the poem's second section. In his self-sacrificing connection with the bird, Saint Kevin thus achieves a kind of transcendence in which

he prays

A prayer his body makes entirely
For he has forgotten self, forgotten bird
And on the riverbank forgotten the river's name.

By the end, this very "network of eternal life" Saint Kevin has plugged himself into absorbs the saint, the bird, the river, even the memory of these things. As the poem moves between hypotaxis and parataxis, then, it makes a larger argument about pain, faith, and transcendence that allows me not only to track Heaney's images but to feel some part of the ultimate self-negation Saint Kevin's sacrifice requires.

Does the Poem's Syntax Reflect Its Argument?

Syntax, as you can see, can enhance or replicate a poem's arguments. It's not just an architect of rhythm but a carrier of thought—one that works almost invisibly on the reader, who responds to the poem's feelings almost before she can articulate the poem's events. It took me, for example, quite a while to figure out why I felt so breathless the first time I read W. B. Yeats's "An Irish Airman Foresees His Death," a short lyric that, on first read, seems deceptively direct:

> I know that I shall meet my fate
> Somewhere among the clouds above;
> Those that I fight I do not hate,
> Those that I guard I do not love;
> My country is Kiltartan Cross,
> My countrymen Kiltartan's poor,
> No likely end could bring them loss
> Or leave them happier than before.
> Nor law, nor duty bade me fight,
> Nor public men, nor cheering crowds,
> A lonely impulse of delight
> Drove to this tumult in the clouds;
> I balanced all, brought all to mind,
> The years to come seemed waste of breath,
> A waste of breath the years behind
> In balance with this life, this death.

Yeats's persona poem is, on the surface, about an unnamed airman who accepts, and perhaps even longs for, death. Yeats's aviator is one of an imagined number of Irish soldiers fighting for England and the United Kingdom during the First World War, a man whose "country is Kiltartan Cross,/ [his] countryman Kiltartan's poor." Yeats reminds us that the Irishman does not see himself as an English subject, though, since the Irish at that time were also fighting for independence. Though aware of his nationality, the aviator does not state that he is one of these Irish freedom fighters, just as he does not appear to imagine his combatants as mortal enemies. "Those that I fight I do not hate," he states, "Those that I guard I do not love." The aviator's indifference to everyone and everything is equaled by his detached observation that his own death, too, will be treated with indifference. It is not for nation, glory, ethnic identity "nor duty . . . nor cheering crowds" that he fights, but rather "[a] lonely impulse of delight." The aviator "balanc[es] all, [brings] all to mind," until the years behind and before him thin to an equal line. To underscore this point, Yeats's final lines are themselves perfectly balanced in imagery and syntax, even as they are also rhetorically linked. The final sentence of this poem is both an example of **epanalepsis**, which repeats a word or phrase from the beginning of the sentence at the very end of it, as well as **antimetabole**, in which a phrase is repeated in reversed order, so that the final four lines function like a pair of stacked mirrors:

> I balanced all, brought all to mind,
> The years to come seemed waste of breath,
> A waste of breath the years behind
> In balance with this life, this death.

The final line ends on the oppositional image of "this life, this death" separated only by a comma, a **caesura** or rhythmic break that makes a hard stop before beginning the last foot of the line's tetrameter to create a precarious metrical balance: a readerly hovering between life and death, without any clear sense of resolution.

And that's really the point of the poem, of course: the perilous line between life and death the aviator traverses. Like Heaney's poem, Yeats's elegy is about transcending the self, and what we're willing to risk to achieve this transcendence. Yeats's poem formally enacts for me the aviator's desire, so that I too feel breathlessly poised between anticipation and resolution as the poem draws to its close. Poems don't just tell us what to think, they make us feel that thinking in our bodies. In that, the knowledge poetry gives us is, ironically, preverbal even though poems are composed of words. But those words, in their precisely disordered order, their interlocking sounds and rhetorical devices, create patterns that heighten our emotional response. Repurposing Emily Dickinson for a moment, I know I'm in the presence of a poem when I feel not just think my way through a piece of language, and I know I'm in the presence of a good poem when the poem's formal and syntactic choices elevate its argument. This is a lesson all writers can take to their work: In what ways are our narratives elevated or undermined by our sentence structures? Are these sentences varied enough to produce, or effectively constrain, tension? Do they merely describe actions or do they also enact them? Syntax is never an additional concern to the reader of a poem, it's one of the primary ways she experiences it, as any poem becomes a complex, rhythmic interplay between sentence and line, turning figurative language into vivid reenactment.

EXPERIMENTS

- Choose a poem from the list below. How would you characterize the speaker's syntax? Where does the syntax grow simpler or more complex? What kind of relationship, if any, do you see between the poet's sentence structure and her lineation? Is the poem organized in any way around particular types of clauses or phrases? What relationship do you see between the poem's syntax and the speaker's physical or emotional situation?

- Take any of the prose poems below and rewrite it so that its sentence structures and style are significantly different. If the sentences are hypotactic and complex, make them simple or paratactic. If any sentences include direct discourse, write them in indirect discourse. If certain sentences are written in active voice, try the passive, and vice-versa. If written in the first person, try writing in the third. Compare your rewrite with the original. What has changed in the poem's tone and pacing? What information in the poem is lost or newly gained?

- Spend some time closely observing someone at work. Now write a poem depicting this person, as clearly as you can, using sentence structures that duplicate for you the rhythms of her movements and activities at work. Alternative exercise: Write a poem depicting a physical job you regularly do yourself. How can your syntax capture the feeling of that work?

SUGGESTED WORKS TO CONSIDER

Robert Creeley, "I Know a Man"
Carl Phillips, "A Kind of Meadow"
Victoria Chang, "OBIT [Ambition]"
Carolyn Forché, "The Colonel"
D. H. Lawrence, "Snake"
Walt Whitman, "When I Heard at the Close of the Day"
William Shakespeare, "Sonnet 29"
Maureen McLane, "syntax"
Robert Frost, "Directive"

Harryette Mullen, "[Kills bugs dead.]"
Beth Ann Fennelly, "Two Sisters, One Thinner, One
    Better Dressed"

All poems can be found either at the Poetry Foundation or the
Academy of American Poets websites.

CHAPTER FIVE

What Kind of Lineation Does the Poet Employ?

I've spent a lot of time thinking about how sentences produce their own music, and you can see that syntax might enhance other features of conventional lineation, such as rhyme and rhythm. But line and sentence don't have to work together at all to be effective. In fact, we tend to forget the sentence in favor of the line, which visually announces itself as the poem's most important feature. But while our eyes may track lines, our ears track syntax, and our syntactic choices shouldn't be that different from the careful decisions made around sound, rhythm, and enjambment, in part to hear where our sense of the sentence diverges from that of the line. And ultimately it's important to distinguish what a **line** itself is: a unit of meaning, a measure of attention, as Ed Hirsch writes in *A Poet's Glossary*.

The Difference Between Sentence and Line

A sentence is different from a line of verse because every sentence carries within it a sense of a beginning, middle, and end—even if the sentence itself is a fragment. Thus, the sentence contains its own complete movement, usually the movement of thought as it

is captured within a particular moment of time. The line, however, moves according to its own requirement, often entirely independent of the sentence: it can connect the individual sentence's
moment of time to other time signatures in the poem, or it can
enhance (or suppress) some of the sentence's rhetorical effects. An
autonomous line in a poem completes a thought and is also **end-
stopped** with punctuation, even if the sentence itself is a fragment
or grammatically incomplete. This can create the sense of a poem
being doubly punctuated, as we must stop both grammatically and
visually, which we see in some of these famous lines:

> Shall I compare thee to a summer's day?

> I am a little world made cunningly.

> I too, dislike it: there are things that are important beyond
>   all this fiddle.

When the meaning of a sentence carries over from one line to
the next, this is called **enjambment**, a French ballet term meaning "to step over" or "to throw a leg over," as it allows us to carry
the idea or thought of a sentence on to the next line.

With poems written in conventional form, lines break according to predetermined requirements based on the repetition of
metrical feet and/or rhyming patterns, as you can see in villanelles, sonnets, sestinas, and blank verse. But with free-verse
poems, lines are broken according to patterns that satisfy the
poet's own sense of movement, meaning, visuality, and breath. In
that case, lineation functions for a reader in much the same way
that sheet music functions for a musician: it's a way of scoring the
poem, suggesting how a poem might be performed by others.

Occasionally lines break apart sentences in ways that increase
tension and intonation, deepening the meaning of what would

otherwise be a simple phrase, such as William Carlos Williams famously did in his poem "To a Poor Old Woman," especially in his second stanza.

TO A POOR OLD WOMAN

> munching a plum on
> the street a paper bag
> of them in her hand
>
> They taste good to her
> They taste good
> to her. They taste
> good to her
>
> You can see it by
> the way she gives herself
> to the one half
> sucked out in her hand
>
> Comforted
> a solace of ripe plums
> seeming to fill the air
> They taste good to her

Here, each line becomes a new evaluation of the words "good" and "taste," drawing out the sentence's sensual undertones through line breaks. In essence, enjambment encourages me to slow down and experience some of the same pleasure this woman takes in eating plums by "tasting" the different readings of the sentence itself. In that, the poem also plays with tone, moving from physical delight to religious benediction, as the final line highlights a phrase that suggests a blessing on the woman herself: "good to her."

Williams refuses to use much punctuation in "To a Poor Old Woman"—the entire poem contains within it only one period, which occurs at the poem's midway point—suggesting that lineation itself is enough to provide us both a sense of pause and closure, even as it also creates tension for the reader to continue on through the rest of the stanza. Some poets, like W. S. Merwin or Mark Bibbins, abandon punctuation entirely, understanding how line breaks and visual or medial caesuras help a reader determine the endings of clauses, even within longer, complex sentences. Here's a section of Mark Bibbins's long poem "13th Balloon" as an example:

Not long ago the Pope decreed

that unbaptized babies would

no longer be banished to Limbo

and that their little souls languishing

there would be released

Imagine them getting the papal memo

and rising in unison   unsure

of where to go

except up   twirling like colossal flocks

of river martins

in dark enormous coils   their outlines

becoming eventually lighter

then translucent   then clear

Here I know that "twirling like colossal flocks" modifies
how the babies' souls would move upward, in part because Bibbins isolates the phrase on its own **hemistich**, or half a line.
But notice that Bibbins's complete image actually extends for
several more lines, which he then proceeds to unpack clause
by clause, isolating "their outlines" on its own hemistich to
indicate visually that we have a new subject to focus on, as it
is these outlines that become "lighter/ then translucent then
clear." This last image, of course, refers finally back to the
babies' souls, but we have to travel many lines and images back
to remember this. In Bibbins's image, babies' souls rise and
twirl, they become like flocks of river martins, which themselves are described as "dark enormous coils," bit by bit fading
from sight. The whole stanza is two sentences, one of which is
extremely complex in its unspooling imagery and, if it were a
single sentence of regularly punctuated prose, might be hard to
swallow. Instead, Bibbins uses line breaks to isolate each clause
and subject, helping the reader to absorb this information in
discrete bites, each one brief enough to let us savor the changes
these souls finally undergo.

While enjambment can unpack and clarify complex images,
it can also allow for the surprising amplification or even reversal
of a sentence's unfurling thought, as you see in this quote from
"Weeds" by Diane Seuss:

Don't debauch
yourself by living
in some former version of yourself
that was more or less naked.

And sometimes lines can break up a sentence into regular units arbitrarily selected by the poet, as in the syllabic poems of Marianne Moore, or this quote from "Sho," a poem by Douglas Kearney, which also counts syllables as part of its form:

> Some need some Body
> or more to ape sweat
> on some site. Bloody
>
> purl or dirty spit
> hocked up for to show
> who gets eaten. Rig . . .

Lines can mimetically reproduce the poem's content, too, like this fragment from Robert Lowell's "To Delmore Schwartz," in which he describes the two poets getting drunk together in lines that trip and slur down the page:

> In the ebb-
> Light of morning, we stuck
> The duck
> -'s web-
> Foot, like a candle, in a quart of gin we'd killed.

Lines can lift away from the page's left-hand margin to be center- or right-justified. They can break internally to create a visual caesura, as Bibbins's poem does, or to concentrate the reader's attention on a particular word or phrase. Or, as you might find in the contrapuntal poems in Tyehimba Jess's *Olio*, interior line breaks might divide a single poem into two separate ones whose lines can be read both horizontally and vertically, thus creating both sonic and visual counterpoint.

Line breaks place greater visual and sonic weight on both

ending *and* initiating words in each line, since the reader's eye rests in these areas; it's one reason that poets generally argue for lines not to end on prepositions or conjunctions but on nouns and verbs, so that lines don't appear to trail off. As for me, I think tension can be generated by more than just visuality since, again, we read for sound as well as sense and sight. Sometimes lines of unequal metrical or rhythmic length can whet the reader's appetite for conclusion, which occurs in these opening lines of Linda Gregerson's "The Resurrection of the Body":

> She must have been thirteen or so, her nascent
> > breasts
> > just showing above the velcro strap
>
> that held her in her chair.
> > Her face
> > translucent, beautiful,
>
> as if a cheekbone might directly render
> > a tranquil
> > heart. And yet
>
> the eyes were all dis-
> > quietude.

In verse where lines are of equal metrical or visual length, ending a line on "yet" or the particle "dis" might not push the reader on so powerfully to the next line, but notice how visually unstable and sonically disjunctive Gregerson's **tercets**, or three-lined stanzas, are. For whatever reason—likely rhyming closure—English poems tend toward **quatrain** stanzas; tercets can look and feel unfinished to an English reader. And here each of Gregerson's tercets focuses on a particular aspect of the girl being described, sometimes even isolating a body part onto a single line. The reader is, line by line, allowed more visual access to the girl, who emerges in our mind's eye via Gregerson's poetic strip tease as the tercets linger first on her breasts, then her face and cheekbones, then her heart, and finally her eyes. Gregerson's lineation creates a sense of coy anticipation, but also disruption since, of course, we are looking at a beautiful adolescent whose "eyes were all dis-/ quietude," meaning that although the girl may appear the passive object of our prurient interest, her eyes reflect a more unruly, perhaps impenetrable, truth. In fact, the girl is intellectually handicapped, in a ward filled with other such children: we see this fact unfold across the tercets, the incremental details of Gregerson's scene thus resurrected into a complete story by the end of the poem.

You could say, and some critics have, that formal verse works both functionally and symbolically toward conclusion. In contrast, then, free verse might allow for more irresolution, something Denise Levertov suggested in her essay "On the Function of the Line," in which she declares that free verse is, by nature, "more exploratory." By this she doesn't mean that free-verse poems resist any and all sense of closure, only that because their lines follow the shape of thought and breath rather than preestablished patterns, conclusion itself becomes less pronounced. For her, free verse represents a process of thought, whereas formal verse focuses *on the results of* thinking.

I can personally think of a dozen sonnets that would contradict or at least complicate Levertov's argument, and I'll be talking about some of them later in a chapter on constrained forms. For me, formal verse can use rhyme to create expectations of conclusion that the poem's own rhetorical movements counteract or even undermine. So perhaps it's better not to insist that certain patterns of lineation consistently do any one type or kind of work and focus instead on what kind of relationship develops between sentence and line in this or that specific poem, as well as what kinds of narrative resolution or tension these relationships offer the reader.

One of my own favorite examples of the difference between sentence and line is "Musée des Beaux Arts" by W. H. Auden, a poem composed of only two stanzas and three sentences, which together total twenty-one lines. From this description alone, you would rightly intuit that Auden's poem must rely heavily on enjambment, something apparent from Auden's very first stanza:

MUSÉE DES BEAUX ARTS

About suffering they were never wrong,
The old Masters: how well they understood
Its human position: how it takes place
While someone else is eating or opening a window or just
    walking dully along;
How, when the aged are reverently, passionately waiting
For the miraculous birth, there always must be
Children who did not specially want it to happen, skating
On a pond at the edge of the wood:
They never forgot
That even the dreadful martyrdom must run its course
Anyhow in a corner, some untidy spot
Where the dogs go on with their doggy life and the
    torturer's horse
Scratches its innocent behind on a tree.

Auden's lines throughout this poem are of wildly different lengths, and they appear to break haphazardly. A close reader will notice, of course, that Auden's lines actually end on a series of close or full rhymes, such as "wrong" and "along" in the first and fourth lines, or "course" and "horse" in the tenth and twelfth, though almost no one hears them when the poem's read aloud. Partly this is because of Auden's high use of enjambment, partly it's because the rhymes themselves don't appear in a consistent pattern (some rhymes, like "understood" and "wood" have five lines that separate them, for instance), and partly it's because of Auden's unequal line lengths themselves: we tend to hear rhymes when they are regular and also when the lines in a stanza are **isometric**, meaning they have equal rhythmic units. A Shakespearean sonnet is an example of an isometric poem, since all fourteen lines have five feet of iambic pentameter. We easily can track Shakespeare's rhymes because his patterning is more consistent than Auden's, whose **heterometric** lines can be as long as twenty-two syllables or as short as five, while the entire first stanza is only a single sentence. This causes his rhymes to disappear from our ear while they may be visually registered by our eyes.

Because Auden continually disrupts any conventional pattern, we don't follow rhyme or rhythm for sense but instead follow the information contained within his incredibly dense and hypotactic syntax. We trace his train of thought as it wends through the poem by paying attention to the relationship between clauses, not sound. What details take precedence and why? In the first stanza, I see a whole series of images—everything from the birth of Christ to a walk in the woods to children skating on a pond. Those familiar with art history might recognize these as the subjects of other Dutch paintings, which Auden reminds us of in the opening of the poem: "About suffering, they were never wrong,/ The old Masters," he writes, then plunges ahead to so many new and different scenes that I almost lose track of the sentence's main argument, which is that suffering's "human position" lies in the corner of our consciousness, half-hidden, if never totally forgotten. That sentence (and argument) takes up the whole first stanza, but Auden's syntax never lets me stay in one place for too long;

his sentence pushes on, distractedly, until I reach the second and final stanza:

> In Breughel's Icarus, for instance: how everything
>   turns away
> Quite leisurely from the disaster; the ploughman may
> Have heard the splash, the forsaken cry,
> But for him it was not an important failure; the sun shone
> As it had to on the white legs disappearing into the green
> Water, and the expensive delicate ship that must have seen
> Something amazing, a boy falling out of the sky,
> Had somewhere to get to and sailed calmly on.

Here the poem wends toward its sad conclusion: the image of Icarus slipping silently into the sea, ignored by sailors whose ship "[h]ad somewhere to get to and sailed calmly on." This "amazing" sight of a boy falling from the sky should surely have drawn their attention, but the sailors are so focused on their own private joys and miseries that they miss it. That was the joke of Breughel's painting *Icarus Falling from the Sky*, and that's the general argument of Auden's poem too since we drift past the many painterly scenes depicted in that first stanza, so caught up in the spell of Auden's sentence we may be surprised to arrive at Icarus at all, just as we may be surprised to see that Auden's visually free verse lines are structured around rhyme.

Auden's poem is **ekphrastic**, meaning that it responds to a piece of visual art, but while the poem is full of descriptions of paintings, I'd argue that the poem isn't really about Breughel or art but the particular distractions of the museum experience itself. Notice that Auden's title is "Musée des Beaux Arts," not "Icarus Falling from the Sky," and his circuitous syntax in that first stanza mimics our own haphazard wandering through a hall of Dutch masters—a few seconds here and there to appreciate a detail or a portrait before we stroll on to the next. Auden, through his complex interplay of sentence and line, is in effect making his readers fall prey to the same sin of inattention he and those Dutch masters have accused humanity of: we, too, are absorbed by the mundane, whether in life or in the museum, and in our desire to look at the next pretty thing—or just our desire to finish the poem—we cease to see the suffering in front of us.

Are the Lines Broken for Particular Visual Effect?

In general, lines are visual markers with sonic effects: we may, if these things accompany the end of a line, hear a poem's lineation because of punctuation or rhyme, but largely we *see* where lines begin or end by studying the page, and we weight the pause in our breath accordingly. Some poets, like George Herbert or Apollinaire or the Brazilian Noigandres poets, have capitalized on the line's visual element through concrete forms that treat the line as material itself. In the case of Apollinaire, we might find that the visual image created by his lines disrupts or even contends with the textual imagery contained within those very lines, as in "Heart, Crown and Mirror," in which the shape of the poem visually depicts, alternately, a heart, a crown, and a mirror, while the text of the poem encourages us to envision other objects entirely, such as when Apollinaire's text for the heart states, "My heart is like an inverted flame." Even the mirror doesn't function like a true mirror, since in its center is printed the name "Guillaume/ Apollinaire," reflecting not the reader of the poem, then, but the writer, who does not—and cannot—visually appear on the page itself.

Some concrete poems highlight, through their visual forms, sonic effects, such as Eugen Gomringer's "Wind," which uses the repetitive re-lineation of the word "wind" to make it appear multidimensional, as if the letters of the word had been tossed about by a storm. Or, by experimenting with typography, scale, and textual placement, as in Stéphane Mallarmé's "Un Coup de Des," poems can communicate meaning through what we'd call "extra-textual" effects, breaking down whatever perceived barrier exists between word and image in our minds. Essentially, concrete poems act as objects themselves, not interpretations of objects, reminding us that when confronted with a visual image, we explain its meaning to ourselves in language, whereas when reading a text, we picture its description as visual images in our minds.

In that, visual or concrete poems always challenge conventional forms of reading. As an example of this, I like to show students David Hinton's poem *Fossil Sky*, a book-length poem printed on an enormous fold-out map in which the lines of the poem, encircled by the blue outline of a globe, crisscross, wind, and weave together, to get them to think about what maps and poems share when it comes to good "reading" practices. Here's a small snippet of what Hinton's poem looks like:

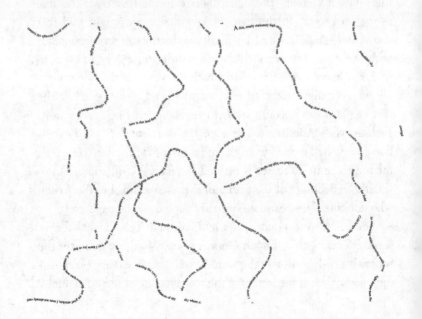

Even from this textual fragment, you can sense that Hinton's map refuses to act like one, despite how its printing and physical layout recalls a conventional map. Hinton's text defies all expectations of how geographic maps should functionally be read. Conventional maps include place names and natural or political boundaries. They're located in an implicit time and history, since borders and places often change, whether due to time, war, colonization, or environmental change. Maps don't privilege human sense-perception of place so much as our historical knowledge of it; they are narratives we can read and reread in order to reliably find our way to chosen locations, not necessarily desired experiences. Maps, in that sense, allow multiple readers to reach the same physical conclusion. We use maps to duplicate journeys, as well as to plot journeys we may take only once. Maps are thus highly plastic documents that offer us a wide possible variety of subjective experiences, even as the information they include is deliberately limited, two-dimensional, stripped of sensory detail.

By taking on the map as a poetic form, Hinton invites me to imagine how his poem will chart a specific place. But if I start to read Hinton's poetic text, I'm lost as to which place I'm meant to envision, which time I'm inhabiting, even which sense or perspective I'm supposed to engage. This is partly to do with the fact that Hinton's poem "maps" walks he's taken in the same area over months, but it's also to do with Hinton's text and lineation. Hinton's lines can be as short as a single word, such as "laughing," "carbon," or "oxygen," and as long as thirty-one syllables. The descriptions range from the sound of a hawk's cry—"pKreeerr" repeats randomly across the poem—to more abstract and personal statements like "And if it is meaningless to pose the particular against the fierce and ancient abstractions driving human history." Some lines focus on the intimate space of the speaker's bed, some lines focus on nearby bodies of water ("rivers flow away"). Other lines evoke physical sensations that would never be included on a map, such as "heat waves ris[ing] over dried grasses." If I follow all the directions and perspectives suggested by Hinton's poem, I find myself in the air, on the ground, in a house, by a river, in a history book, in a bird's body, inside the Earth's core.

Based on its lineation, it's not clear where I'm meant to start reading *Fossil Sky*; indeed, as I turn and move the poem around on my table, I find myself leaping across lines, picking up an image here or there, stalking another that catches my attention. Hinton's lines themselves cross and layer over one another, squiggle across the page and trail off into white space. They resemble animal prints through the brush, or the meandering of a river, or the swooping motions of a hawk. They materially suggest a range of different types of physical and even spiritual movement at the same time the lines themselves are constrained in a two-dimensional print world. I personally can't possibly duplicate any one of my reading experiences of *Fossil Sky* unless I had a much better memory than the one Covid has now gifted me with: each time I pick up the poem, I experience its world differently.

If Hinton's poem blurs map and poem, it also blurs my physical senses to create a total sense of place in which the speaker and I get to reside. No reader, of course, could possibly use this map to navigate a "real" landscape, even as it speaks to us *of* a landscape Hinton experienced on his own. And isn't that the problem inherent to any poem: that what we represent in language can never truly be reexperienced by a reader? Looking at Hinton's poem, I see its lines work on the premise of radical inclusion: to try to represent the world as we actually experience it, all senses, all perspectives, all possible bodies we encounter must be invoked. In that, Hinton's poem, perhaps like any poem, is a map of *impossibility*. Notice that even the title, *Fossil Sky*, places two things together that, in reality, can't coexist. Sky can't be trapped and fossilized, nor can a fossil be as changeable as a skyscape. Hinton is trying to get us to conceptualize two distinctly different states of being that any map itself flirts with representing: stasis and change, the actual world and our representation of it.

Breaking Down Lineation

The majority of poems don't attempt anything as playfully challenging to our reading as *Fossil Sky*, which is one reason I like sharing it. Before showing students the poem, however, I begin by asking what we generally expect from maps; in particular, I ask what kinds of details maps usually include or exclude, and how we each read the details we find on maps. Then I spread Hinton's poem out on a table or the floor and let the students walk around it. I have them take notes to track where and how they start reading, to discuss what directions the poem allows them imaginatively to look or move about in, what kinds of objects (or experiences) the poem includes. I ask how Hinton's poem is and is not "like" a map, and then I ask how they would characterize the shape of the poem's lines. Is each line a poem? Are all the lines together a poem? How does Hinton's lineation differ from the lineation they've seen in other poems? How might it be similar? Do these lines allow for any narrative coherence, not just discontinuity? Do they create or preserve any particular patterns? How would they characterize where a line ends or begins? And finally, how does it change their idea of what it means to "read" a poem?

"Ago": An Exercise

Readers, when faced with *Fossil Sky*, recognize that Hinton's poem allows them to choose where, when, and even whether the lines connect to create any one narrative. In that, they recognize that his lineation is profoundly important to their individual experience of the poem. But *Fossil Sky*'s lineation, while more visually and narratively flexible than that of most free-verse poems, doesn't operate under entirely different assumptions either about how lineation creates meaning apart from or alongside of the meaning of the text's language. When we re-lineate even the most conventionally structured poems, we can see how different choices around line endings create almost totally different poems. As an example of this, I give students a poem they must experience three different ways, the first time as a prose poem, the second time as a lineated poem that replicates the line endings an average or novice poet might choose, the third time as the published poem itself. The poem I use for this exercise is Nick Flynn's "Ago," from his first book *Some Ether*, though almost any poem with unusual lineation would work.

This is the prose-poem version of "Ago" that I present my students:

I don't even know how a telephone works, how your voice reached all the way from Iron River, fed across wires or satellites, transformed & returned. I don't understand the patience this takes, or anything about the light-years between stars. An hour ago you cupped your hands in the tub & raised them up, an offering of steam. Now we're driving 66 mph & one maple is coming up fast, on fire. I begin, *It's like those fireworks over the East River*, but it's not enough to say this. By the time I find the words it will already be past, rushing away as if falling into a grave, drained of electricity, the world between *something is happening* & *something happened*. Think of an astronaut, big silver hands & gravity boots, the effort spent to keep from flying off into space. Think of the first time your grandparents listened to a phonograph, the needle falling to black vinyl, a song without a body. Think of the names you see on a map, think of these towns & rivers before they were named, when "Liberty" & "New Hope" were a large rock, a stand of birches. It's what I'm afraid of, the speed with which everything is replaced, these trees, your smile, my mother turning her back to me before work, asking over her shoulder, *how does this look?*

Take a moment and read this poem out loud to yourself. Try to identify what you think the poem's central images are, and what—if any—sense of the speaker you get while reading. What does the speaker seem to want? What does he seem to fear? Based on how you sense the speaker's tone, how do you imagine the poem to move: quickly or slowly? What are some key phrases or sentences that strike you as you move through the paragraph?

Most readers immediately identify the speaker's anxiety about time and change, focusing on phrases like, "By the time I find the words it will already be past, rushing away as if falling into a grave," and "the speed with which everything is replaced," both of which give the poem the feeling of being rushed. They also sense the speaker's fascination with rapidly changing kinds of technology—the "big silver hands & gravity boots" of the astronaut, for example, along with scattered references to telephones, satellites, electricity and the phonograph.

Assuming that you agree with these readers' assessments, take another moment and write this passage out as a lineated poem by hand. Don't merely indicate line endings with a / placed between words but take time to write each line and see your choices laid out as they would appear on the page. Carefully consider how you will translate your sense of the poem's central anxiety and its tonal movement through your lineation.

After you've written out the poem, read it out loud to yourself to hear how your choices sound. When I do this exercise in class, I actually provide students a possible version of the poem that I've drafted specifically to reflect the kinds of endings I tend to find in first drafts. Again, I read this version aloud, and ask students what they notice about my line breaks. Below is my own re-lineation of the poem. Read it out loud to yourself and take note of what phrases my version highlights. How would you characterize *my* lineation's speed and movement?

I don't even know how a telephone works,
how your voice reached all the way from Iron River,
fed across wires or satellites,
transformed & returned.

I don't understand the patience this takes,
or anything about the light-years between stars.
An hour ago you cupped your hands in the tub &
    raised them up,
an offering of steam.

Now
we're driving 66 mph & one maple is coming up fast,
on fire. I begin, *It's like those fireworks over
the East River,* but it's not enough to say this.

By the time I find the words
it will already be past,
rushing away as if falling
into a grave, drained of electricity,

the world between *something
is happening* & *something happened.*
Think of an astronaut,
big silver hands & gravity boots,
the effort spent to keep from flying off into space.

Think of the first time your grandparents listened
to a phonograph, the needle falling
to black vinyl, a song without a body.

Think of the names
you see on a map,
think of these towns & rivers

before they were named,
when "Liberty" & "New Hope"
were a large rock, a stand of birches.

It's what I'm afraid of,
the speed with which everything
is replaced, these trees, your smile,
my mother turning her back to me before work,
asking over her shoulder,
how does this look?

Likely your lineation is different from mine, which is good. Students generally hate this version I've created because the poem feels, when read aloud, sluggish. The lines almost always end on punctuation, effectively double-stopping each line, slowing the poem's movement to a crawl. Breaking on punctuation also limits the verbal or syntactic play available to the reader, so that the language of the poem itself—already so plainspoken it verges on prose—here becomes entirely prosaic. The poem's lyricism isn't found in any particular rhythmic flourishes or startling imagery but in its rapid change of scene and time. The poem wants to leap across the many situations it offers us but notice how each stanza except for one in my version is end-stopped, which locks the poem down into what feel like discrete, almost disconnected, memories. **Stanza** means "little room" in Italian, and here you can see I've created a structure of rooms that have no connection with one another or easy movement between them, except between stanzas five and six. Readers effectively get siloed, stanza by stanza, scene by scene. If I spend time looking at the different scenarios Flynn includes in his poem, there is no *logical* reason why thoughts about the speaker's relationship with "you" should necessarily be triggered by his inability to describe how a telephone works. I'm also unsure what Flynn means to modify by "this" and "it" in the phrases "it's not enough to say this," "I don't understand the patience this takes," and "By the time I find the words/ it will already be past": a lack of clarity made even more mysterious by the fact that the lines break to reinforce syntax. Considering students, upon first reading of the prose version of the poem, are easily able to identify the poem's nearly frenetic energy and fears of transience, this version I created for them feels not only lethargic but rooted in phrases that themselves lack clarity, in that sense, showcasing a weakness hidden in the poem.

Having compared this version to their own reading of "Ago," I then show the students Flynn's published poem.

AGO

I don't even know
        how a telephone works, how your voice reached
all the way from Iron River, fed

across wires or satellites, transformed

& returned. I don't understand
        the patience this takes, or anything
about the light-years between stars.

        An hour ago
you cupped your hands in the tub & raised them up,
        an offering of steam. Now

we're driving 66 mph
& one maple is coming up fast, on fire. I begin,
        It's like those fireworks over

the East River, but it's not enough

to say this. By the time I find the words
　　　　it will already be past, rushing away as if falling

into a grave, drained
of electricity, the world between *something is happening*

& *something happened*. Think of an astronaut, big silver hands
& gravity boots, the effort spent

　　　　to keep from flying off into space. Think of

the first time your grandparents listened
to a phonograph, the needle falling to black
vinyl, a song without a body. Think of the names

　　　　you see on a map, think of these towns & rivers
before they were named, when "Liberty" & "New Hope"

were a large rock, a stand of birches. It's what

　　　　I'm afraid of, the speed with which everything
is replaced, these trees, your smile, my mother
　　　　　　　　turning her back to me before work,
asking over her shoulder,
how does this look?

As you can see, Flynn's version opens up the poem entirely. Here Flynn, anxious about "the speed with which everything is replaced," eschews punctuation-induced lineation and blocky, end-stopped stanzas. Instead, the poem splits into tercets and couplets and even single lines, darting nervously away from the left-hand margin in fragmentary phrases that highlight the speaker's terror of the space that surrounds him, space that is often represented technologically but also felt as existential confusion, as in the opening:

> I don't even know
>> how a telephone works, how your voice reached
> all the way from Iron River, fed
>
> across wires or satellites, transformed
>
> & returned. I don't understand
>> the patience this takes, or anything
> about the light-years between stars.

Break according to punctuation, as in my version, and these lines become a Luddite's cry of despair, not a revelation of empirical dread. Throughout the poem, Flynn's lines end mid-clause on phrases of disorientation that reinforce the speaker's psychic distress rather than the more mundane troubles that syntactically conclude his sentences. Thus we "know" through his endings that it is the speaker's subjective confusion that troubles him, not his inability to explain to anyone how a telephone works. Notice, too, how often the lines end on words that suggest an almost physical yearning and sense of change—"reached," "fed," "transformed," "I begin," "it's not enough"—or else a dissolve into uncertainty: "falling," "I don't understand," "falling to black." Flynn's syntax itself hasn't been clarified—I still couldn't tell you what "this" or "it" definitively refers to in the first part of the poem—but in this version, I don't care. The lines don't let me linger on such questions because they rush across Flynn's sentences. When students read this version aloud, they can't help but speed up *and also* pause at unexpected moments. They understand, because they feel, the speaker's anxious reaching for something solid and dependable, whether that be in language or in the relationship he has with "you," whose smiles—like everything else in life—can be so easily replaced, and who holds in her cupped hands nothing more solid than "an offering of steam."

Flynn's lineation takes into consideration the endings *and* beginnings of lines, of course: notice how many lines are indented, creating a longer rhythmic pause and thus a greater sense of anticipation at the end and start of each part of the clause than the sentence itself would warrant:

> By the time I find the words
> > it will already be past, rushing away as if falling
>
> into a grave, drained
> of electricity, the world between *something is happening*
>
> & *something happened*. Think of an astronaut, big silver hands
> & gravity boots, the effort spent
>
> > to keep from flying off into space. Think of

The indented line break in the lines "by the time I find the words/ it will already be past" has me actually *feel* the time in which something can slip away, much in the same way I feel a sense of falling myself between that first and following stanza. Likewise, I can see the phrase "to keep from flying off into space" actually drift off into the space of the page. Here, Flynn's line and stanza breaks mimetically reproduce the ideas and anxieties he wants to express, leading to the ultimate reason for the speaker's confusion. At the end of the poem, look at how Flynn lists all the things that, in his life, have been so speedily replaced:

> > > it's what
>
> > I'm afraid of, the speed with which everything
> is replaced, these trees, your smile, my mother

> turning her back to me before work
> asking over her shoulder,
> *how does this look?*

This catalogue Flynn includes—"these trees, your smile, my mother"—suggests these things all may be ephemeral, while the line ending itself places greatest visual and rhetorical weight on "my mother." It's at this moment I understand that the speaker's mother has herself been "replaced," or, more aptly, that she has disappeared from the speaker's life. I know from other poems and books he's written that Flynn's mother committed suicide when Flynn himself was a teenager. Though he doesn't announce this information in "Ago," a quiet but devastating sense of loss permeates the final movement of the poem. It's in the line break that the speaker is able to pronounce his mother gone, while the lineation throughout the first part of the poem registers his nervousness at how temporal are the conditions of this world: a recognition that, in Flynn's version, becomes suggestively tied to the loss of the mother herself. Indeed, the final lines of the poem initially speed through people and images, making them at first equivalent in the quickness of their disappearance but finally slowing down to isolate the speaker's memory of his mother, as you can see in the poem's final stanza and its image of the speaker seeing his mother getting dressed before work. Compare Flynn's version with mine, and you'll feel the difference:

> It's what I'm afraid of,
> the speed with which everything
> is replaced, these trees, your smile,
> my mother turning her back to me before work,
> asking over her shoulder,
> *how does this look?*

Here, my stanza thuds along to its numb conclusion. It lacks the tension and poignancy of Flynn's version, which makes the mother the final cause and locus of the poem. I may have broken the final two lines in a manner similar to Flynn's, but because I haven't isolated them on their own stanza, they don't carry the same visual weight, nor do they slow down my reading in the same effective ways.

For me, "Ago" is an elegy in which the line breaks—almost more than the words themselves—do Flynn's emotional work. When you compare your own version with Flynn's published poem, you might notice some similar choices at work, but many more differences. It's possible that you even prefer your lineation at times because it adds a note of clarity to a phrase or two that gets lost in the original. No poem's choices are inevitable, which is also the point of doing this exercise. We shouldn't treat the final version of any poem as predetermined but understand how our reading is quietly altered by selection, and that small decisions have large textual effects. All poems are essentially patterned choice, and within these patterns exist multiple ways of opening up a poem.

When we start considering the effects of meter and rhythm, we also have to ask how these elements change our ideas of and feeling for the line itself. Each metered line has its own rhythmic thumbprint; if tension occurs in the free-verse poem because of the interplay between line and sentence, tension in metrical verse occurs because of rhythmic variation within the line itself. On top of this, metrical rhythms deviate *across* lines, thus we might see the poetic line in formal verse as being in a persistent tug-of-war with sentence, rhyme, consistent rhythmic pattern, *and* rhythmic deviation. What this means is that, if poems overall offer us multiple points of entry as readers to make meaning, the line itself contains various ways to hear and read sound. It is the line, perhaps of all the poetic elements, that most directs our ear. Lines can, as in Auden's poem, elevate or silence rhymes; they can, when end-stopped, provide moments of rest. They can speed up or slow down our reading; they can elevate the effects of metrical irregularity; and they can, when longer lines are placed against short ones, constrict and release tension. It is the movement across lines that helps poems lift away from dull statements of fact to revelation, helping us feel as if the poem is discovering its meaning at the moment that we read it. Lineation as it interacts with syntax, rhythm, even the page itself isn't an accident of inspiration, then, but a dynamic invitation. For it is through the variety of rhythms that lines produce that poems map the plenitude of human experience, tapping into the range of our physical senses and knowledge to help us speak with as many voices as possible.

EXPERIMENTS

- Take a sentence and lineate it at least three different ways to see what different kinds of meaning you can get from it. This might be a sentence you've overheard, a line from a novel or newspaper article, or a commonly used expression or statement. For example, you might use the question, "How are we feeling today?" and lineate it like this:

  How are we feeling
  today? How are
  we feeling
  today?
  How are we

  feeling today?
  How
  are we
  feeling today?

- Take a found document, such as a newspaper article, an archival letter, advertisement, or page of a novel and lineate it. In what ways does your lineation change the original quotation's tone, situation, or even your understanding of the stated facts?

- Find a poem from the suggested works below that uses found text and examine how the poet's imagery and lineation changes for you the text's original meaning or function. For example, does the original text suddenly seem satirical? More serious? Mysterious? What kinds and type of information does the poem's lineation highlight? Does the found poem appear now to be speaking to an audience different from the one intended by the original text?

- Find a poem from the suggested works below that has unusual lineation and put it into a prose block. Now try lineating the prose block at least two different ways, to compare and contrast the resulting effects. In one version, you may want to re-lineate the poem to make it move more quickly, while in another you might want to reinforce rhymes and sounds that were previously hidden. Perhaps you want to emphasize (or upset) the poem's sentence structures. You might have groups of people working at this same task, since they will arrive at different forms. Now compare your versions with the author's published version. What new meanings or tones emerge from the text based on these different styles of lineation?

- Oftentimes lineation works with or against punctuation, but what about a poem where punctuation has been entirely removed? Write a poem in present tense without punctuation about falling asleep, and consider how your line endings might duplicate this experience for the reader.

SUGGESTED WORKS TO CONSIDER

Charles Reznikoff, "Domestic Scenes"
Langston Hughes, "Advertisement for the
    Waldorf-Astoria"
Tracy K. Smith, "The United States Welcomes You"
John Giorno, "An Unemployed Machinist"
William Carlos Williams, "It Is a Living Coral"
C. K. Williams, "They Call This"
M. NourbeSe Philip, "Ferrum (excerpt)"
Dana Levin, "Watching the Sea Go"
William Stafford, "Traveling Through the Dark"

All poems can be found either at the Poetry Foundation or the Academy of American Poets websites.

CHAPTER SIX

What Word Choice and Diction Does the Poet Use?

S mall changes in a poem can make enormous differences. Take out a parenthetical phrase and the sentence falls slack. Break a line on another word, and suddenly the anxiety of the poem hinges on a mother's death, not a lover's leaving. But what about the words we choose themselves? Why select one word and not another that carries a similar meaning? Why does a poet choose to write in a casual diction where we might expect an elevated one?

Here's a poem whose unusual phrasing and word choice force me to slow down and ask myself just these kinds of questions. It's an excerpt from the long poem "feeld" by Jos Charles, from her first book by the same title:

i

thees wite skirtes / & orang
sweters   / i wont / inn the feedynge marte /
wile mye vegetable partes bloome /
inn the commen waye / a grackel
inn the guarden rooste /   the tall
wymon wasching handes /
or eyeing turnups

/ the sadened powres wee rub /   so economicalie /
                    inn ı virsion off thynges /
                    alarum is mye nayme
                                    / unkempt & handeld
                    i am hors /
                    i am sadeld /   i am a brokn hors

You, like me, might be startled at first by the strangeness of the poem's language. You might even assume this passage was written in Middle English, though if you've studied Middle English, you'll notice that the word choices aren't actually consistent with that language system, though they "read" like Middle English because of Charles's spellings and neologism, such as "feedyng marte" for supermarket, and her arcane-sounding syntax, such as "alarum is mye nayme." Obviously, this is a way of defamiliarizing English to English speakers, to make us "feel" our way into the strangeness of our own language.

But *why* should we feel its strangeness? Here I have to consider the scene Charles has created in the poem, which focuses on an unnamed speaker grocery shopping in a "feedyng marte" where her own "vegetable partes bloome / inn the commen waye" among women "wasching handes / or eyeing turnups." The supermarket isn't just a place for the speaker to shop but to see and be seen, and it takes on a distinctly sexual or at least gendered tone in that description of the women "eyeing turnups," and also in the line "the sadened powres wee rub /   so economalie." Sex, gender, money, and shopping all blur together for me in this place, where the speaker alone is "unkempt & handeld." The speaker also compares herself to a broken horse, something ridden for the pleasure of others, all wildness driven out.

But not all wildness really, since the unruliness of the speaker's language calls attention to itself, refusing to blend in or become invisible. Interestingly, I first described this poem to myself as "non-transparent" in its language, a perhaps unconscious play on the other subject of the poem as it unfolds, which is trans identity and how it intersects with language. In the second part of the poem, Charles continues her comparison of the narrator with the horse, suggesting that the "bit" that reins in the horse might also give it some kind of security:

> the bit provydes
> its horse / the rocke
> provyded a boye
> blessynge gode

If I read language as the "bit," then language becomes one way that gender identity gets maintained and reinforced. It is "the rocke / provyded a boye / blessynge gode"—lines I take to mean that if language stabilizes and tames the horse, it also becomes a way of taming a boy. It is a "blessynge" provided to him, or a gift given to him provided that he himself is "blessynge gode"— suggesting that language only functions positively if he is either religiously devout or *socially* "good." In either case, language is a social and socializing condition, one that Charles clearly rejects in this poem in which she subverts language for her own purposes. "[I] kno / no new waye/ 2 speech," she writes, just as she goes on to state, "a tran i kno doesnt dye / just shye off 27."

As with the multiple translations suggested by "gode," there's a play here on "dye" and "die"; as a reader, I begin to sense the mortal stakes at play in this poem about, among other things, gender transitioning, and resistance to suicide and survival. In the third section of the poem, Charles writes:

>   its
> such   a   pleasure to b alive / inn this trembled soot / u
>   lent / shock is a struktured responce/ a whord lost inn
>   the mouthe off keepers / & u thrum at the mothe / a dozen
> bes

Because of the way Charles spells "to be" as "b" here, when she writes in a later line the phrase "a dozen bes," this could refer equally both to bees and to a dozen human lives. Shock itself here is a "struktured responce/ a whord lost inn/ the mouthe off keepers," suggesting for me the close relationship between social behavior and language—what I am shocked by is an acculturated response that only gets lost in the mouth of "keepers," a play on "beekeepers" as I see in the unfolding line, which suggests both actual beekeepers and people who persist and thrive. I personally see these "keepers" as other trans individuals like Charles, who resist death or cultural erasure.

Charles's neologisms mine the connotation and denotation of words we comprehend largely through sound, oftentimes to make sexual innuendos. "[I] wantd / ı secrete but fore the rod," Charles writes, suggesting that a penis—a "rod"—makes her secret impossible, while also connecting the idea of discipline with phallic imagery itself. Similarly, in a Marvellian twist, the narrator's "vegetable parts bloom" in the "feedynge mart" where tall women "eye" phallic turnips, recalling for me Allen Ginsburg's "A Supermarket in California," which imagines queer poetry icons Garcia Lorca and Walt Whitman "poking among the meats in the refrigerator and eyeing the grocery boys." As in Ginsburg's poem, gender, sexuality, poetry, and the market collide and collapse together. In Charles's poem, sex and gender permeate everything, even as they get mixed up and refracted in surprising ways.

So why choose this diction? It may be reductive to assign all these spellings and diction choices simply to Charles's identity as a trans woman, yet the poem also reminds me that the speaker longs for a language that may be more accurate to an experience which she herself must learn to articulate. "[I] kno new waye/ 2 speech," Charles writes, in this unruly amalgam of texting speech and fake Middle English. Just as Middle English is a transitional language from Norman French, Anglo-Saxon, and modern English, so text-speak is a transitional language hovering somewhere between "proper" English and colloquialism, mediated by technology. Charles has chosen—or, better, singularly created—a language that exists in between the real and the imagined, between history and technology, and it is the collision of these various linguistic streams that produce a "speech" adequate to her singular experience.

On French and Old English Etymologies

Charles's poem may be initially startling in the ways it digs into the English language, but all poems play with and rely upon English's polyphonous registers. English has two etymological channels running through it: Anglo-Saxon and French. The French comes to us via the Norman conquest of England in the eleventh century, which profoundly changed the direction of the English language, since French became the language of government and the new Anglo-Norman nobility. England, of course, had already been conquered by the Romans and Germanic tribes, and so English is a hash of French, Latin, and Scandinavian influences, all of which can be found not only in Middle English's grammatical structures but in its idioms. French itself is a Romance language that evolved from Latin and Greek and, because it quickly became the language of law and the upper class, helped forge not only a two-tier social system in England but a linguistic pattern that continues today in legal contracts and polite phrases that remain etymologically French and Latinate. Meanwhile, our "earthier" or "ruder" words descend from Germanic and Anglo-Saxon roots. Readers who haven't studied either French or Latin can recognize Latinate or French words based on the fact that they tend to be polysyllabic; any word ending in "–ion," for example, is from a Romance language, thus revealing its Latin origin.

Basically, as speakers and writers of English, we move between the Germanic and Romantic, between Anglo-Saxon and French, and we do this unconsciously. You can express almost anything two ways: one politely, by mining etymologically French words, or rudely, by mining Germanic-root words. But the shift between these language families oftentimes causes a shift in rhythm, too, as you can see in Robert Frost's famous "Mending Wall," in particular the neighbor's repeated platitude, "Good fences make good neighbors," which the poem's curmudgeonly neighbor replies whenever Frost's narrator questions him about the necessity of rebuilding the wall between their properties.

MENDING WALL

Something there is that doesn't love a wall,
That sends the frozen-ground-swell under it,
And spills the upper boulders in the sun;
And makes gaps even two can pass abreast.
The work of hunters is another thing:
I have come after them and made repair
Where they have left not one stone on a stone,
But they would have the rabbit out of hiding,
To please the yelping dogs. The gaps I mean,
No one has seen them made or heard them made,
But at spring mending-time we find them there.
I let my neighbor know beyond the hill;
And on a day we meet to walk the line
And set the wall between us once again.
We keep the wall between us as we go.
To each the boulders that have fallen to each.
And some are loaves and some so nearly balls

We have to use a spell to make them balance:
"Stay where you are until our backs are turned!"
We wear our fingers rough with handling them.
Oh, just another kind of out-door game,
One on a side. It comes to little more:
There where it is we do not need the wall:
He is all pine and I am apple orchard.
My apple trees will never get across
And eat the cones under his pines, I tell him.
He only says, "Good fences make good neighbors."
Spring is the mischief in me, and I wonder
If I could put a notion in his head:
"*Why* do they make good neighbors? Isn't it
Where there are cows? But here there are no cows.
Before I built a wall I'd ask to know
What I was walling in or walling out,
And to whom I was like to give offense.
Something there is that doesn't love a wall,
That wants it down." I could say "Elves" to him,
But it's not elves exactly, and I'd rather
He said it for himself. I see him there
Bringing a stone grasped firmly by the top
In each hand, like an old-stone savage armed.
He moves in darkness as it seems to me,
Not of woods only and the shade of trees.
He will not go behind his father's saying,
And he likes having thought of it so well
He says again, "Good fences make good neighbors."

If you look up the etymology of both "good" and "neighbor"
which appear in Frost's famously repeated last line, you'll see they
come from Old English. I'll discuss metrical scansion in more
detail in Chapter 8, but for those who are already adept at meter,

if you scan the line itself you can see that Frost's **blank verse** (unrhymed iambic pentameter) turns into a string of spondees with a single, unstressed sixth foot at the end of the neighbor's reply, also called a **feminine ending**:

Hĕ **sáys** | ăgáin, | |'**Góod fén**|cĕs **máke**| **góod néigh**|bŏrs.'

Frost's neighbor in the poem is tight-lipped, rigid about rituals. Frost's speaker, in contrast, is lighthearted, playful; at one point he muses that the walls between their properties are falling apart not from disuse but something more supernatural, like elves. Not that he believes in elves, of course; still, Frost's narrator wants to suggest, mischievously, that the walls themselves aren't necessary, and that perhaps the truly natural state is one without borders or boundaries to begin with. After all, their property lines haven't been drawn in order to separate livestock but trees: "He is all pine," Frost writes, "and I am apple orchard," a line that metrically reproduces the men's temperamental differences in the spondee "all pine" and the more impish trochaic reversals in "apple orchard."

That said, if Frost's narrator imagines that "something" supernatural is hard at work on this wall, the poem reveals that the neighbor's warning might have merit—not to combat mystical or paranormal forces like elves or faeries, but something more innate to human nature itself:

> I see him there
> Bringing a stone grasped firmly by the top
> In each hand, like an old-stone savage armed.
> He moves in darkness as it seems to me,
> Not of woods only and the shade of trees.

Frost here acknowledges that mending walls may be arbitrary and rote, but walls are necessary due to the violence innate in all humans. When Frost's narrator imagines the neighbor, he sees him as a prehistoric savage, a man grasping a stone not for wall-building but as a weapon. Interestingly, the phrase "old-stone savage" blends the Germanic with the Latinate: "savage" and "armed" both come from old French, thus Latin, but the rest of the line is Germanic. "Darkness," too, is Germanic in origin, as well as the words "grasped," "woods," "shade," and "tree." Frost's lines become increasingly monosyllabic—usually a good sign the words are themselves coming out of Old English, Dutch, or German—and spondaic. You can practically hear a man beating a stone on the ground—or another man's head. For those attuned to meter, you might scan the stresses in these lines like this:

Bríngĭng | ă **stóne** |**grás**ped **fírm**|lў bý | thĕ **tóp**

Ĭn **éach** | **hánd**, || lĭke | ăn **óld-**| **stóne sá**|văge **árm**ed.

Hĕ **móves** | ĭn **dárk**|nĕss ás | ĭt **séems** | tŏ **mé** . . .

At the poem's lyric crisis—that is, at the narrator's admission of the violence that finally animates and structures human relationships—the poem switches out of a regular iambic rhythm toward a more trochaic and spondaic one, while also using more Germanic-inflected words.

A similar pattern occurs in Robert Browning's famous "My Last Duchess." "My Last Duchess" is an ekphrastic persona poem in which the Duke of Ferrara describes a work of art that may or may not be the actual portrait of Lucrezia de' Medici, while the artists he references—Claus of Innsbruck and Fra Pandolf—are entirely imagined. In reality, I'd argue that the real work of art here is the duke himself, a man whose facility with language would rival Michelangelo's with a brush.

MY LAST DUCHESS

FERRARA

That's my last Duchess painted on the wall,
Looking as if she were alive. I call
That piece a wonder, now; Fra Pandolf's hands
Worked busily a day, and there she stands.
Will't please you sit and look at her? I said
"Fra Pandolf" by design, for never read
Strangers like you that pictured countenance,
The depth and passion of its earnest glance,
But to myself they turned (since none puts by
The curtain I have drawn for you, but I)
And seemed as they would ask me, if they durst,
How such a glance came there; so, not the first
Are you to turn and ask thus. Sir, 'twas not
Her husband's presence only, called that spot
Of joy into the Duchess' cheek; perhaps
Fra Pandolf chanced to say, "Her mantle laps
Over my lady's wrist too much," or "Paint
Must never hope to reproduce the faint
Half-flush that dies along her throat." Such stuff
Was courtesy, she thought, and cause enough
For calling up that spot of joy. She had
A heart—how shall I say?—too soon made glad,
Too easily impressed; she liked whate'er
She looked on, and her looks went everywhere.
Sir, 'twas all one! My favour at her breast,
The dropping of the daylight in the West,
The bough of cherries some officious fool
Broke in the orchard for her, the white mule
She rode with round the terrace—all and each
Would draw from her alike the approving speech,
Or blush, at least. She thanked men—good! but thanked

Somehow—I know not how—as if she ranked
My gift of a nine-hundred-years-old name
With anybody's gift. Who'd stoop to blame
This sort of trifling? Even had you skill
In speech—which I have not—to make your will
Quite clear to such an one, and say, "Just this
Or that in you disgusts me; here you miss,
Or there exceed the mark"—and if she let
Herself be lessoned so, nor plainly set
Her wits to yours, forsooth, and made excuse—
E'en then would be some stooping; and I choose
Never to stoop. Oh, sir, she smiled, no doubt,
Whene'er I passed her; but who passed without
Much the same smile? This grew; I gave commands;
Then all smiles stopped together. There she stands
As if alive. Will't please you rise? We'll meet
The company below, then. I repeat,
The Count your master's known munificence
Is ample warrant that no just pretense
Of mine for dowry will be disallowed;
Though his fair daughter's self, as I avowed
At starting, is my object. Nay, we'll go
Together down, sir. Notice Neptune, though,
Taming a sea-horse, thought a rarity,
Which Claus of Innsbruck cast in bronze for me!

Here Browning's narrator, the duke of Ferrara, negotiates with
another nobleman's emissary the marriage of a new wife to replace
his last duchess, a woman many readers would suspect he's killed
off for being too friendly, or perhaps too indiscriminate in her
attentions to men other than the duke. Ownership and control
are important to the duke, as we can see by the fact that everything in the poem is (or is treated as) an object he can display at
will. Even the duchess is present in the poem only via the duke's

recollection of her and her portrait, which he commissioned. In Browning's poem, woman, art, and objects are interchangeable but, as with "Story About the Body," there's a third art at play in this poem ostensibly about art: rhetoric, as demonstrated by Browning's deft switching between etymological registers.

If I were to isolate certain crisis points of the poem—that is, places where I find the duke's language to become particularly pointed—some interesting patterns emerge. Here are three such moments in the poem where I think the etymological underpinnings of Browning's word choice matter:

A.
                              Such stuff
Was courtesy, she thought, and cause enough
For calling up that spot of joy. She had
A heart—how shall I say?— too soon made glad,
Too easily impressed; she liked whate'er
She looked on, and her looks went everywhere.

B.
                              —and if she let
Herself be lessoned so, nor plainly set
Her wits to yours, forsooth, and made excuse—
E'en then would be some stooping; and I choose
Never to stoop. Oh, sir, she smiled, no doubt,
Whene'er I passed her; but who passed without
Much the same smile? This grew; I gave commands;
Then all smiles stopped together.

C.
The Count your master's known munificence
Is ample warrant that no just pretense

> Of mine for dowry will be disallowed;
> Though his fair daughter's self, as I avowed
> At starting, is my object.

In section A, with the help of a dictionary, I can see that Browning's duke employs a number of Germanic, Old English, or Dutch words. "Spot" and "glad," for instance, come from Dutch and Old English respectively, and it's clear the words aren't merely meant to describe the Duchess's blush. "Spot" in particular suggests a stain, perhaps a moral one, something that clearly annoys the duke since he uses the phrase "spot of joy" twice in the poem. "Joy" comes from Old French, thus Latin, meaning "delight" but also "erotic pleasure." Obviously, the duke here suggests something sexual about the satisfaction the duchess takes in other people's interest in her, something promiscuous about her own noticing of other people and objects, as he then adds, darkly, "[S]he liked whate'er/ She looked on, and her looks went everywhere."

The duke's implication is blatant, and embellishes the insult he's already made when imagining Fra Pandolf's own blandishments to his wife:

>   [P]erhaps
> Fra Pandolf chanced to say, "Her mantle laps
> Over my lady's wrist too much," or "Paint
> Must never hope to reproduce the faint
> Half-flush that dies along her throat."

"Lap" is another Germanic word, suggesting both the spilling of the fabric over the duchess's lap, but also something like oral pleasure: a tantalizing bit of innuendo made even more lecherous by Browning's enjambment. By the end of the sentence, these hints become explicit, since the Germanic "to die" was a common euphemism for orgasm used since the Renaissance, while the more respectable (and Latinate) word "reproduce" directly connects images of artistic representation with human procreation itself.

Something similar occurs in passage B, where another pileup of Germanic root words suddenly appears, "forsooth," "stooping," "stop" and "smile" being the most notable. Throughout the poem, the duke succumbs to moments of psychological crisis or confession by repeating particular words rooted in Old English or German: notice how Browning's repetition of the words "stoop" and "stooping" here reveal the duke's fury at having to lower himself to "lesson" his wife. There's a sonic play, I think, on the words "lesson" and "lessen" that Browning either accidentally or deliberately employs, which speaks to the duke's rage at the thought he is somehow not being taken seriously, by his wife or anyone else around him. The duke is a power-mad snob, as well as a murderer, which he makes clear not in direct imagery but in his reference to the "commands" (a Latinate word) that he gives, which "stops" his wife's smiles "altogether." Scan these lines, and you'll also notice this plethora of monosyllabic, Germanic words produce a spondaic, thumping beat: "Thĕn **áll | smíles stóp**ped | tŏgét|hĕr." As with passage A, Browning essentially lets the roots of his word choice do the talking—or killing—for him.

All this, however, changes dramatically by the poem's end. Notice this rush of polysyllabic, Latinate words that suddenly occurs in passage C:

> [Y]our master's known munificence
> Is ample warrant that no just pretense
> Of mine for dowry will be disallowed

"Munificence," "pretense," "disallowed," and even "dowry" all have French and/or Latinate roots. Here, the duke switches abruptly from sexual and violent language to courtly language. Having made his implicit accusations and threats in the previous passages, he can now return to politesse. This is contractual language, of course, because the duke wants to redirect the conversation from threatening to bartering. His shift in diction isn't accidental, however; the duke's rhetoric deliberately slides from Germanic to Latinate registers to underscore his point, which is one reason I find his aside—"Even had you skill/ [i]n speech—which I have not"—so bitterly funny. In reality, the duke is incredibly skillful with language, which Browning's own deft movements between English's different registers underscores. The poem, ostensibly about the imagined portrait of a duchess, finally becomes a portrait of misogynist control.

Browning's swiveling between Germanic and Latinate words is common both to English poetry and daily speech. As with syntax, it's actually rare—even a mark of poor writing—when a text hews strictly to one register. That said, when a poem does do this, it may be trying to draw our attention to how we have linguistically framed the ideas represented in the poem at hand. As an example of this, I like to look at Myung Mi Kim's "[accumulation of land]," a poem that demonstrates, through its accretion of fragmented Latinate phrases, war's final, dehumanizing effects on families.

[ACCUMULATION OF LAND]

accumulation of land   maintain household bear   labor of
                                                    house child

cooking reserve line   belonging to   elaborate isolation

familias implements   enemies captured in war   bearing
                                                   child rearing

production heirs number   and rear household
                           family contains

counting herds possessions   fellow feeling crude
                                   isolate care

family contains in germ   bearing rearing   accumulation of land

implements of production   cooking reserve line of   the
                                               number belonging

counting possessions   heirs   the captured

isolated household bear   rear heirs

feeling crude   belonging to   fellow feeling crude

Kim's disorienting lineation forces me to choose how to read:
vertically or horizontally? In columns or as a single fragmented
sentence? Thinking forensically about the poem, I notice several
words work here as verbs, nouns and adjectives, such as "elaborate" or "feeling" or "crude": only spoken emphasis might clarify
intention. In public readings, Kim has said all options of meaning are possible, and has performed the poem multiple ways to
highlight the differences a changed visual order and syntactic
stress might engender. Regardless of where I start and how I cat-
egorize parts of speech, however, the poem's repetitiveness suggests a particular logic. Each word or phrase in the poem appears
at least twice except "maintain," "germ," "enemies," and "war,"
though the sense of these echoes throughout, as children and
women are transfigured into captives of a pernicious, martially
inflected social system. This system turns families into domestic products bound by legal, not emotional ties, children become
"heirs" that work for others' benefit, "implements of production"
that "belong" to parents by necessity rather than love. Motherhood, too, is both a physical and economic practice that keeps
the mother emotionally removed from her offspring, as Kim

plays off the word "labor" in the poem, turning it from a reference to childbirth to work, and finally to overbearing loneliness, just as the word "bear" evolves from childbirth to the endurance of private suffering.

It's a bleak view of family life to say the least, and Kim's use of almost exclusively Latinate words to describe basic domestic functions—cooking, for instance, becomes something done on "a reserve line"—strips the poem of sentiment or empathy. Kim even uses one purely Latin word—"familias"—in place of "family" itself, making the poem seem suddenly written in a foreign language. Kim's Latinate word choice highlights the contractual nature of family life while also making English newly strange to a reader who may or may not herself be a native speaker of English.

Readers may wonder why I see this poem as attached to war, a reading I've assembled partly based on Kim's biography. Born in South Korea in 1957, four years after the armistice that put a halt to the Korean War, Kim immigrated with her mother to the United States at age nine. Here Kim learned English, a fact that may be one reason she's so attentive to the language's etymological and political strains. In Kim's hands, English is at once opaque and excruciatingly specific, so that I'm never quite sure what particular event, person, or object she has imagined. This sense of disorientation, rather than weakening Kim's poems, for me enacts the experience of learning a new language: a language that cannot, no matter how fluent one becomes, approximate the trauma of having one's original culture forgotten.

Kim's poem—so coolly impersonal that it feels antiseptic—may seem impenetrable to readers who believe poetry should first express private emotion, but when reading this poem, ask yourself three questions: First, if you were writing about your own family, what kind of language and diction would you choose to use? Second, how would you characterize the language that Kim relies upon? Third, when faced with "[accumulation of land]," where do you start reading?

In answering these questions, you start to see the reason why we find Kim's poem so sterile in its register, something that gets heightened by its visual fragmentation. These aspects of the poem push us to assemble patterns of meaning that speak to and against each other. By doing this, you soon recognize that Kim's poetry only flirts with incoherence: you can begin to feel the depersonalizing aftermath of war through Kim's diction.

What Sounds and Tones Do You Hear?
Making Sense from Nonsense

Frost's and Browning's shifts in diction attend important shifts in the narrative meaning and characterization within their poems; in that, the etymological differences between certain words become part of these poets' representational strategies. But Kim's and Charles's poems do something different—they skirt the line between sense and nonsense to ask larger questions about how language-making itself becomes attached to specific identities. This raises an important question: What about poems that include words with *no* traceable etymological roots at all, that might even be composed of words that refuse to make sense? For this, we have to think about the ways that words mean not just according to the dictionary but according to their *sound*.

When I talk about sound and meaning in poetry, you might first think of rhyme. In that, you're hardly alone: Robert Frost called rhyme the "sound of sense," while Alexander Pope argued that "sound must seem an echo to the sense." We talk about aspects of rhyme and meter as extensions of the poem's thinking and tone, even critically disparaging poems where form and sense divide. Imagine someone trying to write an elegy in a limerick, for example, and you get what I mean. We have it so ingrained in our minds that sound and sense must cohere that we take it for granted that sound itself can allow for particular interpretations; in fact, sound might be one initial way we interpret a poem, becoming, as Frost suggested, the possibility of sense itself.

For example, how would you read this?

TOTENKLAGE

Ombula
take
bitdli
solunkola
table tokta tokta takabla
taka tak
Babula m balam
tak tru tü
wo um
biba bimbel
o kla o auwa
kla o auwa
la auma
o kla o ü
la o auma
klinga o e auwa
klinga inga M ao Auwa
omba dij omuff pomo auwa
tru-ü
tro u ü a o ü
mo-auwa
gomun guma zangaga gago blagaga
szagaglugi m ba o auma
szaga szago
szaga la m blama
bschigi bschigo

bschigi bschigi
bschiggo bschiggo
goggo goggo
ogoggo
a o auma

It may not appear so, but this *is* a poem, at least according to its author, the German poet and Dada Manifesto author Hugo Ball. Ball wrote "Totenklage," or "Death Lament," in 1916, the same year he created his manifesto, and you can see it's a stream of nonsensical sounds, many of which repeat exactly or are only slightly altered in their repetition. In many ways, "Totenklage" epitomizes Ball's manifesto, which argued that poets "were always writing words but never writing the word itself, who are always writing around the actual point." In effect, Ball wanted to abandon sense to create a completely new poetic language, one that wasn't invented by others but innate to Ball himself. "I let the vowels fool around," Ball declared, "I let the vowels quite simply occur, as a cat meows . . ."

You might treat this poem as one long piece of caterwauling, but the artists who have performed "Totenklage" over the last century have drawn from it a remarkable amount of meaning and nuance. One performance by Hanna Aurbacher on the *Futura Poesia Sonora* record, for instance, features the sounds of a woman wailing, her thin, high voice alternately gulping down each syllable of the poem as if choking on grief, throbbing with pain and terror. You can hear Aurbacher's version on YouTube (just as you can hear Marie Osmond perform Ball's 1918 sound poem "Karawane" on the Penn Sound website for an even more out-of-body experience) and clearly intuit how she interprets Ball's language. Ball wrote both "Totenklage" and the Dada Manifesto in the midst of World War I, so perhaps it's no surprise that Aurbacher translated the poem as an outpouring of grief—whether for dead soldiers and civilians or for a lost beloved.

WHAT WORD CHOICE AND DICTION DOES THE POET USE?   185

Aurbacher's performance is fascinating and disturbing, but what draws me back to "Totenklage" is not that it creates any one meaning out of Ball's sounds but that this same poem—because it lacks definable words that give it a specific time, place, and even elegiac subject—can be performed by other poets to produce very different interpretations. Listen to the Canadian poet Christian Bök perform "Totenklage" in 2005 (a clip you can also find on the Penn Sound website), and you'll hear Bök growl the poem deep from his throat and chest, creating a low hum that undergirds each syllable. Where Aurbacher focused on the poem's "o" and "a" vowels, making their sounds high-pitched and wailing, Bök instead clips his consonants, turning each "s" into a "z" sound, transforming a possible WWI lament voiced by a single woman into something that resembles an ancient and choral Tibetan religious rite.

Aurbacher's and Bök's wildly different performances remind me how slyly we can suggest time, occasion, sex, and even culture or race through sound. While both performances retain a deep, mournful feeling, the relationship between speaker and grief changes according to how I hear each poet embody Ball's invented language. One poem feels immediate, intimate; the other ritualized and impersonal. Listening to these different versions of "Totenklage" recently in class, one student asked how an American poet might perform the poem after our long war in Afghanistan. Could we, she asked, change Ball's poem again to suggest something like a military anthem or patriotic march? I replied that it seemed possible: as both Aurbacher and Bök demonstrated, sound itself is open to interpretation. The duration of the syllables, the particular ways a poet might suppress or heighten certain fricatives were ultimately the choice of the performer, who could create a multitude of laments from the same nonsensical phrases.

Some readers might take umbrage at Ball's experiments, insisting that—because the poem resists using *any* known language—it ceases to be a poem. Sound poems, they might argue, are limited creatively, since how "artful" can random choices like Ball's be? After all, aren't poems meant to communicate legible emotion that others can translate into an experience they also share? But poems have always played along the slippery line between what can be said and what can't, what we intimately intuit versus what we can articulate, and poems like Ball's exploit that shifting edge. To perform "Totenklage" yourself pushes you to embody something that becomes, at heart, pure feeling. You yourself become the translation of the poem, experiencing, bodily, whatever forms of grief you find contained in it—and isn't that what some of the most conservative readers of poetry insist that reading poetry fundamentally requires?

And of course readers who find Ball's poem a dubious experiment might want to reread this beloved poem:

JABBERWOCKY

'Twas brillig, and the slithy toves
    Did gyre and gimble in the wabe:
All mimsy were the borogoves,
    And the mome raths outgrabe.

"Beware the Jabberwock, my son!
    The jaws that bite, the claws that catch!
Beware the Jubjub bird, and shun
    The frumious Bandersnatch!"

He took his vorpal sword in hand;
    Long time the manxome foe he sought—
So rested he by the Tumtum tree
    And stood awhile in thought.

And, as in uffish thought he stood,
    The Jabberwock, with eyes of flame,

Came whiffling through the tulgey wood,
And burbled as it came!

One, two! One, two! And through and through
The vorpal blade went snicker-snack!
He left it dead, and with its head
He went galumphing back.

"And hast thou slain the Jabberwock?
Come to my arms, my beamish boy!
O frabjous day! Callooh! Callay!"
He chortled in his joy.

'Twas brillig, and the slithy toves
Did gyre and gimble in the wabe:
All mimsy were the borogoves,
And the mome raths outgrabe.

Lewis Carroll's "Jabberwocky" thrills in part *because* of what we cannot define, even as we perfectly understand the poem's meaning. If Ball's sound poems are, on the surface, pure nonsense, Carroll's "Jabberwocky" is what we'd call **near-nonsense**, since its syntax and the bulk of the poem's words can be clearly tracked by any reader, who is then invited to fill in the meaning of invented words like "mimsy," "uffish," "vorpal," and "tulgey" with her own imagining. Carroll's poem also gains from its regular metrical forms and balladic rhymes, which offer the reader's ear both closure and structure. In effect, the poem's metrical and sonic regularity acts as a ballast, a safe container for readers to feel emotional completion, even if no absolutely understood narrative can be reached via the definition of the words themselves.

The linguistic experiments of "Jabberwocky" and "Toten-klage" are an extension of the sonic playfulness we expect of any poem, especially ones that use onomatopoeia or other mimetic devices, either to represent outbursts or animals, or to give a line some particular emotional resonance, as you can hear in Wilfred Owen's poem "Strange Meeting," with its repeated *a, ow, oh,* and *or* sounds.

STRANGE MEETING

It seemed that out of battle I escaped
Down some profound dull tunnel, long since scooped
Through granites which titanic wars had groined.

Yet also there encumbered sleepers groaned,
Too fast in thought or death to be bestirred.
Then, as I probed them, one sprang up, and stared
With piteous recognition in fixed eyes,
Lifting distressful hands, as if to bless.
And by his smile, I knew that sullen hall,—
By his dead smile I knew we stood in Hell.

With a thousand fears that vision's face was grained;
Yet no blood reached there from the upper ground,
And no guns thumped, or down the flues made moan.
"Strange friend," I said, "here is no cause to mourn."
"None," said that other, "save the undone years,
The hopelessness. Whatever hope is yours,
Was my life also; I went hunting wild
After the wildest beauty in the world,
Which lies not calm in eyes, or braided hair,
But mocks the steady running of the hour,
And if it grieves, grieves richlier than here.
For by my glee might many men have laughed,
And of my weeping something had been left,
Which must die now. I mean the truth untold,
The pity of war, the pity war distilled.

Now men will go content with what we spoiled.
Or, discontent, boil bloody, and be spilled.
They will be swift with swiftness of the tigress.
None will break ranks, though nations trek from progress.
Courage was mine, and I had mystery;
Wisdom was mine, and I had mastery:
To miss the march of this retreating world
Into vain citadels that are not walled.
Then, when much blood had clogged their chariot-wheels,
I would go up and wash them from sweet wells,
Even with truths that lie too deep for taint.
I would have poured my spirit without stint
But not through wounds; not on the cess of war.
Foreheads of men have bled where no wounds were.

"I am the enemy you killed, my friend.
I knew you in this dark: for so you frowned
Yesterday through me as you jabbed and killed.
I parried; but my hands were loath and cold.
Let us sleep now. . . ."

Owen assembled "Strange Meeting" from a series of slightly askew rhymes, each couplet sonically blurring into the next: "untold/distilled/spoiled/spilled" and "world/walled/wheels/wells" muddying the poem's heroic couplet form into something that at times better resembles the interlocking tercet rhymes of **terza rima**. By violating the expectation of "perfect" rhymes, Owen deflates the "heroic" aspect of his couplets and emphasizes instead the painful and morally slippery ground these two young men both traversed in war. You can even hear how Owen also plays off a single agonized sound over a series of lines in the third stanza, "grained" turning to "ground," "moan" turning to "mourn," reinforcing the poem's sounds of lament.

This is interpretive information carried less immediately in the meaning of the words than in their sonic effects, though if I examine the etymologies of these words, I discover that "grained," "ground," "moan," and "mourn" all stem from the Germanic or Middle English sides of our linguistic heritage; in fact, very few of the end words in "Strange Meeting" come from French or Latin at all, as if Owen were deliberately unearthing the most elemental, anguished roots of our language.

Language as Performance

I've spent a lot of time here talking about the roots and sounds of words, which themselves convey emotional information that may or may not be immediately legible to a listener. In that, poems are always asking us to pay attention to the hidden valences of language, sometimes making these implicit opportunities explicit, with an eye to critique not just what is being said but how we have historically framed or even codified certain ideas within types of language. That kind of critical poetic play has been the province of postmodern or avant-garde poets in particular, who want us to pay attention to the estranging effects of even our most bland social utterances. I'm thinking especially of the sound poems of Tracie Morris, which sometimes tap into documentary or found language to create richer, powerful confrontations with history. Her poem "Africa(n)," for example, is composed of just a single sentence: "It all started when we were brought here as slaves from Africa." Morris starts by speaking this sentence much like a professional lecturer might, cleanly and clearly, without emotion, but on her second repetition, she begins to stutter on the words "started" and "as." Morris's pitch rises in the third repetition, as if she's going to try to sing the line, but soon the song splutters out, slurring on the opening phrase "It all started" as Morris's voice rises frantically in an attempt to finish her sentence. By her fourth repetition, this sentence has collapsed to one phrase: "when when we when when we when when we," Morris sing-stutters. As she continues to perform, the sentence becomes unintelligibly jumbled, the phrases backtracking and splicing together, eliding verbs and subjects, finally rearranging the sentence itself. "It all started Africa," Morris says at one point, then changes this to "when we were Africa," then changes it again to "It all started with Africa," then to "It all started when we were Africa," then finally collapses to a single repeated pronoun: "It it it it it it." As the poem progresses, Morris can't or won't even say the word "slaves" entirely, eliding and splicing it to a single, nonsensical sound: "slah." At the poem's end, the recitation has become a series of syncopations: "when we when whe whe we when whe whe we when," Morris hiccups, stopping with the phrase, "It all started when we."

You can listen to Morris perform the poem on both YouTube and Penn Sound, and it's fascinating to watch her face as she recites/sings it, as her expression changes from that of a professional lecturer to a traumatized witness. The poem is deliberately unbearable to listen to, as it violates so many of our expectations of "good" or "proper" public speech, the first being that expression itself should be comprehensible and also a complete thought. But what begins as a complete statement, if not a fully articulated thesis, soon devolves into verbal glitches that reveal the speaker's buried emotion. As she fractures and rearranges phrases, Morris forces her listeners to confront slavery's horror by making the sentence perform what narrative history would suppress with bland fact. Sound, Morris shows us, is not just interpretive but a critical apparatus. We can encode race, gender, culture, even a sense of community in the ways we pronounce a word. We can also make history, in its articulation, more palpable, personal, and dimensional.

I know it's strange to write about what can't actually be experienced on the page, but so much of what interests me about poetry lifts away from print or calls to the page as a space of performance itself. Poetry is, at heart, dramatic, as our first poems were composed to be sung, not written, and I think we limit ourselves as readers if we confine our experience of poetry only to poems that have been composed primarily for conventional forms of publication. Though I don't write sound poems myself, I've learned a lot from Bök's and Morris's work, from the ways their performances invite me to turn a sentence or sound over, jewel-like, examining it for flaws and surprising illuminations. As I wrote before, it's not that different a practice from the forensic reading we demand of more conventionally legible poems whose words reveal hidden histories within the dictionary. And to ignore the pleasures of making and listening to nonsense does disservice to the ways many of us come to poetry to begin with: not because of what poems say to our brains so much as how they ring in our ears. I had no idea that Gerard Manley Hopkins's poem "The Windhover" was about Christ when I was fifteen and first encountered it, but I knew its words made me feel giddy and electric and alive, a bit like that falcon Hopkins described as it wheeled through the air. I defy anyone to read that poem aloud and not be moved by its sonic swoops and dives, its electric rhythms and strange, archaic phrasings.

When we read or write poetry, it's imperative to read poems aloud, in part to hear the beauty of the language but also to hear how the poem's thinking unfolds. We catch up to the meanings of poems, we rarely comprehend them in an instant. Sometimes, this process of catching up takes a lifetime. One of the first books of poetry I ever read was Czesław Miłosz's *Winter Bells*, which I bought in high school, having fished it out of a $1 sale bin at my local bookstore, where I also found a copy of Sylvia Plath's *Ariel* and Louise Glück's *House on Marshland*. I had absolutely no idea who these poets were, whether they were good or bad or even alive; it wasn't a mark of precocity but price that made me choose them. I would have gone home with Charles Bukowski or Rod McKuen if they'd been in that bin. But those three poets formed the spine of my poetry reading that year, and throughout my junior year in high school, as I slavishly imitated Miłosz in English classes, not because I understood his poems, but because they sounded beautiful to me. My teachers must have been baffled by finding the work of a teenage girl who sounded like a war-torn, fifty-year-old Polish émigré in their grading stack, but I passed my classes and went on to fish more books of poetry out of sale bins—Galway Kinnell and Seamus Heaney and Linda Bierds and Lucille Clifton among them—again, not because I much understood them or knew of their cultural importance but because of the newness of the language they offered me. That's what poetry gives us, after all: a gorgeous estranging of the familiar. They remake what we might otherwise grow indifferent to, allowing us to feel, for a moment, not just like explorers of our words but creators of language itself.

EXPERIMENTS

- Take a poem and excise crucial words from it, then give it to someone else to choose words that "complete" the poem. You can choose to excise any poem you like, but I often use two poems: Wilfred Owen's "Dulce et Decorum Est Pro Patria Mori" and Gerard Manley Hopkins's "God's Grandeur," since both ask readers to consider the poets' rhythmic and/or metrical patterns as well as tone, imagery, meaning and diction. Hopkins's poems in particular are full of novel words for students, but which have real spiritual and etymological depth. Below is my excised version of Hopkins's poem. Fill in the blanks with your own words, then compare Hopkins's published version with yours. If Hopkins uses any words that seem particularly unusual, look up the etymology of the word to see if there might be any other connections you can find between the word Hopkins chose and the imagery that surrounds it.

GOD'S GRANDEUR

The world is _____ with the grandeur of God.
   It will flame out, like _____ from shook _____;
   It _____ to a greatness, like the _____ of oil
_____. Why do men then now not _____ his rod?
Generations have _____, have _____, have trod;
   And all is _____ with trade; _____ , _____ with toil;
   And _____ man's _____ and shares man's _____: the soil
Is _____ now, nor can _____ feel, being shod.

And for all this, nature is never spent;
   There lives the dearest _____ deep down things;
And though the last _____ off the black West went
   Oh, morning, at the brown _____ eastward, _____—
Because the Holy Ghost over the bent
   World _____ with warm breast and with _____ bright wings.

- Examine a poem from the suggested works list below that seems interested in the etymology of a particular word or words. Look up the meanings of the ways in which the original meanings of these words might have larger implications for the reader now.
- Write a poem that tells a story that includes or is entirely composed of nonsense words, or that highlights specific sounds or sonic connections between words. How

can sound influence our understanding of your speaker's emotions or situation?

- Write a poem composed of a single sentence in which the sentence syntactically breaks down over the course of the poem. How do your sonic or syntactic disruptions highlight a meaning hidden within the sentence itself? How might these disruptions change how we imagine your speaker?

- Examine a draft of one of your own poems. Are there any places in which Latinate or Germanic words predominate? What is taking place at that moment in the poem? What kind of tone does this etymological register create? Can you switch out some of your Latinate words for Germanic ones, and vice versa? What happens to your understanding of tone, event, image, or character in the poem when you make those changes?

SUGGESTED WORKS TO CONSIDER

E. E. Cummings, "r-p-o-p-h-e-s-s-a-g-r"
Kurt Schwitters, "Ursonate" (samples on Penn Sound)
Brenda Iijima, "Skyland"
Orlando White, "water"
Gertrude Stein, "Guillaume Apollinaire" and "Picasso"
Heather McHugh, "Etymological Dirge"
Eduardo Chirinos, "A Brief Treatise on Etymology"
Brandon Som, "Chino"
Solmaz Sharif, "[Persian Letters]"
Paul Muldoon, "Anseo"

Except otherwise noted, all poems can be found either at the Poetry Foundation or the Academy of American Poets websites.

CHAPTER SEVEN

What Rhymes Do You Hear?

I f sound is one of the most powerful encounters we first have
with poetry, then rhyme is one of the most consistent methods
we have of managing it. Rhyme creates a sense of magic, which
is why chants, spells, charms, and nursery rhymes are replete
with it, and why it profoundly shapes oral literary culture, functioning both as a mnemonic device for the poet and a source of
pleasure for the listener. I like to think of Anne Carson's take
on what sound and rhyme might have meant to people living in
such a preliterate society, where senses other than sight helped
them organize and absorb complex information about the world.
As Carson imagined it:

> An individual who lives in an oral culture uses his senses
> differently than one who lives in a literate culture, and with
> that different sensual deployment comes a different way of
> conceiving his own relations with his environment, a dif-
> ferent conception of his body and a different conception of
> his self.*

---

* Anne Carson, *Eros the Bittersweet* (Dallas: Dalkey Archive Press New
York, 1998), 45.

I used to teach literacy skills to men coming out of the Washington State Prison system, and while none of the men I worked with had achieved more than a fourth-grade reading level, each possessed an astonishingly large body of memorized songs. One man, rather than writing weekly short paragraphs for our meetings, made mix tapes instead, recording snippets of sound and diaristic entries about his impressions of the books we read, as well as memories from his childhood. It wasn't that these men were illiterate, their literacy just functioned—and flourished—in different ways. What they heard and how they spoke revealed more about the ways their minds worked than what their hands could quickly put to paper. Some people might see sound and rhyme as part of poetry's elaborate construction, serving ultimately as elaborate game playing. But I think rhyme comes closer to how Carson envisioned it: as part of bodily expression itself and, in that, a way of coming into one's identity.

We might believe that because so much of English-language poetry is formal and because our earliest oral poems, such as ballads and songs, rely heavily on rhyme, that rhyme is innate to the Western tradition. In reality, rhyme was rare in classical poetry, and in the Germanic languages overlooked in favor of **alliteration**, a form of rhyme that depends on the repetition of initial vowels or consonants in words rather than the exact duplication of sounds. Rhyme in English starts showing up in the late Middle Ages and takes such a strong hold on literary verse by the Renaissance that Sir Philip Sidney, in his *Defense of Poesie*, calls rhyme "the chiefe life" of poetry itself. Even now, some readers so strongly associate rhyme with poetry that they refuse to recognize as verse any poem that lacks it. But rhyme is a historical development and cultural accident. Not all poetic traditions require rhyme, and our understanding of and terminology around rhyme itself have changed over the centuries. Rhyme isn't simply two words that sound alike but patterns of sound that break down into the following categories:

Alliteration: The repetition of the same sound or letter at the beginning of neighboring words

Consonance: The repetition of the same consonantal sounds in a series of adjacent words

Assonance: The repetition of the same vowel sounds in a series of adjacent words

Slant rhyme or **near rhyme**: Rhymes of one or more syllables that aren't exact (cartwheel/windmill)

Full rhyme or **end rhymes**: Rhymes of one or more syllables that are exact (cat/hat)

Rime riche or **identical rhyme**: Rhymes of two or more syllables where matching consonants appear before the last accented vowel (compare/despair), or of homographs (cleave/cleave), or of homophones (pair/pear)

Masculine rhymes: Rhyme words of different syllables rhyming on the final syllable (abound/round)

Feminine rhymes: Words of different syllables rhyming on the initial syllable (soreness/ doorless)

Eye rhymes: Words spelled similarly but pronounced differently (dove/move).

Rhymes don't occur only at the ends of lines, either, but can be scattered throughout a poem. Rhyme's many kinds and types also mean that different examples of rhyme can be—and often are—mixed and matched, such as when a poem uses end rhymes, internal rhymes, and alliteration, as in Percy Bysshe Shelley's "The Cloud," which uses regular internal rhymes, as well as alliteration and sibilance:

> I sift the snow on the mountains below,
> And their great pines groan aghast;
> And all the night 'tis my pillow white,
> While I sleep in the arms of the blast.

And here is a tongue-twister you already likely know:

> How much wood could a woodchuck chuck
> If a woodchuck could chuck wood?
> As much wood as a woodchuck could chuck,
> If a woodchuck could chuck wood.

This short seventeenth-century poem attributed to "Mother Goose" is replete with rhyme: there's consonance and assonance, full rhymes and direct repetition, rime riche and alliteration. Almost every word rhymes in some fashion with another, which is one reason it's so hard—and fun—to rattle off.

But while sonic play is fun in poetry, the question remains why we rhyme in poetry at all. We rhyme to tell jokes, to make didactic points, to remember complex narratives, to sell things, to make puns, and to memorialize ourselves. Rhyme on its own carries limited meaning; it is primarily through its interaction with rhythm, lineation, and metrical pattern that it gains significance, which is why I'll spend more time in the next chapters on formal verse closely examining specific rhymes. But although rhyme has no single function in poetry, in a multi-stanza poem, it bears a strong relationship to our sense of closure. Formal verse even structures stanzas around particular patterns of sound; once one pattern ends, another rhyming pattern begins, and with it a new stanza. Some **quatrains**, or four-line stanzas, create closure through what we call **envelope rhymes**, in which the first and fourth rhyming lines enclose the second and third rhyming lines, in an ABBA pattern, such as you see in Alfred, Lord Tennyson's "In Memoriam":

Strong Son of God, immortal Love,
    Whom we, that have not seen thy face,
    By faith, and faith alone, embrace,
Believing where we cannot prove;

Thine are these orbs of light and shade;
    Thou madest Life in man and brute;
    Thou madest Death; and lo, thy foot
Is on the skull which thou hast made.

Other common quatrain rhymes include the ABAB **inter-laced** or **alternate rhyme** pattern, and the AABB **double-couplet** pattern. One of the most intriguing patterns of rhyme is the **unbounded** or **ballad** quatrain, which follows the ABAC or ABCB pattern and thus contains within it a jarring "flaw" that can function like a deliberately dissonant note in a song. For me, it adds an air of tension or anticipation, since by momentarily abandoning the presumed rhyme scheme, we long to hear the pattern right itself again. In Gwendolyn Brooks's ballad "Sadie and Maud," for example, note how that third line creates a brief pause in each stanza, almost as if the line had an extra metrical foot.

SADIE AND MAUD

Maud went to college.
Sadie stayed at home.
Sadie scraped life
With a fine-tooth comb.

She didn't leave a tangle in.
Her comb found every strand.
Sadie was one of the livingest chits
In all the land.

Sadie bore two babies
Under her maiden name.
Maud and Ma and Papa
Nearly died of shame.

When Sadie said her last so-long
Her girls struck out from home.
(Sadie had left as heritage
Her fine-tooth comb.)

Maud, who went to college,
Is a thin brown mouse.
She is living all alone
In this old house.

That pause is created by our expectation that the third line should rhyme with the first, since the ABAB quatrain is one of the most common ballad and hymnal rhyme schemes. When the third line doesn't meet that expectation, it sticks in our ear. But Brooks's unrhyming third line also duplicates some measure of the poem's story—Sadie, the wild girl who doesn't go to college and has two children out of wedlock, doesn't fit in with her family's more conservative, middle-class ambitions. Sadie is not like her sister, Maud, who goes to college and thus fulfills those ambitions, but at the personal cost of loneliness. The two girls in Brooks's poem are sisters whose lives are meant to "rhyme" or reflect upon the other's. And yet their lives don't rhyme at all, at least not exactly; both sacrifice something in pursuit of some fulfillment (Sadie loses her family's respect, while Maud loses out on a family altogether), though the poem spends three of the five stanzas detailing Sadie's life. Sadie, in her unorthodox zest for experience and sensation, attracts more attention, in and outside of the poem.

Brooks's ballad carries with it a whiff of moral judgment, the result both of its form, which suggests neat resolution through its rhyme and meter, and the juxtaposition of Sadie and Maud. The surprise of the poem, however, is that no comfortable judgment upon or about these girls can ultimately be made: neither Sadie nor Maud makes the "right" choice, since both girls' desires are, in some fundamental way, judged by society, including by the reader who might be encouraged to read Maud's celibacy as a chastisement. If Brooks makes any clear moral pronouncement in her poem, it might be against whomever would look askance at that "livingest chit" Sadie, whose only sin was to love life and pass that particular love on through her girls, free to strike out now on their own. In contrast, Maud is a "thin brown mouse" who lives alone. Perhaps this as her ironic penance for "nearly [dying] of shame" over Sadie's choices, but considering how we're supposed to look askance at the criticism of Sadie, why should we then judge Maud for failing to have a family herself, thus becoming another "wrong" kind of woman? In reality, Brooks's ballad shows us that there is no "right" woman in a world of conservative Black family and class values, and the genius of her unbounded quatrains is that, even as the rhymes right themselves, each stanza reminds the reader that something is—if briefly—irreconcilable. In that, form merges with content, duplicating the estranging and complex feelings I have for Sadie and Maud.

Are the Stanzas Organized by Rhyme?

In general, stanzas organized around patterns of rhyme create contained units of sense, tone, or narrative. A change of rhyme might accompany either a change in thought or change of stanza, as well as an evolution of theme, subject, or argument. Isolated couplets create the sense of finality and closure, which is why they tend to occur at the ends of stanzas and poems, while quatrains function as rhetorical building blocks, useful for extending an image or the poem's plot. **Terza rima** tercets, in which the first and third lines' ending words rhyme while the second line's ending word sets the rhyming pattern for the following stanza, allow for a poem's continuous unfurling: in that, it functions beautifully for extended narratives such as Dante's *Divine Comedy*, whereas the tightly structured quatrains and couplet sequence of Shakespearean sonnets curtail story in favor of lyric reflection and perception. Rhyme's effects are also enhanced by line length and syntax, which, when all three are combined together, produce rhythm. Put rhymes closer together in simple syntax or end-stopped lines, for example, and the poem sounds more song- or chant-like, even comedic. Spread farther apart across lines or metrical feet, or placed in hypotactic syntax, however, and rhymes tend toward the rhetorical. For example, the ballad's short, closely rhymed quatrains in "Sadie and Maud" allow for its quick advancement of plot, while the longer-lined stanzas of Keats's "Ode to a Nightingale," whose ten-line stanzas resemble the Petrarchan sonnet's rhyming patterns, provide more space for meditation. In Keats's ode, each stanza ends with a CDECDE rhyme scheme, which allows Keats to create a sense of connection but not closure, as the sestet pulls away from the more tightly resolved ABAB interlaced rhymes of the opening quatrain to create a sense of irresolution, which you see in both the questions and the rhymes that appear in the poem's final stanza:

> Forlorn! the very word is like a bell
>> To toll me back from thee to my sole self!
> Adieu! the fancy cannot cheat so well
>> As she is fam'd to do, deceiving elf.
> Adieu! adieu! thy plaintive anthem fades
>> Past the near meadows, over the still stream,
>>> Up the hill-side; and now 'tis buried deep
>> In the next valley-glades:
> Was it a vision, or a waking dream?
>> Fled is that music:—Do I wake or sleep?

Here, Keats's rhymes fade yet linger, just like the nightingale's song itself on Keats's consciousness. We hear them still, as a cascading echo. But space rhymes *many* lines apart, as Auden did in "Musée des Beaux Arts," and some readers might argue that the poem lacks rhyme at all.

Just because a poem is absent a conventional rhyme scheme, however, doesn't mean it isn't attuned to how rhyme functions. Here's a poem with no sonic rhymes at all but which is, oddly, entirely rhymed. A. E. Stallings's poem "Alice in the Looking Glass" is a sonnet whose title alludes to the famous Lewis Carroll novel, though by the end of the poem, it's clear that the "Alice" in the mirror refers not to Carroll's heroine but Alicia Stallings herself:

ALICE IN THE LOOKING GLASS

No longer can I just climb through—the time
Is past for going back. But you are there
Still conning books in Hebrew, right to left,
Or moving little jars on the dresser top
Like red and white pieces on a chessboard. Still
You look up curiously at me when I pass
As if you'd ask me something—maybe why
I've left you locked inside. I'd say because
That is where I'd have reflections stay,
In surfaces, where they cannot disquiet,
Shallow, for all that they seem deep at bottom;
Though it's to you I look to set things right—
(The blouse askew, hair silvering here and here)—
Where everything reverses save for time.

If Stallings's first rhyme in the poem is Alice and herself, a quick scan of the end words of this sonnet reveals that every word is also part of a conceptual pair. If we divide the poem at the seventh and eighth lines, for example, I see that they end on "why" and "because" respectively. If I work backwards from these lines to the end and beginning of the poem, I see each end word is rhetorically related to another through reversed logic: why/because, stay/pass, disquiet/still, bottom/top, right/left, here/there. The poem then begins and ends on an eye rhyme: time/time. Stallings thus plays with our ideas of rhyme by showing how words might be paired not through sound but rhetorical sense. The poem itself is all about reversals: Stallings muses on her reflection in the mirror, which recalls simultaneously both her younger and current self. The mirror image is, of course, the reverse image of ourselves in life, and yet even as they suggest our reversals, they cannot actually reverse our own aging. Stallings admits this to her reflection in the mirror, the thing to which she "look[s] to set things right—/(The blouse askew, hair silvering here and here)—" even as she recognizes that time itself can never be reversed. That reversal can only happen in the sonnet, which "turns" at the midway point—an unusual volta in a Shakespearean sonnet, though closer to the Petrarchan one—so that the poem feels as if it divides in two, one half reflecting on the other, mimetically reproducing the effect of looking in a mirror.

Stallings's poem creates an odd and ingenious sense of movement: even as the poem narratively progresses forward, its *conceptual* rhymes move us backward. Her poem thus allows me to experience two kinds of time simultaneously, duplicating the rush of nostalgia I might feel when confronted with my own aging appearance in the mirror. Stallings's poem reminds me that rhyme—even conceptual rhyme—is a powerful way to create movement and change in verse, whether that occurs in a poem's syntax or narrative, or in the sense of catharsis a reader experiences. Simply put, you feel good when you hear an expected rhyme complete itself and you feel something off when it doesn't. For example, notice how George Herbert's rhyme in his poem "Denial" sticks in our ear, mimicking the poem's own focus on disorder, alarm, discontent, the result of God's unwillingness or inability to hear the speaker's devotional pleas, which in effect "breaks" Herbert's verse, just as it breaks his heart.

DENIAL

When my devotions could not pierce
Thy silent ears,
Then was my heart broken, as was my verse;
My breast was full of fears
And disorder.

My bent thoughts, like a brittle bow,
Did fly asunder:
Each took his way; some would to pleasures go,
Some to the wars and thunder
Of alarms.

"As good go anywhere," they say,
"As to benumb
Both knees and heart, in crying night and day,
Come, come, my God, O come!
But no hearing."

O that thou shouldst give dust a tongue
To cry to thee,
And then not hear it crying! All day long
My heart was in my knee,
But no hearing.

Therefore my soul lay out of sight,
Untuned, unstrung:
My feeble spirit, unable to look right,

Like a nipped blossom, hung
Discontented.

O cheer and tune my heartless breast,
Defer no time;
That so thy favors granting my request,
They and my mind may chime,
And mend my rhyme.

In Herbert's poem, rhyme symbolizes spiritual as well as a
sonic union, one he effects for the reader in his ending couplet,
even as it may not be truly finished in the spiritual realm that
lies outside his poetic control. Man and God may never automatically "rhyme" in our material world. Rhyme is the desired
completion of a pattern, and pattern—whether of sound, imagery, syntax, thought, or rhythm—is what signals we are in the
poem's territory.

Do Any Sounds or Phrases Repeat?

Pattern is, of course, a result of conscious repetition, whether
through repeated sounds via rhythm or rhyme, repeated syntactical structures, or through repeated images or refrains such as
this one, by the fifteenth-century French poet François Villon,
here translated by Galway Kinnell:

BALLADE

The goat scratches so much it can't sleep
The pot fetches water so much it breaks
You heat iron so much it reddens
You hammer it so much it cracks

A man's worth so much as he's esteemed
He's away so much he's forgotten
He's bad so much he's hated
We cry good news so much it comes.

You talk so much you refute yourself
Fame's worth so much as its perquisites
You promise so much you renege
You beg so much you get your wish
A thing costs so much you want it
You want it so much you get it
It's around so much you want it no more
We cry good news so much it comes.

You love a dog so much you feed it
A song's loved so much as people hum it
A fruit is kept so much it rots
You strive for a place so much it's taken
You dawdle so much you miss your chance
You hurry so much you run into bad luck
You grasp so hard you lose your grip
We cry good news so much it comes.

You jeer so much nobody laughs
You spend so much you've lost your shirt
You're honest so much you're broke
"Take it" is worth so much as a promise
You love God so much you go to church
You give so much you have to borrow
The wind shifts so much it blows cold
We cry good news so much it comes.

Prince a fool lives so much he grows wise
He travels so much he returns home

He's beaten so much he reverts to form
We cry good news so much it comes.

Refrains are lines, parts of lines, or even groups of lines that repeat in a poem, usually at the end of stanzas. Whole repeated stanzas are—amusingly—called **burdens**, while fragments of repeated lines, including individual words or inexact repetitions of a single line are called **repetends**. Villon's poem uses both repetends and an end refrain, suggesting some of the earliest uses of the refrain itself, which is to create a chorus-like effect, allowing the audience to chant back or join the poet at crucial moments in the poem. Villon's poem also uses apostrophe to address the listener and, in that, point out the universal conditions of life that he and his audience share. You can tell from Villon's poem that he knew his listeners were poor, struggling but ambitious, just as often to be unlucky as lucky in life: something true of Villon himself, a brawler, robber, and murderer who reportedly earned little in riches or reputation from his poems. Villon's refrain "We cry good news so much it comes" becomes—to my ear—alternately desperate, embittered, bemused, and resigned as his poem unfolds, just as the phrase "so much" repeated in the middle of each line sounds increasingly like a strained cry. What keeps these repetitions from becoming monotonous is the fact that the actions in the poem themselves aren't the same, nor do they produce the same results. Many of the lines even read like moral riddles: "You love a dog so much you feed it," Villon declares, just as earlier he reminds us "You want it so much you get it/ It's around so much you want it no more." We "talk so much" that we "refute ourselves," at the same time we "strive for a place so much it's taken." Thus we who admit to finding ourselves included in the poem's address are both sympathetic victims of fate, and also the patsies of our own quixotic desires. We aren't to be blamed for our foibles, exactly, but we aren't to be trusted either. Villon's poem is a clear-eyed, if satiric, take on the vanity of human wishes, and part of its charm is that Villon also implicates himself.

As I said before, the refrains' meaning changes through repetition, which allows readers to feel the nuances contained within the same language, and it's why "Ballade" achieves so many modulations of tone. In this, I'm reminded of John Hollander's argument in *Melodious Guile* that refrains "have memories—of their own prior strophes or stretches or text, of their own preoccurrences, and of their own genealogies in earlier texts as well." Villon's repetitions speak back to each other while also building on their previous arguments: we remember our first encounter with the refrain and the meaning we assigned it. Thus, refrain serves to underscore the poem's sense of paradox and irony, giving "Ballade" its biting, yet sympathetic, wit.

On Anaphora

The use of refrain in "Ballade" calls back to one of our most ancient forms of repetition in lyric poetry: anaphora. **Anaphora** occurs when a particular word or phrase repeats either at the beginning or the end in every sentence of a poem, and it's a device often used to structure devotional poems and religious rituals. You see it in the Psalms or *The Descent of Inanna*, and most delightfully in Christopher Smart's long poem "Jubilate Agno," which marries the ecstatic, joyous hymn of religious praise with the catalogue or list poem, as Smart enumerates the many qualities, behaviors, and actions of his cat, Jeoffry. Here's the opening of the poem:

> For I will consider my Cat Jeoffry.
> For he is the servant of the Living God duly and daily
>   serving him.
> For at the first glance of the glory of God in the East he
>   worships in his way.

For this is done by wreathing his body seven times round
    with elegant quickness.
For then he leaps up to catch the musk, which is the blessing
    of God upon his prayer.
For he rolls upon prank to work it in.
For having done duty and received blessing he begins to
    consider himself.
For this he performs in ten degrees.
For first he looks upon his forepaws to see if they are clean.
For secondly he kicks up behind to clear away there.
For thirdly he works it upon stretch with the
    forepaws extended.
For fourthly he sharpens his paws by wood.
For fifthly he washes himself.
For sixthly he rolls upon wash.
For seventhly he fleas himself, that he may not be
    interrupted upon the beat.
For eighthly he rubs himself against a post.
For ninthly he looks up for his instructions.
For tenthly he goes in quest of food.
For having consider'd God and himself he will consider
    his neighbour.
For if he meets another cat he will kiss her in kindness.
For when he takes his prey he plays with it to give it a chance.
For one mouse in seven escapes by his dallying.

Anaphora in Greek means "carrying up or back," and its insistent repetition lends a poem an air of prophetic utterance. When anaphora is tied to the cataloguing of a subject's parts, it implicitly declares every part of that subject—whether it be a person, divinity, animal, or idea—worthy of reverence. Walt Whitman, William Blake, and Allen Ginsberg (a devotee of Blake) often used anaphora as a way to elevate humble or even socially degraded figures in their poems. For example, in the second part of *Kaddish*, Ginsberg's book-length elegy for his mother, Naomi, Ginsberg repeatedly blesses the memory of Naomi by specifically blessing the fact of her mental illness, her aging body, and his own homosexuality:

In the world which He has created according to his will
    Blessed Praised
Magnified Lauded Exalted the Name of the Holy One
    Blessed is He!
In the house in Newark Blessed is He! In the madhouse Blessed is
    He! In the house of Death Blessed is He!
Blessed be He in homosexuality! Blessed be He in Paranoia!
    Blessed be He in the city! Blessed be He in the Book!
Blessed be He who dwells in the shadow! Blessed be He!
    Blessed be He!
Blessed be you Naomi in tears! Blessed be you Naomi in fears!
    Blessed Blessed Blessed in sickness!
Blessed be you Naomi in Hospitals! Blessed be you Naomi in
    solitude! Blest be your triumph! Blest be your bars! Blest be your
    last years' loneliness!
Blest be your failure! Blest be your stroke! Blest be the close
    of your eye! Blest be the gaunt of your cheek! Blest be your
    withered thighs!
Blessed be Thee Naomi in Death! Blessed be Death!
    Blessed be Death!
Blessed be He Who leads all sorrow to Heaven! Blessed be He
    in the end!
Blessed be He who builds Heaven in Darkness! Blessed Blessed
    Blessed be He! Blessed be He! Blessed be Death on us All!

Ginsberg's ecstatic blessings here crescendo to include blessing death itself: a surprising but, within this poem's trajectory, organic reversal of our usual revulsion toward mortality. Just as Naomi's "withered" and physically ailing body had become something to consecrate, so too do Ginsberg's homosexuality and the "madhouse" in which both Naomi and Ginsberg himself were occasionally institutionalized become holy: these social deaths in 1950s America parallel actual ones that are, in memory, revered. All these details become part of Ginsberg's litany of blessings and so expand our definition of what—and who—can be considered sacred. In this, Ginsberg's elegy shares a relationship with Smart's poem, which raises up a common domestic pet—a housecat!—to the level of the divine:

> For he knows that God is his Saviour.
> For there is nothing sweeter than his peace when at rest.
> For there is nothing brisker than his life when in motion.
> For he is of the Lord's poor and so indeed is he called by
> benevolence perpetually—Poor Jeoffry! poor Jeoffry! the
> rat has bit thy throat.
> For I bless the name of the Lord Jesus that Jeoffry is better.
> For the divine spirit comes about his body to sustain it in
> complete cat.

As with Adrienne Rich, who uses anaphora in "Dedication" to catalogue the various readers she imagines for her poem, Ginsberg's elegy becomes broader, more democratic. It's not just Naomi that Ginsberg mourns and celebrates here, but anyone who shares Naomi's outsider position. The paratactic catalogue itself—rather than being a meaningless list—elevates the significance of each line and suggests radical equivalence among the different things being described.

Does the Poem Use Parallelism?

If anaphora creates a rhythmic, almost trancelike state in the reader, it also relies upon **parallelism**: a structural pattern in which phrases, clauses, or even whole sentences are repeated in a passage of verse. Parallelism often relies on opposition or amplification of an image or idea, which you see in Psalm 23, in which the comparison between a shepherd and God becomes amplified by the descriptions that follow the initial metaphor: "The Lord is my shepherd; I shall not want. He maketh me to lie down in green pastures: he leadeth me beside the still waters." Parallelism suggests an elemental transference between the statements themselves, which is one reason why "Jubilate Agno" can leap across so many different aspects of Jeoffry's behavior, appearance, and personality without sticking to a chronological or logical narrative. Each line in Smart's poem is a statement unto itself, and yet the poem moves easily from observation to observation. Smart's use of anaphoric parallelism allows us to see how his cat's hunting techniques share something with the cat's spiritual awareness of the world, a point Smart embroiders upon throughout the poem until Jeoffry doesn't just *share* qualities with Christ; to Smart he *becomes* an aspect of Christ himself. Stated so bluntly, this might be hard for certain readers to swallow, but through his use of parallelism, Smart lets us feel the magic, the mystery, and finally the spiritual power of this comparison.

You find parallelism in a variety of poems, both free verse and formal, from the *Kalevala* to Robin Coste Lewis's long poem "The Voyage of the Sable Venus," which stitches together documentary catalogue language of art objects through history that have depicted Africans and Black people. Here, however, Lewis's use of repetition and parallelism is not for an ecstatic but a critical effect. In this short passage, for example, Lewis describes a series of objects on the left-hand side of the page, while on the right-hand side she notes how these objects have been shaped to resemble Black female bodies:

> water jar
> bowl
> ointment spoon
>
> > > in the form of swimming
> > > > black girl
>
>
> mirror
> with handle
>
> > > in the form of a carved standing
> > > > black girl

Lewis here makes real object and figural representation confront and mirror each other. In that, Lewis's parallelism is both visual and syntactic, since Lewis, by splitting the lines, demonstrates how the syntax wants us to treat the objects and girls as equivalent, while the visual spacing insists that each should stand alone.

Lewis's poem also uses repetitions that tonally change both the meaning of and our response to the repeated word itself. In one passage, for instance, Lewis repeats the word "relief" down the page, turning the word from an art-historical term to a cry for respite:

> Site relief
> Relief fragment
>
> Relief
> Relief
> Relief
> Relief

As with Villon's refrains, Lewis's repetitions are designed to make us feel how the same word can change meaning over the course of a poem, deepening its sensibility and tone while also returning us to the poem's essential themes. In Lewis's poem, the repetition of "relief" reminds me of the poem's final purpose, which is to give both the writer and reader some breathing space from the seemingly endless negative representations of Black people in art and the museum. Her use of repetition and parallelism are architectural parts of the poem's argument and also ways to speak back against these very constructions.

Are There Actions or Images That Rhyme?

While we associate rhyme with sound, I would also argue that rhyme can conceptually organize a poem, since repeating images and actions often link disparate stories or periods of time, creating narrative unity out of lyric fragmentation. Imagine, say, a poem that begins with a meditation on an orange tree in the yard of a couple undergoing a disastrous divorce and ends with a suitor arriving on the speaker's doorstep, an orange blossom tucked in his breast pocket. How we feel about that suitor is now contingent on what we remember about the divorcing couple, the two stories tied together through the repeated image of orange blossoms. The fiction writer Charles Baxter calls this a **rhyming action**, and while he locates this device in novels and short stories, he argues that it initially comes from poetry. Ballads, Baxter argues, love repeating events, in which the doubling narratives take on an air of prophecy. We might see a touch of fatalism, for example, in the conceptual rhymes that organize Stallings's "Alice in the Looking Glass," and in the shared gesture of frustration that Alexander Pope makes with Miss Blount at the end of his epistolary poem to her. In many ways, it's the same work behind metaphoric conceit: how does a particular image get returned to over the course of the poem, and how does this return shape the final trajectory of the poem?

Here's an example of just such a ballad replete not just with rhyme but rhyming actions. It's a wartime elegy written by the English poet and World War II veteran Keith Douglas titled "Vergissmeinnicht," or "Forget Me Not."

VERGISSMEINNICHT

Three weeks gone and the combatants gone
returning over the nightmare ground
we found the place again, and found
the soldier sprawling in the sun.

The frowning barrel of his gun
overshadowing. As we came on
that day, he hit my tank with one
like the entry of a demon.

Look. Here in the gunpit spoil
the dishonoured picture of his girl
who has put: *Steffi. Vergissmeinnicht*
in a copybook gothic script.

We see him almost with content,
abased, and seeming to have paid
and mocked at by his own equipment
that's hard and good when he's decayed.

But she would weep to see today
how on his skin the swart flies move;
the dust upon the paper eye
and the burst stomach like a cave.

For here the lover and killer are mingled
who had one body and one heart.
And death who had the soldier singled
has done the lover mortal hurt.

Douglas's poem contains within it two different gazes: the
gaze of the English soldiers, returned after battle to find the body
of a German combatant decomposing, and the imagined gaze of
the German's girlfriend, Steffi, whose photo is tucked inside the
gunpit. Alive, the German soldier had been a ferocious combatant, able to "hit [their] tank . . . like the entry of a demon." Three
weeks in the sun, however, his "sprawling" body has decom-
posed, "overshadow[ed]" by the "frowning barrel of his gun."
Though the German's gun remains technically able to penetrate
another tank, the soldier who manipulates it has been rendered
forever impotent. In that, the tank's physical integrity becomes
a cruel reminder of the soldier's sexual corruption: the soldier
"mocked . . . by his own equipment/ that's hard and good when
he's decayed."

If the German soldier was once the British gunners' former
"demon" lover, death reduces him to inhuman remains: a "paper
eye" and a stomach "burst" open "like a cave." I'm most fasci-
nated, however, by Douglas's choice of the word "dishonoured" as
it has been applied to the photograph of Steffi. Is the photo "dishonoured" because the German has been killed in combat, thus
rendered "less" of a man? Is it a reference to the way in which the
German likely used his girlfriend's photo in private, as both his
own pornographic image and an object of romantic attachment? I
think the word suggests both these meanings, especially since, in
death, the German soldier himself has become another "dishonoured" image akin to Steffi's photo: a pornographic object and a
romantic memory, but also a symbol of masculinity emptied of its
physical power.

In its overall structure, Douglas's poem "rhymes" war with

sex, as the dead soldier is both "killer and lover," public warrior and private citizen, whose divided roles become united in death which "mingle[s]" them into one man "who ha[s] one body and one heart." The final mortal wound, however, is not suffered by the German but by his girlfriend, here imagined by the poem's British speakers. By seeing the German through the eyes of his girlfriend, these soldiers return to him some sliver of humanity. To denigrate the German's masculinity is ultimately to denigrate their own, since the same imagery could just as easily be applied to them in death. I think this is the reason Douglas's rhymes harden and regularize in that fourth stanza: "paid" and "decayed" sudden, full rhymes in comparison with the slant rhymes that populate the rest of the poem, which at times appear to cascade rather than alternate through the stanzas. The poem slides between various quatrain forms, its rhymes becoming blurry echoes of each other so that no two lines easily "pair": "gun," "on," "one," and "demon" are all slant rhymes that collapse the second stanza to the single sound of something like a gun distantly firing. Because Douglas doesn't stick to one rhyming pattern—the poem morphs from ABBA to AAAA to AABB to ABAB—it destabilizes my narrative and formal expectations. Douglas's poem moves less by regular pattern than clusters of sound reminiscent of Wilfred Owen's collapsing rhymes in "Strange Meeting," the shifts of its sounds echoing the shifts of its tone.

This is one reason why that fourth stanza and its cruel aside stick out to me. "Paid" and "decayed" are simple rhymes, their lines' rhythms almost comically singsong compared to the other lines of the poem, as if to suggest the immaturity of the speaker's observation. The switch from the Englishmen's to Steffi's perspective also brings me up short, allowing me to imagine a different identity for the German while forcing me to imagine Steffi herself now dead, as her boyfriend's death becomes the blow that deals her own "mortal hurt." If her lover doesn't survive, Steffi can't either, and yet her death, unlike the German's, won't be mourned but taken as a fact. In that sense, "Forget Me Not," the command Steffi writes to her boyfriend, accretes meaning as the poem continues, a repeated command that refers not just to Steffi, not just to the dead German, not just to the English soldiers, but perhaps to the larger question of who we do and don't remember in war.

But if each quatrain structure isn't consistently repeated, the poem's narrative is certainly patterned. If the British soldiers sense some part of their own story contained in the dead German's body, if Steffi's death comes hard on the heels of her dead lover's, that is because war makes their own lives "rhyme" with each other as death repeats itself across nations and relationships. Victim, combatant, lover, ghost: the dead soldier is all of these things and more to those who remember him. "Vergissmeinnicht," in its mirroring action and end rhymes, reminds us that, in war's devastation, the fate of individuals isn't distinct.

Reading poems that utilize rhymes and rhyming actions might reasonably make readers wonder whether we choose our rhyming patterns or they choose us. The answer to this, of course, depends upon the poet. I know several poets who think so naturally in form they slide easily into distinct patterns whenever they write. Others accidentally uncover a rhyme during writing, and slowly excavate and burnish that discovery over drafts. Still others give themselves formal exercises to "shock" their imaginations into connections they might otherwise not make. As for me, I've come to rhymes in my poems through all these ways, but I've learned to trust the editing process to help me land on a pattern, in particular by concentrating on what sounds still excite me draft after draft, what feels good in the mouth when read out loud. Rhyme in a poem may function as an organizing device and, in that, requires something conscious about its construction, but it is ultimately the result of creative play. And play is important to remember when it comes to reading and writing poems. As a writer, I know that I produce unconsciously even as I edit consciously, and rhyme—whether sonic or conceptual—is part of the spell that makes it possible for me to create. The inevitability that rhyme suggests arises out of game-playing and chance, a trick I might use to test out all the valences and meanings—the memories—of the devices I duplicate. Like Villon's refrains or Douglas's mirroring sounds and actions, rhymes help us see how repetitions don't *really* repeat but expand their meanings, even as these repetitions connect different aspects of the poem together. Through its dream logic, rhyme becomes a process of change, then, as we alter our understanding of a poem's echoes so that even as we return to its same obsessions, desires, fears, and sounds, we confront them each time as different readers.

EXPERIMENTS

- Take a poem from the list below and pay close attention to its sounds. What are all the different kinds and types of rhyme that you hear? Are there also rhyming actions, phrases, or images that occur in the poem? How do these various rhymes combined accrue meaning as the poem continues?
- Write a poem that uses a refrain from a line you find in a newspaper article or headline. How many different meanings and tones can you get from repeating this refrain?
- Write a poem in which the same sound gets repeated in as many ways as possible.
- Write a poem whose title uses a refrain from a song you love. Consider how that refrain connects with a series of different memories or events from your own life. How might you use that refrain to reflect your own personal changes over time?

SUGGESTED WORKS TO CONSIDER

William Blake, "The Chimney Sweeper"
Edgar Allan Poe, "The Raven"
Robert Frost, "Stopping by Woods on a Snowy Evening"
Atsuro Riley, "Caw"
Anthony Hecht, "More Light! More Light!"
Wilfred Owen, "Strange Meeting"
Muriel Rukeyser, "Ballad of Orange and Grape"
Claire Wahmanholm, "O"
Sylvia Plath, "Daddy"
Kimberly Johnson, "Farrow"

All poems can be found either at the Poetry Foundation or the Academy of American Poets websites.

CHAPTER EIGHT

Does the Poem Employ Meter?

Analyzing rhyme on its own is limited without understanding its interaction with the poem's movement and flow, and understanding, too, the difference rhyme plays in free-verse poems with a strong sense of rhythm versus poems written in a conventional meter. All poems have rhythm, and that's because rhythm can be created many different ways—through the repetition of phrases and sounds, through a particular type of word choice or style of syntax, and through the tension constrained or released by lineation, all of which are easy to note forensically. In free-verse poems, rhythm is most often reinforced by line endings, even the visual shape of the poem on the page. But in culturally received poetic forms, rhythm is also produced by **meter**, which is the regular repetition of stressed and unstressed syllables in a line of verse. **Prosody** is the study of poetic meter, and **metrical scansion** is what we use to graphically represent changes of sound in a line of metrical verse by marking particular syllables as stressed and others as unstressed. In formal poems such as sonnets or blank verse, metrical scansion marks the beat caused by intonation, which is based on the way that words themselves are pronounced. It's pronunciation that determines where we mark a syllable as stressed or unstressed in our metrical scansion and ultimately how we hear metrical regularity and change.

Simply put, this means that the most important skill all readers of poetry require to scan a line of verse is a sense for how English words are pronounced. But though this sounds simple, lots of readers—perhaps too accustomed to speaking these words in conversation—insist they can't hear stress or aren't consciously attuned to hearing stress. On top of that, it's technically false to say that some syllables are stressed and others aren't. If a sound is made and heard, obviously *some* stress has occurred. The question is which syllables in a word receive *more* stress than others: that's what determines what we graphically mark as stressed, or unstressed, in a line.

Try saying these words out loud:

> Endlessly
> Tundra
> Astride
> Handshake

In each case, which syllable receives the most emphasis for the entire word to be correctly pronounced? Once you can determine which syllable (or syllables) within the word receive the most stress, then you can treat the other syllables as (technically) unstressed. Stressed and unstressed syllables are graphically marked with a (´) or a (˘) over their corresponding vowels, like this:

> **Énd**ĕsslў
> **Tún**dră
> Ăst**ríde**
> **Hánd**sháke

Notice that "endlessly" starts with a strong stress syllable, followed by two unstressed syllables. "Tundra" is a stressed syllable followed by an unstressed one. "Astride" is an unstressed syllable followed by a stressed one. Some readers might get tripped up on "handshake," since the word is double stressed. English has a number of disyllabic words of equal stress, such as "toothache" and "sunshine," and in metrical verse we call these **spondees**. But the other words are, in order, examples of a **dactyl**, a **trochee**, and an **iamb**. Each of these is a poetic rhythm that is the basis of a specific and common metrical **foot**, which refers to a repeated sequence of meter composed of two or more stressed or unstressed syllables. Add other feet like each of these to the ones above, and suddenly you have a line of metrical verse; in other words, a beat or consistent rhythm that characterizes your poem.

We call a line monometer, dimeter, trimeter, tetrameter, or pentameter based on whether the line has either one to five feet of a particular foot. A line of verse can be as short as a single iambic foot or as long as six dactylic feet. We graphically represent the ending of a foot with a | mark, and it's important to remember that metrical feet follow patterns of stressed and unstressed syllables, *not* the beginnings and endings of words themselves, or even the syntax of the line. Only occasionally does a change in punctuation also track a change in feet. In general, punctuation within a line of verse signals a **caesura**, which is a rhythmic or rhetorical break in the flow of a line, one that can also be signaled by extended visual space between its phrases. Deriving from the Latin *caedere* meaning "to cut," a caesura can occur just after or inside of a metrical foot and is graphically represented by || in metrical scansion.

Metered verse generally relies on the predominance of one type of foot over another throughout the poem, such as sonnets, which are largely iambic. But anyone with a good ear can hear that poets switch out metrical feet in verse forms all the time: it's actually the *rare* sonnet that's written entirely in iambic pentameter. When an occasional foot is different from what characterizes the regular meter of a particular line of verse, we call that **substitution**. Sometimes, a line might substitute several feet. A single line of a sonnet, for example, might be composed of two feet of iambs, one dactylic foot, an anapest, and a spondee all strung together, which is why it's never a good idea to only count syllables to see if a line is iambic pentameter, since the combination of various regular and substituted feet can produce more than ten total syllables. If any true oddities occur, they tend to appear at the end of the line, where you may find an extra stressed or unstressed syllable, called (alternately and dubiously) the **masculine** or **feminine ending**. We characterize a poem as "iambic" or "dactylic," then, based on the preponderance of one type of meter over others. And we should pay careful attention to when the regular meter of a poem changes its rhythm, whether within a line or within a stanza, because that alteration may accompany some significant change in the poem's tone and meaning.

Here's a mnemonic poem I use to recall the most common metrical feet:

> The iamb marches slow and strong,
> Trochees rush and tumble.
> While the anapest runs like the hurrying brook,
> Dactyls are stately and classical.

Scan this poem for stress, and you'll quickly realize that each line is written in the metrical foot referenced in the line itself. These meters, along with spondees, comprise the most common metrical feet in poetry. In the poem above, you can see that the first line is four feet of iambs, the second is three feet of trochees, the fourth is four feet of anapests, and the last is three feet of dactyls, which looks like this:

> Thĕ **í**|ămb **már**|chĕs **slów**| ănd **stróng,**
> **Tró**chĕes | **rúsh** ănd | **túm**blĕ.
> Whĭle thĕ **án**|ăpĕst **rúns** | lĭke thĕ **húr**|ry̆ĭng **bróok,**
> **Dác**ty̆ls ăre | **stá**tely̆ ănd | **cláss**ĭcăl.

We can say, then, that the first line is iambic tetrameter, the second line is trochaic trimeter, the third line anapestic tetrameter, and the last line dactylic trimeter.

The poem is written in a 4–3 beat common to ballads and hymnals. But what I love about this poem is the fact that it also unites poetic rhythm to readerly expectation. Essentially, different metrical feet have different sonic and even emotional or literary effects on us: trochees tumble, iambs march, anapests rush, and dactyls come to English from classical epics like the *Iliad*.

The poem is also a mirror of itself—iambs and trochees are reverse-image rhythms of each other, just as anapests and dactyls are reverse images of each other. Though they aren't featured in this poem, spondees, too, have a mirror-image: the pyrrhic, which is two unstressed syllables. We call iambs and anapests "rising rhythms" because we start with unstressed syllables and move upward to stressed ones, whereas trochees and dactyls "fall" from stressed to unstressed syllables. When someone says a line of poetry has a rising or a falling rhythm, we know that this refers to a preponderance of an iambic or trochaic meter.

This is a lot of information to take in at once, and it is only relevant to **accentual-syllabic verse** poems. Accentual-syllabic verse is the result of two different prosodic systems meeting—and mixing—in English. Just as the English language contains within it two different linguistic branches—the Germanic and the French/Latinate—so, too, does English prosody contain within it the ghost of two different metrical systems that accompanied those linguistic traditions: **accentual verse**, which comes from Anglo-Saxon poetry, and **syllabic verse**, which comes from French. Syllabic verse counts numbers of syllables and disregards stress. Accentual verse, by contrast, doesn't count syllables but stresses, and is also marked by alliteration. In accentual verse, whole words, regardless of their number of syllables, receive a single stress: it's the metrical system in which *Beowulf* and certain nursery rhymes like "Pat-a-cake" were written, and it persists in the sprung rhythm of Gerard Manley Hopkins's poems, in contemporary poems like Gwendolyn Brooks's "We Real Cool" or Richard Wilbur's "Junk," and in hip-hop.

Accentual-syllabic verse, as you can see, combines these two verse traditions by counting out syllables *and* stresses. While the number of stresses (or **accents**) may change, the total number of syllables themselves remains largely (but not always) fixed because they adhere to specific metrical patterns. Thus, a line of iambic pentameter, strictly rendered, tends to be a line of ten syllables, five of which are stressed.

Syllabic poems in English are rare but written, and there's some debate as to whether English-speakers ever really "hear" the rhythms of syllabic verse, so attuned are we to the rise and fall of stress as we read across lines. Some critics have argued that iambic pentameter itself is the "natural" rhythm of English, as it dominates our verse forms, thus to write in either syllabics or accentual verse alone is to fight against our innate inclination, though the popularity of hip-hop would belie this. Marianne Moore, Robyn Schiff, and Douglas Kearney have all written syllabic verse, and it's almost impossible to find a performance poet working today whose work doesn't call back to the strong-stress rhythms we associate with *Beowulf*. While the bulk of English poems written from the Renaissance to the late nineteenth century are accentual-syllabic, modern and contemporary poems have largely explored the free-verse line, and by doing so explored different avenues of rhythm-making, based less on abstract metrical regularity and more on the nuances we hear in daily speech and also self-invention.

A lot of people initially struggle to hear the difference between accentual-syllabic meters and accentual or syllabic rhythms, and part of this may be due to the fact that we rarely read or recite poems out loud; certainly, almost no one moves her body while reading it. But there is, I believe, something physical about the rhythms of poetry, and sometimes it helps not just to memorize and read poems aloud but to tap our hands and feet while doing so, as if we were following a song. Some readers take an almost mathematical approach to assigning stress to words, remembering where accents fall not because they hear it with their own ears but because they've memorized it based on scanning previous poems. There are many tricks for hearing stress outside of pronunciation, of course: for instance, we tend to stress monosyllabic words that are verbs and nouns, and we tend to hear as unstressed any definite and indefinite articles and conjunctions because they're filler words in a sentence. But generally speaking, we have to listen to how we pronounce words and also the cadence that develops once these words are placed beside each other to determine how we scan a line of poetry, and whether we characterize that poetry as accentual or accentual-syllabic.

One day, in a fit of pique, I played my class the songs "DNA" by Kendrick Lamar and "Walkin' After Midnight," by Patsy Cline back to back. I'd been struggling to help my students hear the difference between a stressed and an unstressed syllable, and how we could tell when a poem was working within an accentual-syllabic system versus an accentual one. Listening to "DNA" and "Walkin' After Midnight," students could hear instantly that Cline sang to accentuate both stress *and* syllable, while Lamar rapped to hit only specific stresses. The performers' styles reinforced their particular rhythmic patterns—the guitar on Cline's recording plucked and swung to the lyrics' walking gait while Lamar's voice hammered each line home with a driving, downward beat—but students could recognize that a line of Lamar's song could contain within it a much larger number of syllables and words than Cline's yet still contain only four to five strong stresses. Whether consciously or not, these two artists had capitalized on our deepest roots of English prosody, and the fact that we treat and recognize both songs as equal forms of lyric expression reveals how intrinsically familiar we are with both of these verse systems.

Before moving on to explain more specifically the difference between rhythm and meter, there's a third metrical system
that you should be aware of that existed, very briefly, in English,
and that's **quantitative meter**. Quantitative meter comes most
directly from Latin and Greek prosody, in which each syllable is
assigned a value that's dependent on its length of sound, a quantity usually based on its proximity to a diphthong, consonant, or
other vowel in a word. Few English poets have attempted it, and
only as an admiring nod to classical Greek and Latin poets. You
can find an example of quantitative meter in Edmund Spenser's
"Iambic Trimetrum" if you're curious, but you won't find any
examples of it in contemporary poetry, since it's a nearly untranslatable verse form for poets unused to measuring the "length" of
sound itself. Go ahead and make a note of quantitative meter,
then happily forget all about it.

The Difference Between Rhythm and Meter: Counterpoint and Substitution

Because metrical poems have such a strong beat to our ears, we
might want to treat rhythm and meter interchangeably, but—
again—the two are different. As the critic Laurence Perrine
writes, "[R]hythm is the flow of sound; meter is the patterns in
sounds." This is why free-verse poems often have a strong sense
of rhythm with no regular patterning of stresses and syllables,
and why we can feel in accentual poems a consistent beat across
lines of wildly different lengths.

Here's another way of saying it: Meter *always* produces rhythm
in poetry, but rhythm itself doesn't require meter. The two songs
I played for my class are, technically, without any regular meter,
but they each have a strong sense of rhythm that *calls back* to a
specific verse system in English. Rhythm can be created through
almost any kind of continuous pattern of repetition, which is why

poems that use refrains, rhymes, or specific types of syntax also carry powerful rhythmic weight. But when poems rely on specific meters to create their rhythms, they establish patterns of sound that become so regular to our ears that we may not immediately sense—or may not immediately *want* to sense—when meter and rhythm divide. And sometimes these established metrical rhythms run counter to the ways that we ourselves would, under other conditions, want to hear stress in a word or phrase.

For example, take a moment to scan this poem:

> There was a young maid from Aberystwyth
> Who bought grain from the mill to make grist with.
> The miller's son Jack
> Laid her flat on her back
> And united the organs they pissed with.

This is a limerick written by Algernon Charles Swinburne, and you can see it's a leaping run of anapests with the occasional feminine ending. It's also an example of just how strong rhythms, once they get into our ears and bodies, can become. Based on what I've just written about pronunciation and stress, you might want to stress the words "bought" and "make" in the second line and "laid" in the fourth because they're verbs and we'd naturally stress them in speech. But get into the rhythm of the piece, and suddenly you find yourself stressing "grain" rather than "bought," and "flat" rather than "laid" to keep with the poem's rising, light-footed pace. Limericks are funny because of the anapests, and we hesitate to alter a pattern that ends in a joke.

At these moments in his limerick, Swinburne uses what we might call **counterpoint,** which is when we assign a metrical value to a foot or set of syllables according to the metrical expectations of the verse, as opposed to how it would naturally be stressed in speech. Some critics would argue against counterpoint in favor of exactitude; we should always scan a line according to how we would pronounce the words outside the poem in order to fully appreciate the line's rhythmic variation and nuance. Others would argue that, for ease and practicality, counterpoint is natural, and that we should scan a poem based on its established metrical pattern, recognizing that at these moments in the poem, the rhythm of a line has shifted only to our ears. I'm of both minds: I think exactitude is more important to poems invested in the revelation of character, story, and the evolution of argument and tone. Counterpoint is essential for poems like limericks or ballads to function, since they are invested in regularity—whether of music or rhythm, or refrain or jokes. I allow myself to change my mind on this point based on how I read the poem before me. Basically, does an exact reading of the meter matter more or less to how I understand what is being said in the poem?

Theodore Roethke's poem "My Papa's Waltz," for example, offers an easy and fascinating opportunity to see how a forensic analysis of meter might benefit a reader's larger understanding of the poem. From the start, Roethke's poem announces itself as a waltz and, as such, keeps a regular 3–3 iambic beat and interlaced rhymes throughout its four stanzas. From the first stanza, I could make every line follow a conventional iambic rhythm like so:

Thĕ **whís**|kĕy **ón** | yŏur **bréath**

C ŏuld **máke** | ă s**máll** | bŏy **dízz**|ў;

Bŭt **Í** | hŭng **ón** | lĭke **déath**:

Sŭch **wá**|ltzĭng **wás** |nŏt **éas**|ў.

Reading the first stanza, I might be tempted to scan "a small boy dizzy" as two feet of iambs followed by a feminine ending; I certainly wouldn't be faulted for it. And yet, I prefer to stress "boy" because I would stress it in speech and I hear it stressed in the poem, thus I now make the second line two feet of iambs, then a spondee, then a feminine ending. By doing this, the line itself feels like it pulls up short then falls away, mimicking the kind of dizziness the boy himself might feel when dancing with his drunk father. Likewise, I want to scan "hung on" as a spondee because I hear two strong stresses, which reinforce the boy's desperate grip. Thus, the exact way I'd scan the first stanza would look like this:

Thĕ **whís**|kĕy **ón** | yŏur **bréath**

Cŏuld **máke** | ă **smáll** | **bóy díz**|zў;

Bŭt **Í** | **húng ón** | lĭke **déath**:

Sŭch **wá**|ltzĭng **wás** |nŏt **éas**|ў.

Scanning the rest of the poem reveals that the "difficult" waltzing rhythm established in the first stanza soon gives way to something far more irregular, revealing the emotional stakes in this family dynamic reflected in the father's dancing here:

Wĕ **rómped** | ŭn**tíl** | thĕ **páns**

Slíd frŏm | thĕ **kít**|chĕn **shélf**;

Mў **mó**|thĕr's **cóunt**|ĕn**ánce**

Cŏuld **nót** | ŭn**frówn** | ĭt**sélf**.

Thĕ **hánd** | thăt **héld** | mў **wríst**

Wăs **bát**|tĕred **ón**| óne **knúck**|lĕ;

Ăt é| vĕrў **stép** | yŏu **míssed**

Mў **ríght** | **éar scráped** | ă **búck**|lĕ.

Yŏu **béat** | **tíme** ŏn | mў **héad**

Wĭth ă **pálm** | **cáked hárd** | bў **dírt,**

Thĕn **wáltzed** | mĕ **óff** | tŏ **béd**

Stíll clíng|ĭng **tó** | yŏur **shírt.**

By now the poem has lots of little slippages, such as the falling, trochaic start of the second stanza's second line which reflects the "sliding" of pots and pans from the shelf, while the pileup of spondees in the third and fourth stanzas—in "one knuckle" and "right ear scraped," "beat time," and "palm caked hard"—reinforces the father's physical force and size, while also hinting at something darker: the possibility of the father's violence, implied both in the image of the son's ear being "scraped by a buckle" when the father himself missteps and in the father's "beat[ing] time" on his son's head. That violence is also there in the hard, driving beat that moves the poem by the end, as evidenced by the stanza's accrual of monosyllabic words, most of them deriving from Anglo-Saxon or Germanic roots.

Oftentimes, we know things in poems not just by explicit images but careful switches in rhythm and diction; this poem is filled with such changes. In the third line of the third stanza, Roethke writes "At every step you missed": a line that, to make it fit into a regular metrical pattern, would have to employ **syncope** or "cutting" the second *e* in the word "every," so that it would be scanned like this: "**év**'rў." Most of us reading the poem aloud might naturally do this. But I prefer drawing out that second *e* and scanning the first two feet as an iamb followed by an anapest in order to reflect the argument of the line itself—the poem, like the father, "misses" a step of the waltz, a rhythm that then "scrapes" the reader's ear in the reading of the line.

A lot of weight, too, is placed on the word "countenance" in the second stanza: a masculine rhyme with "pans" in that first line, thus another sonic "sliding" in the poem. "Countenance," of course, refers to the mother's sour expression, but it's also a fancy, Latinate word that, while matching the meter of the line beautifully, reveals something about the mother's disposition. If the father is someone with dirt-seamed palms and rough habits, someone who "romps" rather than waltzes and whose drinking leads him to sudden, violent outbursts, the mother is here depicted in one word as being not only of a different temperament but possibly of a different social or educational class. The mother stands in opposition to the father; she knows what the likely outcome of all this horseplay will be, something the narrator refuses to fully acknowledge, though he hints throughout at his father's coming death. If his father is drunk on whiskey, the child is drunk on his father's attention; to a certain extent, the child wills himself to overlook his father's behavior. I hear that willfulness in the spondaic opening of the final line: the fact the son waltzes off to bed "still clinging" to his father's shirt.

Shifting Meters, Shifting Tones

While Swinburne's limerick is a good example of counterpoint, I'd argue that Roethke's poem is an example of substitution, since his poem entirely tracks a regular iambic rhythm with only occasional "slippages" of metrical feet. Substitution and counterpoint happen frequently in metrical verse, but there are also poems that employ different metrical line lengths (called **heterometric lines**) within the same stanza in order to produce larger effects of *tonal* counterpoint. These heterometric lines can inject a sudden note of humor, seriousness, or of dissonance into the poem, which you can see in W. B. Yeats's poem "The Wild Swans at Coole," a lovely poem composed of six-line stanzas that combine lyric song with melancholic reflection.

THE WILD SWANS AT COOLE

The trees are in their autumn beauty,
The woodland paths are dry,
Under the October twilight the water
Mirrors a still sky;
Upon the brimming water among the stones
Are nine-and-fifty swans.

The nineteenth autumn has come upon me
Since I first made my count;
I saw, before I had well finished,
All suddenly mount
And scatter wheeling in great broken rings
Upon their clamorous wings.

I have looked upon those brilliant creatures,
And now my heart is sore.
All's changed since I, hearing at twilight,
The first time on this shore,
The bell-beat of their wings above my head,
Trod with a lighter tread.

Unwearied still, lover by lover,
They paddle in the cold

Companionable streams or climb the air;
Their hearts have not grown old;
Passion or conquest, wander where they will,
Attend upon them still.

But now they drift on the still water,
Mysterious, beautiful;
Among what rushes will they build,
By what lake's edge or pool
Delight men's eyes when I awake some day
To find they have flown away?

Scan these lines, and you'll notice how the first four lines of each stanza follow a traditional ballad's iambic tetrameter/trimeter beat, as established by the poem's opening: "Thĕ **trées** | ăre **ín** | thĕir **áu**|tŭmn **béau**|tў,/ Thĕ **wóod**|lănd **páths** | ăre **drў**." But Yeats reverses that rhythmic and metrical expectation in the longer fifth line, which unfurls suddenly into pentameter—"[ŭ]**pón** | thĕ **brím**|mĭng **wá**|tĕr ămóng | thĕ **stónes**." This pattern, too, is then brought up short by the stanza's final line, which returns to iambic trimeter: "Ăre **níne**|-ănd-**fíf**|tў **swáns**." The effect of this is to create a momentary sense of discordance in each stanza, as the poem's rhythm is repeatedly and briefly disrupted, then "righted" again at the last. This discordance for me is heightened by the fact that the ending foot of the fourth line is a spondee— "**stíll skў**"—which creates a metric pause before the launching of that fifth line. The songlike pattern established at the poem's opening thus turns to something more meditative, a series of irregularities that slows the reader down and adds a note of melancholy to the poem.

This tonal counterpoint plays with ideas of emotional closure itself, I'd argue, since the poem constantly offers—and rejects— sonic completion. The mostly full rhymes throughout the poem offer some closure, of course, since the first four lines of each stanza follow an interlaced quatrain pattern, while the last two act as rhyming couplets. Each stanza is also end-stopped, again gesturing at psychological completion. And yet even as the poem offers so many levels of closure, the stanzas themselves still feel as if something is amiss. That something, of course, is the metrically longer fifth line, which briefly strains out of song and into meditation and memory, as the speaker returns to a beloved waterway "nineteen years" after "his last count" to find that the swans he's tracked continue to mate and pair, while the speaker remains alone.

The poem opens on archetypal images of middle age: the trees "are in their autumn beauty," while "the woodland paths are dry." The landscape reflects the speaker's maturity—that period of stasis between youth and old age in which the speaker can reflect upon his own changed circumstances, which feel more poignant when compared with the unchanging life pattern of the swans themselves, creatures whose own hearts (unlike the speaker's) "have not grown cold." We don't know what has specifically occurred in this speaker's life, what particular lover has rejected him (or lovers, since by this period of his life Yeats had been put aside both by his longtime object of obsession, Maud Gonne, and also her daughter, Iseult). We don't know what personal dreams he's abandoned, either, though we can feel the aching envy the speaker has for these swans for whom "[p]assion or conquest, wander where they will/ [a]ttend upon them still." That ache is felt in the poem's symbolism of the swans, the fact that the speaker knows someday he, too, will "awake some day/ to find that they have flown away," but we also feel it in that metrical shift. If the swans suggest youth, vigor, passion and desire, Yeats's speaker is poised between being full of denied romantic desire and the knowledge that someday soon he may not desire at all. Which is worse? Having one's passions thwarted, or not feeling anything? The poem's metrical toggling between resolution and irresolution suggests that, struggle as he might, some sense of completion—whether that be through literal or figurative death—will finally settle the question for him.

Is There Any Interplay Between Rhythm and Meter?

Something similar happens in Christian Wiman's poem "Every Riven Thing," which also uses heterometric lines to create tension, even as the poem overall relies upon a changing refrain to connect and advance its stanzas:

EVERY RIVEN THING

God goes, belonging to every riven thing he's made
sing his being simply by being
the thing it is:
stone and tree and sky,
man who sees and sings and wonders why

God goes. Belonging, to every riven thing he's made,
means a storm of peace.
Think of the atoms inside the stone.
Think of the man who sits alone
trying to will himself into a stillness where

God goes belonging. To every riven thing he's made
there is given one shade
shaped exactly to the thing itself:
under the tree a darker tree;
under the man the only man to see

God goes belonging to every riven thing. He's made
the things that bring him near,
made the mind that makes him go.
A part of what man knows,
apart from what man knows,

God goes belonging to every riven thing he's made.

The first thing I note about Wiman's refrain is how he changes its meaning by changing punctuation, thus its logical relationship to the following lines in each stanza. The first time I read the refrain, I understand it to mean that, while God goes, he belongs to every everything He has created. This declaration, however, swiftly evolves to a larger consideration of humans, who themselves—by singing about God—are forced to wonder where "God goes." "Belonging" itself becomes a different part of speech in each of its iterations in the poem, moving from adjective to gerund to adverb, as it finally modifies the manner in which God goes. By the penultimate refrain, I see Wiman has divided the line to focus on what God has created, which includes all things "that bring [God] near" and also the human consciousness that "makes [God] go." God is, as Wiman writes, "A part of what man knows" but also "apart from what man knows": in that, God represents a fundamental break in human logic, even as He is fundamental to faith itself. As we are divided between what we believe and what we can prove, humans thus become another "riven thing" God has made and belongs to. We are God's creatures, even as God becomes our own construction in turn.

That's what the poem, generally, means, but look at how the form reinforces this sense of being "riven." First, the poem is littered with caesuras that disrupt the refrain's iambic flow, so that no two refrains maintain the same rhythm, as you hear in these lines: "**Gód góes.**|| Bĕlóng|ĭng,|| tŏ é|vĕrў rí|vĕn thíng | hĕ's máde" and "**Gód góes** | bĕ**lóng**|ĭng.|| Tŏ **é**|vĕrў **rí**|vĕn **thíng** | hĕ's **máde**." And yet, even as the refrain's syntax and meter are consistently broken apart, the refrain itself still anchors the poem through its repetition.

Second, the stanzas themselves contain a cascade of irregular rhymes, while the lines are heterometric, both in and across stanzas. If I scan the poem for a rhyme scheme, it looks like this: ABCDD ABCCD AABCC ABCCC. Likewise, if I scan the poem metrically, each stanza employs its own pattern. While each stanza starts with a (very unusual) iambic hexameter line, the rest of the stanzas move line by line from iambic tetrameter to dimeter to trimeter to pentameter, or some combination of these. The poem plays with the quatrain shape and rhyme scheme, yet no two stanzas follow the same metrical or rhyming patterns.

On top of that, the poem contains images of paradox or of things divided: "Belonging," Wiman writes, "means a storm of peace," while everything is attached to a shadow "shaped exactly to the thing itself," even though it is obviously *not* the thing itself. And yet these shadows cannot be divorced from the natural objects that cast them, just as God cannot be split from the things He's created and who strain to imagine Him in turn.

So how does Wiman's poem contain all these formal elements that threaten to pull the poem syntactically, and logically, apart? There's a rhythmic, if not metric, regularity that binds these arbitrarily unequal components. It's not merely the refrain that connects the stanzas but also the ways that rhymes themselves play across and inside of the poem, so that in the first stanza, "sings," "being," and "thing" call to each other across the lines, even as the end-rhyming couplet of "sky" and "why" creates a sense of closure. You see something similar in the second and third stanzas as well, where "atoms" and "storm," "will" and "stillness" become slant or feminine rhymes, while "exactly" picks up on the end-rhyming couplet of "tree" and "see." This creates a sonic connection that, to my ear, extends the rhythmic flow of the shorter lines, so that the third line's iambic dimeter in the first stanza sounds, when read aloud, like a longer three- or four-beat line if I rhyme "thing" with "sing."

And of course there's the rhythm created by Wiman's syntax. Notice how few lines in the first three stanzas are end-stopped. In the first stanza, Wiman uses a high degree of enjambment in the first three lines before ending on a colon, which focuses the reader on the clear parallelism of the ending couplet—both material objects and human beings are the "thing[s]" that sing God's existence merely by being themselves:

> God goes, belonging to every riven thing he's made
> sing his being simply by being
> the thing it is:
> stone and tree and sky,
> man who sees and sings and wonders why

Likewise, Wiman's end-stopping the third line of the second stanza makes "stone" rhyme more clearly with "alone," while his use of hypotaxis in the next several sentences means we track the relationship of his clauses rather than his rhymes:

> God goes. Belonging, to every riven thing he's made,
> means a storm of peace.
> Think of the atoms inside the stone.
> Think of the man who sits alone
> trying to will himself into a stillness where

> God goes belonging. To every riven thing he's made
> there is given one shade
> shaped exactly to the thing itself:

under the tree a darker tree;
under the man the only man to see

Wiman in fact regularly inverts his clauses, as in the lines: "To every riven thing he's made/ there is given one shade/ shaped exactly to the thing itself," a complex construction I might be tempted to rewrite for directness:

There is one given shade
to every riven thing he's made
shaped exactly to the thing itself

It's clearer, certainly, but notice how singsong and almost childish this revision sounds in comparison, how the metrical and rhyming regularities make the poem itself feel less urgent. I clunk along to the end of each line; the sentence lacks movement, as the meter is no longer in tension with the syntax. In his version, Wiman's enjambments and inversions only "right" themselves in each stanza at a point of parallelism: "Think of the atoms inside the stone./ Think of the man who sits alone," Wiman writes in the second stanza, just as he repeats a prepositional phrase beginning with "under the" in the third, finally ending with the couplet "A part of what man knows/ apart from what man knows" in his fourth. Wiman's syntax wants to highlight these parallels, which is why these statements appear each time as rhyming couplets. Thus, both rhythm *and* rhyme push toward these places in the poem, acting as brief moments of, if not closure, encapsulation of sense.

Essentially, Wiman allows syntax and rhyme to create *another* rhythm that plays in and alongside the metrically enforced beat of each stanza, binding the poem together and making it feel regular to our ears in ways that belie what the scansion itself tells us. In this, he manages to produce both balance and tension, harmony and fragmentation. Wiman creates—then seals up—small fissures throughout his poem, mimetically reproducing some part of his argument, which is that, though we live fundamentally apart from what we believe, we live and move *as* part of it too.

Is There a Relationship Between Meter and Content? On Organic Form

Wiman's poem delights me because, even as it is masterful *at* form, it's also *his own* form, much like Terrance Hayes's golden shovel is his own form, and the duplex has become Jericho Brown's. Wiman clearly knows how to write a perfect line of iambic pentameter, and I trust that if he wanted to write isometric quatrains, he would have. What he's done in "Every Riven Thing" is thus by choice, and I believe it's important to take those choices seriously. Denise Levertov's essay "Some Notes on Organic Form" makes the argument that form "is based on an intuition of an order . . . of which man's creative works are analogies, resemblances, natural allegories." In an organically formed poem, then, content shouldn't just match up with its form, form itself should become a "revelation of content." Considering how elaborate Wiman's form is, it feels to me an excellent example of organic form, an unveiling of different types of being "riven," much in the ways that Stallings's sonnet becomes a series of interlocking mirrors, or Brooks's ballad makes social critique and story sing as one. These poets have all capitalized upon and even violated some expectation of what their chosen form is and should do, or perhaps created a self-invented or **nonce form** within a received one to better reflect the unfolding thinking around their content.

Recognizing the mechanics of what makes poems such as these exceptional is, after all, the point of prosody. To consider the ways in which sound and sense may bear some fundamental relationship to each other is not an extraneous reading activity, even as it's one we have to train for. Some of the most exciting conversations you will have around poetry are when you discover how form and content connect; they are also the conversations that will make you want to beat your head against a wall. That's because there's a paradox in reading poetry: we are presented ironclad rules about great writing that some poet out there in the world is cheerfully proceeding to break. The fact is, the information I've included here about rhyme, rhythm, and meter are general points that cannot be unthinkingly exported to all poems, even as they provide you a vocabulary with which to discuss the prosody of *specific* poems. When I talk about what makes a poem good, then, I'm talking about poems that follow and perform understood rules closely enough that any reader can appreciate them. But what makes a poem *great* is when the poet has metabolized and moved beyond these rules, creating another kind of form in which to confront experience, one that not only articulates the poet's thinking but becomes a process of thought itself.

I'm aware, of course, that talking about meter in poetry is rare these days because it's intimidating. One reason for this is that all of us might hear a similar rhythm across a poem, but the subjectivity of our ears and our understanding of the poem's meaning allow for sometimes stark variations in how we scan a line. On top of this, poems capitalize on the tension that arises between meter, line, and syntactical segmentation: our ears track rhythm, our eyes track lines, and our brains listen for the beginnings and ends of sentences. This tension can lead some to believe that what ultimately distinguishes a poem from prose is its use of enjambment, which highlights this particular tension and serves to remind readers that when we read and listen to poems, we are essentially hearing at least two different rhythms played at the same time, both against and with each other. This is what the critic and philosopher Giorgio Agamben argued in his essay "The End of the Poem," saying that this tension leads to a fundamental irresolution in poetry, since we hear different types of completion hitting at different moments, whether that's the completion of an iambic pentameter line, the completion of rhyme, or the completion of a thought. Thus readers who want to treat metrical scansion as the math of poetry might be better served by thinking of it as experimental jazz—a song that confounds and subverts its musical expectations, making the regular irregular for the sake of creating movement. And admittedly, I don't know a lot of people who love experimental jazz.

That said, variable ways of scanning a line shouldn't be treated as a crisis but an opportunity: *Why* do you hear stress in this place and not that one? Are there sudden internal rhymes or alliteration? Does one word's sound elevate another through consonance or assonance? What is the poet saying at this moment in the poem? What has immediately changed in the poem's tone, syntax, or action? Meter wasn't designed to make us look stupid but to offer us a way to play in language. As we ourselves become more adept at hearing rhythm, rhyme, and meter, we become more adept at discussing the impact of particular metrical substitutions. Granted: when scanning a poem, if any reader feels more comfortable sticking close to the poem's established meter and ignoring its variations for the sake of ease, that's not only good enough training in prosody but supports many critics' belief about how most verse should be scanned. The close attention I pay to substitution in "My Papa's Waltz" may be something for advanced readers, though I always teach it to introductory ones, since the poem's language and symbolism are easy to grasp, thus the metrical conversation becomes less intimidating. Another poem I have introductory readers scan is Philip Larkin's "This Be the Verse," both because it's funny (everyone's up for scanning a poem with the word "fuck" in it), and because it, too, has an easily perceptible rhythm that offers students a comfortable opportunity to talk about substitution and counterpoint.

But the close reading of meter has another effect on us, I believe, which is that it makes us more attentive writers. Whether that's the writing of our own poems or prose, our attention to metrical variation attunes us to the rhythms of speech. One question I'm always asked by poets after scanning "My Papa's Waltz" is how conscious Roethke had been about his decisions. Do poets writing formal verse think out every line in such precise, even microscopic moves? I can't answer for Roethke, but I suspect most poets can't consciously make such high-level decisions without ruining the flow of the poem. To a certain extent, felicities of metrical variation are just that: happy accidents. But these accidents happen more frequently—and more usefully— the more we practice. Over time, we feel our way into rhythmic alterations based on how we feel the poem's action or thought itself shift. So for those just starting to write metrical verse, I suggest first simply writing out as many lines as you can that interest you, then going back to scan the results. What rhythms appear and reappear? Do the lines feel like they are starting to organize themselves around a particular set of metrical feet? Are stanzas falling into a regular number of lines? What rhymes occur and where do they fall? For some writers, it may be easier to start editing your way to a metrical form once you sense a pattern developing. This form may be one that's culturally inherited, such as blank verse, or it might be one that combines or reinvents particular stanzaic patterns you've seen, such as in "The Wild Swans at Coole." For other writers, however, it may be easier to play with a specific exercise that links form and content, such as writing a sonnet that contemplates the loss of a relationship, or a ballad that spins the sensational tale of a fallen celebrity. But the best practice for writing metrical verse remains reading it, ideally out loud. It is far easier to reproduce any rhythm, and to hear the subtleties of its variations, when these sounds have become part of your listening vocabulary.

Prosody requires a commitment from readers and writers in order for them to gain familiarity with meter, and while I teach it specifically at the intermediate and advanced levels, I start talking about the difference between meter and rhythm with all my introductory poets. Prior to the twentieth century, most poetry in English was written in metrical verse. Without some level of familiarity with meter, then, readers can't advance beyond generalized comments about anyone's work, including their own. But the most important question with regard to prosody remains not how we should scan a line but *why* we hear a line a particular way, and how this hearing elevates certain readings. Form, sound, and sense intertwine; we hear our way into the thinking of a poem as much as we see it unfold through images. Learning to hear may be tough work, but it will be utterly meaningless unless we understand that scansion is fundamentally attached to larger questions of sense. For me, poetry is the genre marked by pattern; in particular, where subject and form are in self-conscious contention *and* agreement with each other, where I'm asked to care as much about how a thing is said as what itself is expressed. That's the delight that separates poetry from prose. For poetry requires not just the communication of an experience or idea to a reader but treats language as an experience itself.

EXPERIMENTS

- Find a poem from the list below whose rhythms interest you. (Note: The list is a mix of syllabic poems, free-verse poems, accentual poems, and accentual-syllabic poems. Determine which type of poem yours is.) How would you characterize your poem's rhythm, and what are the elements of the poem—rhyme, repetition, meter, syllable count, syntax, line breaks, or visual caesuras—that create it? Does the rhythm change for you at any point, and if so, where and why? Is there any relationship for you between the poem's rhythm and its subject matter?

- Find a poem in metrical verse from the list below and scan as many of its lines as you can. What stresses do you hear and where? Is the poem accentual or accentual-syllabic? Does the poem ever deviate from its metrical pattern, and if so, where? Is there a content-based reason that the meter might change at this particular moment in the poem?

- Replete with heroes and villains, ballads traditionally were the form of the sensational romantic or gothic story: highway robberies, ghost stories, love affairs gone wrong. Find a tabloid story that interests you and rewrite it as a ballad. Which quatrain rhyme scheme will you choose to tell the tale?

- Write a dramatic monologue in the voice of a much older person (a grandparent, a politician, a stranger at a bus stop) giving someone advice. Try writing this monologue in blank verse (unrhymed iambic pentameter). If you don't feel comfortable yet counting out each stressed and unstressed syllable, try writing the poem so that it has five stressed "beats" per line to your ear. How do the rhythms of this metrical line shape this person's thinking? What does it reveal about this person's advice or character?

- Write a syllabic poem about an insect that fascinates or frightens you. For this poem, you will develop your own form, as each line must contain a specific number of syllables of your choosing. Each line of your poem can have the same number of syllables or different ones to create a rhythmic pattern that pleases you.

SUGGESTED WORKS TO CONSIDER

Richard Wilbur, "Junk"
Gwendolyn Brooks, "We Real Cool"
Robert Herrick, "Delight in Disorder"
Gerard Manley Hopkins, "No worst, there is none.
    Pitched past pitch of grief."
Philip Larkin, "This Be the Verse"
Edna St. Vincent Millay, "What lips my lips have kissed,
    and where, and why"
Joy Harjo, "She Had Some Horses"
Eduardo C. Corral, "Lines Written During My
    Second Pandemic"
Anne Waldman, "Scallop Song"
Monica Youn, "Blackacre"
Marianne Moore, "The Steeple-Jack"

All poems can be found either at the Poetry Foundation or the
Academy of American Poets websites.

CHAPTER NINE

Does the Poem Have
Conventional Form?

When Denise Levertov said that an organic form is a method of "apperception" that becomes "a revelation of [its] content," she was arguing that all aspects of a poem—its meter, rhythm, tone—become direct expressions of how we perceive things in the moment. In that, organically formed poems don't merely represent content, they become measures of feeling an experience itself. Organically formed poems, then, aren't static but mimetic. This may sound mysterious on first reading, but to me it's meant the difference between someone crashing two cymbals together to represent the sound of a wave hitting the shore versus a symphony in which I feel encompassed by the ocean itself.

When I first found Levertov's essay "Some Notes on Organic Form," I'd assumed she'd wanted to distinguish between closed or culturally received forms of poetry and free verse, but Levertov never argued that free verse had any inherent claim to being "more" or "less" organic to its content. If anything, formal verse just had more known elements that a writer had to take into account, and sometimes those elements could counteract or constrain some measure of feeling the poet needed to explore. I learned this myself, having once agonized over a villanelle that kept failing until I realized that villanelles, with their high degree of repetition and tight rhyme schemes, are lyric and not narrative forms. I'd been trying to stuff a novel's worth of research about Gericault's *The Wreck of the Medusa*—including the story of how Gericault purchased sawn-off body parts from a surgeon just so he could watch them rot—into a poem of only nineteen lines. If a villanelle is a light craft built to skim over waves, I had effectively sunk my own boat.

Once I realized this, I scrapped my attempts and found this line from a *New York Times* article instead: "In the perfect universe of math, we should be less than dead." I chose the line because I didn't understand it when I first read it, and the more I parsed it, the more mysterious it became. My villanelle was an attempt to unpack this statement through repetition, to lay out all its many implications about death, extinction, chance, and even math that the article suggested.

I could use this anecdote as an example of how we might treat conventionally formed poems as fixed containers just waiting to be filled with the right material, but that's a glib, even dishonest, take on form that doesn't allow for the natural experimentation that occurs when we write. In reality, all poems have form, even if that form exists only in the interplay between sentence and line, or between sense and syntax. The question really can't be about matching form up to content if we want to understand what particular forms do and mean to us as readers, and how they are shaped by poets over time. Conventional forms aren't static: the Shakespearean sonnet was not the sonnet Sir Thomas Wyatt imported to England after a stint in Italy, and the Shakespearean sonnet is not the same sonnet Seamus Heaney wrote centuries later, nor the sonnet Ted Berrigan bowdlerized, and certainly not the sonnet that Wanda Coleman, Terrance Hayes, or Diane Seuss all reinvented, to name just a tiny fraction of the poets who have written sonnets over the centuries.

Poetic forms are plastic, even as we understand they depend on limitation. They may require no particular subject matter even as they still—subtly— enforce certain registers and modes. They make demands on us that become most pleasing, ironically, when some part of the demand itself is violated. If poetic forms have meanings outside of their requirements, it may be that they carry cultural and historic weight not even their original proponents imagined. When Heaney takes on the sonnet, for instance, it matters that the son of Irish sharecroppers would write in a form long associated with the culture that colonized his nation. Years ago, I once overheard a poet declare that only fascists would dare to write sonnets: an idea that would be offensive were it not so laughable, though I take his larger point. Verse forms cannot entirely be divorced from their histories and originating cultures in our contemporary reception of them, which is one reason why some poets chose those forms to begin with—as a space of both play and subversion—and why some poets worry now that it's cultural appropriation to write pantoums.

Consider this sonnet by Jericho Brown:

THE TRADITION

> *Aster. Nasturtium. Delphinium.* We thought
> Fingers in dirt meant it was our dirt, learning
> Names in heat, in elements classical
> Philosophers said could change us. *Star Gazer.*
> *Foxglove.* Summer seemed to bloom against the will
> Of the sun, which news reports claimed flamed hotter
> On this planet than when our dead fathers
> Wiped sweat from their necks. *Cosmos. Baby's Breath.*
> Men like me and my brothers filmed what we
> Planted for proof we existed before
> Too late, sped the video to see blossoms

Brought in seconds, colors you expect in poems
Where the world ends, everything cut down.
John Crawford. Eric Garner. Mike Brown.

William Carlos Williams once declared that the sonnet "does not admit of the slightest change to its structural composition," a statement that pretty much every American poet of note has debunked. You can see that Brown's sonnet plays with, but does not exactly replicate the Shakespearean sonnet, as it keeps the fourteen lines and ending couplet, but otherwise abandons the rhyme scheme. Likewise, it keeps to a four-to-five beat-per-line rhythm, though you'd struggle to scan it for regular iambic pentameter. What it keeps, or embroiders upon, is the sense of rhetorical movement, and also the rhythms of the sonnet built through sound and syntax. Notice that the opening flowers—aster, nasturtium, delphinium—share syllables in common, a slow purring "r" sound that calls to the words "dirt," "fingers" and "learning" in the following line. By the third line, however, that "r" sound has disappeared, replaced by crisper "t" sounds in "heat" and "elements," while the fifth through seventh lines contain a series of alliterative words, internal and end rhymes, all of which I've put here in bold:

Summer **s**eemed to bloom again**st** the will
of the **s**un, which new**s** reports cl**ai**med fl**a**med hot**ter**
On this planet than when our dead fath**ers**

If I follow the poem's sonic trajectory, I notice these changes in internal rhymes take place after new flowers are listed: after "Cosmos. Baby's breath," for instance, I hear more *b* and *e* sounds proliferate. But the change in sound also accompanies a change in perspective. If the first four lines—here, what I'd call an unrhymed quatrain—focus on how the claiming (and naming) of dirt and flowers might possess alchemical processes that could "change" the speaker and those like him, the next unrhymed quatrain suggests it is climate change that marks our world as essentially, and painfully, different from that of our "dead father[s']." But the last six lines—the sestet—take the biggest swerve:

> Men like me and my brothers filmed what we
> Planted for proof we existed before
> Too late, sped the video to see blossoms
> Brought in seconds, colors you expect in poems
> Where the world ends, everything cut down.
> *John Crawford. Eric Garner. Mike Brown.*

Here all the images of proof, alchemy, and disaster that opened the poem have coalesced to a much darker meaning. If Brown begins this poem by suggesting that gardening represents particular forms of knowledge and transformation, here "proof" becomes a film Brown and his friends make to show both they and their gardens ever existed, even as they fast-forward these films to watch the flowers bloom and die. At this point, I struggle a bit to follow the line of Brown's thought, since it leaps from the video to "the colors you expect in poems/ [w]here the world ends," a reference, perhaps, to the climate apocalypse hinted at in the second quatrain, but also to the fact that the speaker and his friends, like the murdered Black men named at the poem's end, might not survive due to racist violence. The precise logical connection between all these elements may be vague, but I suspect that's the point: this isn't about reason or the clarifying yet ultimately false knowledge "classical philosophers" might offer, but the rushed experience of a life lived on the verge of various types of extinction. I can't unknot these different scenes and images; I have to flow with and through them, thus be transformed by them, which is why the bulk of this last sestet might be a single sentence, just as the first and second quatrains are each a single sentence. For me, this creates a rhythm of mounting panic, punctuated by the list of flowers' names that both mark the end of each quatrain and pause to give the reader a moment to breathe.

Those flowers, of course, along with the gardening images, allude to the work that Eric Garner did while alive. Garner worked as a horticulturalist for the New York City Department of Parks and Recreation before being choked to death by a police officer during his arrest in 2014. The poem opens with the names of three flowers and ends with the names of three Black men killed by the police, just after the penultimate line's abrupt ending: "everything cut down." This is the final, awful transformation that occurs in Brown's poem, and harkens back not only to Garner's own employment but common pastoral themes often found in sonnets around mortality and youth. That's one of the "traditions" Brown's sonnet implicitly references, though another, more horrifying one is the extrajudicial killing of Black men in America.

To understand what makes Brown's sonnet both conventional *and* unusual, it's important to know something about the sonnet's tradition in English. "**Sonnet**" comes from the Italian, *sonetto*, meaning "a little sound or song." Most readers know that the English sonnet is a short, fourteen-line poem written in iambic pentameter and structured around one of three strict rhyme schemes that comprise the three types of sonnets in English: the Petrarchan, the Spenserian, and the Shakespearean. The Petrarchan sonnet, modeled after Petrarch, the great thirteenth-century Italian sonneteer, divides between an **octave** (ABBABBA) and a **sestet** (CDECDE or CDCDCD, or any version of this that avoids a final couplet). In contrast, the Spenserian sonnet, named for Edmund Spenser, with its cascade of closely interlocking rhymes, effectively creates three couplets (ABABB-CBCCDCDEE), while the Shakespearean sonnet contains three distinct quatrains and a couplet (ABABACDCDEFEFGG).

If a change of rhyming pattern changes suggests a change in thought, you can see that the Petrarchan sonnet has a big change between the octave and sestet. We call this the **volta** or turn in the poem, since the octave (ABBAABBA) has an envelope rhyme scheme, while the sestet allows for variance, even unpredictability. Some critics have suggested that the turn in the Petrarchan sonnet allows for more "acceleration" of thought or feeling, and resists conclusion in the ways that the Spenserian and Shakespearean sonnets—which finish with couplets—invite. I've told students that the Shakespearean sonnet's organization around three distinct quatrains suggests a progression of thought: the first quatrain introduces a subject, the second embroiders or expands upon that subject, and the third offers a rejoinder or introduces some measure of doubt, which the couplet resolves.

The sonnet comes into English through desire and politics—in particular through Sir Thomas Wyatt, ambassador to Henry VIII and former lover of Anne Boleyn, who went to Italy, became entranced by the form, and returned to write "Whoso List to Hunt": a sonnet purportedly written for Boleyn, lost to him to her more powerful suitor, Henry VIII. Wyatt's sonnet imports not only a version of Petrarch's rhyme scheme then, but the Italian sonnet's tendency toward psychological and erotic content, and its use of extended metaphor or conceit. Wyatt's Petrarchan interests were echoed by Henry Howard, the Earl of Surrey, who took the Petrarchan model and changed it to the rhyme scheme that eventually became known as the Shakespearean sonnet, as Shakespeare became the form's most noted early practitioner.

Sonnets have focused on everything from love to the loss of a child to the consideration of one's relationship to God to the crowning of a prince to a translated volume of Homer's poetry. Sonnets have been devotional, political, personal, pastoral, humorous, erotic. Today, there are no set conventions regarding subject matter for the sonnet, but I would argue that whatever its subject, the sonnet retains a durable interest in *thinking through one's relationship* to that subject. The sonnet's compressed form resists narrative in favor of lyric time and movement, though a series of sonnets—whether it be a crown or a sequence—allows for narrative or more chronological progression.

You can see that Brown's elegiac poem is an act of thinking through the cultural and personal meaning of these Black men's murders. To underscore this process, he takes part of the Shakespearean quatrain structure, then moves to the Petrarchan sestet, then ends with a rhyming couplet. In effect, he marries the Shakespearean and Petrarchan models and breaks his sonnet down into thirds, based around three different types of "arguments" or "proofs" in his poem: (1) Gardening as proof of life and change; (2) Climate change as proof of change and death; and (3) Racial violence as the proof of the speaker's own mortal condition. Brown took what he needed from the sonnet traditions we've inherited and made it his own, even as he also clearly converses with other models that have come before.

And I think that conversation is important to the poem's subject; that is, it matters that this is a free-verse sonnet and not a free-verse poem, since "The Tradition" also has a defined community it has envisioned as part of the sonnet's own tradition: Black Americans and, more specifically, Black American men. That is the "we" Brown addresses, though the "you" might be more broadly and even pointedly directed. The sense of deixis here is attached to its verse form, as it connects ideas of "classical" thought, rhetoric, and form with Brown's critique of American racism and how it has affected men like him. In this, Brown has considered how almost every aspect of the sonnet form can not only connect with but enable more of his argument.

And that, I think, is an example of organic form at work. The sonnet is not a container of Brown's conclusions; it enables me to see how Brown reaches those conclusions, measure by measure.

It also reveals how the formal expectations of the sonnet based on its own tradition have pushed Brown toward syntactic patterns that reflect and are also implicitly curtailed by those expectations. Simply put, Brown could at any time have abandoned the tripartite structure of his sonnet to focus on embellishing one train of thought, or he could have had composed his sonnet with much shorter or longer rhythms per line, all in direct service to his content rather than following the sonnet form itself. In that, content and form are *not* the same thing, even as they remain dynamically engaged, something Levertov believed marked the most natural of poems, so that I can see how the sounds and rhythms and even the history of the sonnet form amplifies Brown's evolving thought.

Sonnet Structure and the Volta

Here's another sonnet that might surprise you:

> Poetry, the only father, landscape, moon, food, the bowl
> of clam chowder in Nahcotta, was I happy, mountains
> of oyster shells gleaming silver, poetry, the only gold,
> or is it, my breasts, feet, my hands, index finger,
> fingernail, hangnail, paper cut, what is divine, I drove
> to the sea, wandered aimlessly, I stared at my tree, I said
> in my mind there's my tree, there's my tree I said
>   in my mind,
> I remember myself before words, thrilled at my parents'
> touch, opened milkweed with no agenda, blew the fluff,
> no reaching for comparison, to be free of signification,
> wriggle out of the figurative itchy sweater, body, breasts,
> vulva, little cave of the uterus, clit, need, touch,
>   come, I came

before I knew what coming was, iambic pentameter, did I
feel it, does language eclipse feeling, does it eclipse
    the eclipse

This unrhymed, untitled, and unmetered sonnet by Diane Seuss
from her book of sonnets, *frank*, might not look like any version
of the sonnet I've listed here, which raises an important question:
What is it about a sonnet that makes it a sonnet, no matter how
many of its formal attributes we lose?

With the loss of rhyme in Seuss's poem, you could argue
that you also lose its rhetorical movement, since ideas no longer connect—or conclude—according to the rhyming patterns
of quatrains, couplets, or sestets. Likewise, you could also argue
that, without such regular rhymes or a meter, we lose the poem's
resolution. Certainly, Seuss's poem unspools in one long series
of memories that connect either by sensory or semantic association and word play: "little cave of the uterus, clit, need, touch,
come, I came/ before I knew what coming was," Seuss playfully
writes, just as she connects other clauses together through repetition that function like an anaphoric refrain: "I stared at my
tree, I said/ in my mind there's my tree, there's my tree I said
in my mind."

The sonnet rushes through time and memory without taking
a pause for breath, which makes the poem feel both exhilarat-
ing and overwhelming. That said, I feel two distinctly different
changes that occur in the poem, the first of which appears in the
fifth through the eighth lines:

                                              I drove
to the sea, wandered aimlessly, I stared at my tree, I said
in my mind there's my tree, there's my tree I said
    in my mind,
I remember myself before words

This moment startles because the poem swerves to a moment of self-conscious revelation in which the speaker suddenly articulates to herself *what* she sees (the tree in both her imagination and in her real life), and remembers herself, too, "before words," an important detail because it's words that give the speaker social "signification" as female, details that she also longs to free herself of.

The poem swerves again just before its conclusion, in which the speaker recalls her younger self's desire to "wriggle out of her figurative itchy sweater, body, breasts," noting that as a young girl she was able to achieve sexual pleasure before knowing what it was called. This, for me, is the sonnet's actual subject—not trees, childhood, memory, or sex, but the role that language plays in shaping our responses to memory and our experience of the world. "Did I feel it," the speaker asks, of orgasm but also, perhaps, of the immensity of her desire to escape language's hold. "[D]oes language eclipse feeling," she finishes, "does it eclipse the eclipse"?

At both these junctures, the poem self-consciously wrenches our gaze away from recalled physical scenes to larger, more abstract concerns. Even if Seuss doesn't—because she can't—answer the poem's final question, I feel its overarching importance, and its inevitability. In effect, Seuss relies upon two "turns" in the poem that function much like the voltas that appear in more conventional sonnets. Her turns even appear at fairly expected points: one around the middle, right around where we might find a Petrarchan sestet to start, and one again at the final two lines, where we might expect the Shakespearean couplet. It's these voltas that allow Seuss's speaker to switch from the flotsam of memory to the question of identity, to wheel the poem's gaze back to herself. To me, these moments feel the most ruminative, the closest in tone and style to earlier sonnets. Of course, all poems have turns in them, surprising revelations of character or a new understanding of the crisis that initiated the poem, but a sonnet's condensed lyric time frame means that these turns must happen more decidedly and frequently, occurring at similar junctures not just because of expectations but because of the sonnet's constrained number of lines. If time in a **narrative** poem is determined by the unfolding of cause and effect in story, time in a **lyric** poem is defined by chronological departure, by the poem's focus on voice and the speaker's emotional crisis as the poem associatively leaps and returns. Lyric time not only allows for but demands more movement. You could even see each one of Seuss's images in the poem as a mini turn, since they connect more through sound than sense, functioning as fragmented memories. Seuss's poem teaches me that it's the volta, then, that distinguishes the sonnet from other forms, the final device without which such a compressed structure as the sonnet cannot function.

Form as Thinking

When I look at a poem like "The Tradition," I'm immediately aware that there's a relationship between the poem's form and its content. But when I look at Seuss's sonnet, I don't make such an automatic connection. What is it about the sonnet that spoke to her, that made that formal choice seem inevitable for a rumination on childhood, memory, and identity? With that question in mind, perhaps I have to consider why we write in form at all. Is a poem's form meant to match up with and even constrain its content, or is it meant to shape some part of content that ultimately extends beyond the form itself? In other words, does form restrict, refract, or liberate content? And when do we know a poem's form has been productively altered, perhaps been distilled to essence, not merely failed?

In very good poems, of course, form and content cohere in ways that create emotional resolution for the reader *and* formal closure of the poem. The excellence of Elizabeth Bishop's "Sestina," for example, is based in part on the naturalness with which she repeats the same six words to portray a family consumed by unspoken grief. Bishop's repetitions allow readers to identify what the poem's characters refuse to name; in particular, a young child's sorrow for her dead father or paternal figure, a loss that permeates every object and aspect of the house instead.

SESTINA

September rain falls on the house.
In the failing light, the old grandmother
sits in the kitchen with the child
beside the Little Marvel Stove,
reading the jokes from the almanac,
laughing and talking to hide her tears.

She thinks that her equinoctial tears
and the rain that beats on the roof of the house
were both foretold by the almanac,
but only known to a grandmother.
The iron kettle sings on the stove.
She cuts some bread and says to the child,

It's time for tea now; but the child
is watching the teakettle's small hard tears
dance like mad on the hot black stove,
the way the rain must dance on the house.
Tidying up, the old grandmother
hangs up the clever almanac

on its string. Birdlike, the almanac
hovers half open above the child,
hovers above the old grandmother

and her teacup full of dark brown tears.
She shivers and says she thinks the house
feels chilly, and puts more wood in the stove.

It was to be, says the Marvel Stove.
I know what I know, says the almanac.
With crayons the child draws a rigid house
and a winding pathway. Then the child
puts in a man with buttons like tears
and shows it proudly to the grandmother.

But secretly, while the grandmother
busies herself about the stove,
the little moons fall down like tears
from between the pages of the almanac
into the flower bed the child
has carefully placed in the front of the house.

Time to plant tears, says the almanac.
The grandmother sings to the marvelous stove
and the child draws another inscrutable house.

A **sestina** is a poem of six stanzas of six lines each with an ending three-line stanza, or **envoi**. In the sestina, the same six ending words repeat throughout the stanzas in an intricate pattern whose numerological significance once purportedly held magical meaning. Whether or not Bishop knew of the sestina's possible connection to magic, notice that the stove is called Marvel and also depicted here as "marvelous"; how the "clever" and "birdlike" almanac functions as a poetic as well as agricultural soothsayer, prone to making prophetic statements that could refer equally to the weather as to the father's fated death. Sestinas, attributed to the twelfth-century Provençal troubadour Arnaut

Daniel, were known for their relationship to the courtly love tradition, but Bishop clearly recognized that a form of such densely packed repetition could also amplify grief, in effect duplicating the mourner's obsessive mourning. In "Sestina," all human emotions are displaced onto the stove and almanac, subsumed into the drawing the child makes of a "rigid house" with its "winding pathway," and also of a man "with buttons like tears." Bishop's own father died when she was an infant, while her mother was institutionalized when Bishop was a child. An only child herself, Bishop then went to live with her maternal grandparents in Nova Scotia. Though written in third person, "Sestina" obviously mines certain facts of Bishop's early childhood, and if the child in her poem displaces the intensity of her feelings onto the objects around her, Bishop releases her own feelings through the repetition of six carefully selected words.

And yet is everything ultimately released? Note the poem's final image of the child drawing yet another picture of that "inscrutable house" in the envoi. If I think of the child's act of drawing as an attempt to represent and perhaps reconcile her feelings, then her return to it—like Bishop's return to her repeated words in the envoi itself—both suggests and denies catharsis. In that, the poem is as much about the artistic failures of representation as it is about the sublimation of grief.

Something similar happens in Bishop's villanelle "One Art," which ends on Bishop's parenthetical demands to herself to write down the final loss of a loved one, a grief which subtly and steadily builds, animating her entire poem.

ONE ART

The art of losing isn't hard to master;
so many things seem filled with the intent
to be lost that their loss is no disaster.

Lose something every day. Accept the fluster
of lost door keys, the hour badly spent.
The art of losing isn't hard to master.

Then practice losing farther, losing faster:
places, and names, and where it was you meant
to travel. None of these will bring disaster.

I lost my mother's watch. And look! my last, or
next-to-last, of three loved houses went.
The art of losing isn't hard to master.

I lost two cities, lovely ones. And, vaster,
some realms I owned, two rivers, a continent.
I miss them, but it wasn't a disaster.

—Even losing you (the joking voice, a gesture
I love) I shan't have lied. It's evident
the art of losing's not too hard to master
though it may look like (Write it!) like disaster.

Like the sestina, the villanelle suggests both obsessive return
and self-conscious performance. Here, I see how Bishop's final
stanza focuses on the control she wills herself to execute from
the start of the poem. As her syntax becomes more self-directed
through her use of parentheticals, I become more aware of
Bishop as both subject *and* author of the poem, as the loss of this
"you" threatens to become amplified for Bishop by the loss of
her personal (and writerly) composure. By the end of "One Art,"
I understand that Bishop's choice of the villanelle form doesn't
just allow for compulsive reiterations of loss, it's a way to test out
her assertions across the whole of the poem, "mastering" each
casualty in verse. Throughout her poem, Bishop declares that

"the art of losing isn't hard to master," even as each stanza moves incrementally to larger and more personal disappearances: from the "fluster" of lost house keys and "an hour badly spent," to her mother's watch and "three loved houses," "a continent," and finally, to the loss of the beloved. Each loss is different of course; the poem's refrains revise themselves as they repeat, thus they make increasingly doubtful the speaker's claims. In the end, certain losses *are* impossible to reconcile. Loss itself isn't an art at all, even if writing about and surviving it are.

Villanelles, one of our most elaborate and interlocking verse forms in English, didn't actually begin with any specific rhyme schemes or refrains, only the expectation that these poems, due to their title ("*villanella*" and "*villancico*" mean "peasant" in Italian) would involve pastoral themes. The **villanelle** was in fact a French form with roots in Italian dance songs, evolving over the years into a nineteen-line poem of five tercets, a quatrain, and two repeating rhymes, in which the rhyming first and third lines from the opening tercet recur as alternating refrains across the following stanzas, becoming the ending couplet of the quatrain. It entered the English literary tradition in the nineteenth century as a form of light verse, which Bishop preserves in "One Art" with her self-mocking, ironic tone, which only makes me more aware of the seriousness of her feelings. It's the villanelle's rhyming refrains that are meant to delight, their repetitions made new in each context that create surprising narrative change even as the refrain itself insists upon sameness and return.

This tug-of-war between change and return, sameness and difference, adds a certain piquancy to villanelles in which difference itself becomes the subject of the poem. Here, for instance, is Adrienne Su's villanelle "Personal History," in which the villanelle's repetitions reflect and magnify the speaker's conflicted sense of identity:

PERSONAL HISTORY

The world's largest Confederate monument
was too big to perceive on my earliest trips to the park.
Unlike my parents, I was not an immigrant

but learned, in speech and writing, to represent.
Picnicking at the foot and sometimes peak
of the world's largest Confederate monument,

we raised our Cokes to the first Georgian president.
His daughter was nine like me, but Jimmy Carter,
unlike my father, was not an immigrant.

Teachers and tour guides stressed the achievement
of turning three vertical granite acres into art.
Since no one called it a Confederate monument,

it remained invisible, like outdated wallpaper meant
long ago to be stripped. Nothing at Stone Mountain Park
echoed my ancestry, but it's normal for immigrants

not to see themselves in landmarks. On summer nights,
fireworks and laser shows obscured, with sparks,
the world's largest Confederate monument.
Our story began when my parents arrived as immigrants.

What I love about this poem is the way its imagery and form
suggest parallels but not exact duplications. Su's speaker is,
unlike her parents, "not an immigrant," even as she is shaped by
the immigrant experience. Stone Mountain may be "the largest
Confederate monument" in America, but as it isn't called this, it
becomes "invisible, like outdated wallpaper meant/ long ago to be

stripped." If the speaker's family isn't reflected by Stone Mountain because "it's normal for immigrants// not to see themselves in monuments," the monument, too, is "obscured, with sparks" from summer fireworks, just as its size is, initially, "too big" for the speaker to "perceive on [her] earliest trips to the park." In that, the monument becomes a metaphor for the immigrant family, since their ancestry must be erased in order to assimilate, thus rendering the family culturally invisible—both to Stone Mountain and to American history. Interestingly, the parallel American history represented by this Confederate monument insists on its own cultural specificity and difference, something not allowed the speaker's family, since they visit it in order to be more American, "rais[ing their] Cokes to the first Georgian president," Jimmy Carter, whose own daughter is the same age as the poem's speaker, though racially and culturally different.

Su's poem is filled with symbolic echoes, and to emphasize this, her villanelle's refrains and rhymes echo each other, if distantly. Her initial refrain, "The world's largest Confederate monument," in the fourth stanza becomes "[s]ince no one called it a Confederate monument," just as "[u]nlike my parents, I was not an immigrant" turns into "it's normal for immigrants" in the fifth stanza and finally, "[o]ur story began when my parents arrived as immigrants" by the poem's end. Su's rhymes, too, are largely slant (monument/immigrant; Carter/park), while the poem as a whole is framed by rhyming themes of representation and obscurity. Notice how, if the speaker "learn[s] in speech and writing to represent" her family's experience, the tour guides in the fourth stanza "represents" Stone Mountain not as a Confederate monument but an artistic "achievement."

In its returns and revisions, Su's villanelle shows me how both the speaker and Stone Mountain are cultural outsiders while they remain fundamentally American; the speaker is "like" this monument that still refuses to reflect her family's experience.

Difference is parsed and refracted in Su's repetitions, American identity itself lost and gained and lost again over the course of the poem, since the final fact of her history rests on the line "Our story began when my parents arrived as immigrants." With that line, Su's villanelle returns to the parents' origin story, refusing to assimilate into an American cultural narrative. The speaker remains both citizen and immigrant, alien and native, Su's villanelle an act of mourning for the fact only racial difference makes her an outsider.

Clearly, Su's villanelle becomes not just a perfect container for her content but a mimetic experience of racial mourning itself. But forms don't always have to encapsulate or heighten their subjects so concretely. In some of the most exciting constrained verse, I'd even argue that form anticipates but *cannot* finally shape or control its meaning. I wrote before that, because we know their rules, poetic forms are designed to produce expected conclusions and, in that, the possibility of readerly relief. And yet many engaging formal poems—whether accidentally or deliberately—fall short of achieving this resolution, in which case, the poem's meaning might speak back to or capitalize upon what the form itself can't achieve.

Does the Poem's Form Conflict at Any Point with Its Argument?

Here's a sonnet that, for me, fails even as it succeeds at perfectly reproducing its formal requirements. Shakespeare's Sonnet 30 is, like Bishop's "Sestina," a poem about grief. But while Bishop's poem ends on an image of the child drawing "another inscrutable house," thus suggesting continual grieving, Shakespeare's sonnet promises a neater resolution. His train of thought carefully tracks the sonnet's formal structure, the poem's single, hypotactic sentence turning precisely at the start of each quatrain and couplet on

the linking adverbs "when," "then" and "but," which I have put
in bold:

> **When** to the sessions of sweet silent thought
> I summon up remembrance of things past,
> I sigh the lack of many a thing I sought,
> And with old woes new wail my dear time's waste:
> **Then** can I drown an eye, unus'd to flow,
> For precious friends hid in death's dateless night,
> And weep afresh love's long since cancell'd woe,
> And moan th' expense of many a vanish'd sight;
> **Then** can I grieve at grievances foregone,
> And heavily from woe to woe tell o'er
> The sad account of fore-bemoaned moan,
> Which I new pay as if not paid before.
> **But** if the while I think on thee, dear friend,
> All losses are restor'd, and sorrows end.

Shakespeare's sonnet is symmetrical and carefully balanced,
but even as he breaks his complex sentence up into clauses that
track the quatrains, his syntax pushes beyond the rhymes, meaning that I must find resolution as much through the sentence as
through meter and rhyme, which is partly why the poem tanta-
lizes. But his formal consistency *and* syntactic straining to reach
the sentence's conclusion presents a fascinating paradox: the
metrical and rhyming structure is regular to the point of near-
mathematical precision, while the subject matter itself grows
increasingly unrestrained. As the poem's many remembered
losses—of friends to death, lovers to change, and circumstances
to fate—accumulate, grief grows upon grief. Shakespeare repeats
the sounds and images of intense mourning, threading his sonnet with alliterative *w* sounds, as in the hard, spondaic rhythm
of the line "And with old woes new wail my dear time's waste."
Likewise, he repeats the words "grieve" and "grievances," return-

ing, too, to synonyms for them with "weep" and "wail" and "sorrow." The poem repeats "woe" itself four times, while sonically riffing off its *o* sounds in "sorrow," "old," "o'er," "flow," and "forebemoaned moan," creating a tapestry of pain that raises the poem's emotions to a fever pitch quatrain by quatrain, even as the metrical form itself icily refuses to break. In comparison with all this heightened feeling, however, Shakespeare's concluding couplet feels distant, abstract, as if the speaker were suddenly standing outside himself, trying to offer up this pat solution:

> But if the while I think on thee, dear friend,
> All losses are restor'd, and sorrows end.

Who is this "friend"? And how in the world is the mere thought of him or her supposed to restore the speaker's lost time and dead companions? The couplet reaches for a catharsis I can formally anticipate through the rhymes and completion of syntax, but which I can't actually feel since the poem remains awash in three quatrains of mounting grief.

Looking at Sonnet 30, I'm reminded of Paul Fussell's argument that the sonnet's volta represents a "logical action" as it responds to a question or proposition put forth by the preceding quatrains; it might also, Fussell wrote, function like a "literal turn of the body or head." Shakespeare's volta feels entirely logical to me and, in that, an indifferent turning-away from the feelings that preceded it. I could read his volta as a failure or a challenge, a knowing glance at me, the reader, to see if I believe this sudden change of heart. Can new love adequately redress past losses? Does sorrow actually end? Should it? Perhaps Shakespeare's use of the sonnet is a conscious attempt to write his way out of grief, much like Bishop's villanelle is a performed act of writerly self-control. But personal experience proves that some feelings will not be written out of being felt; perhaps Shakespeare's sonnet, then, is an ironic commentary on the limitation of the form itself.

Failures of Form

Obviously, perfectly observed rules don't require or always produce a form's perfect fusion with its content. I can hear Shakespeare's sonnet as concluded even as I experience his sorrow as ongoing. Was Shakespeare wrong to select a sonnet for content that extends beyond what fourteen lines can express? Or was he attracted to the sonnet not for its concision but for the surprisingly variable modulations of tone its lyric movement allows for? As I wrote before, Sonnet 30, like the bulk of Shakespeare's sonnets, favors hypotactic syntax, which in its complex use of subordination and hierarchy allows me to see contradictions of thought and tone evolve within one sentence. It's not unusual to see moments of exultation follow or precede despair within a single Shakespearean sonnet. What is unusual in Sonnet 30 is that its tone does not swerve from Shakespeare's mourning *until* that final couplet. In that, the malleability of feeling that the sonnet's voltas allow for has been constrained by the poem's sounds of grief.

In many ways, Sonnet 30 reflects the core contradiction inherent to all formal poems: constrained verse may produce sonic resolution even as the content itself is not productively resolved through all its devices. In the best constrained verse, this contradiction might become part of the poem's overarching question. And yet, as Denise Levertov argued in "Some Thoughts on the Line," if formal poems are meant to focus on "the results of thinking," what about formal poems that reside in the process of thought, presenting neither consequences nor conclusions but more unending questions?

Resisting Conclusion

Here is a sonnet that to me suggests such thought-as-process. Like Shakespeare's Sonnet 30, Percy Bysshe Shelley's "Ozymandias" resists finality, but here in both content *and* form, a lack of resolution I find its most appealing aspect.

OZYMANDIAS

I met a traveller from an antique land
Who said: "Two vast and trunkless legs of stone
Stand in the desert . . . Near them, on the sand,
Half sunk, a shattered visage lies, whose frown,
And wrinkled lip, and sneer of cold command,
Tell that its sculptor well those passions read
Which yet survive, stamped on these lifeless things,
The hand that mocked them, and the heart that fed:
And on the pedestal these words appear:
'My name is Ozymandias, King of Kings:
Look on my Works, ye Mighty, and despair!'
Nothing beside remains. Round the decay
Of that colossal Wreck, boundless and bare
The lone and level sands stretch far away."

Shelley here relates a purportedly simple anecdote: a traveler "from an antique land" comes across the statuary remains of "Ozymandias," or Pharaoh Ramesses II, the third pharaoh of the nineteenth dynasty of Egypt. This "colossal Wreck" that comprises Ozymandias's memory now lies in fragments scattered across the desert—a moral and ironic judgment on Ozymandias's rule, since the statue was constructed to suggest his greatness, even as it also depicts his "frown,/ And wrinkled lip, and sneer of cold command." The poem, then, might be read as a cautionary tale about the limits of power, especially the authoritarian kind. But it's also a cautionary tale about the limits of art, since it's through Ozymandias's statue that we sense his presence through the fog of history, fragmentary as it is, as the art that represents him, too, barely survives.

Shelley's sonnet is three sentences, the longest of which is divided with a semicolon at the octave. While this punctuation mark does not technically end the sentence, it acts as a strong pause that also marks the volta we normally expect with the Petrarchan sonnet, where the interlaced rhymes of the octave give way to the more cascading rhymes of the sestet. Shelley mostly follows this model, though his rhyme scheme is not as consistent as the Petrarchan one, as the rhymes proceed like this: ABABACDCEFEGFG. The octave of the sonnet focuses on the appearance of the statue, while the sestet focuses on its message—both the message that Ozymandias had chiseled into it and the message we as readers might take from Shelley's sonnet. But notice how the sinuous opening of this sonnet gives way, at the end, to two shorter sentences, one of only three metrical feet:

> Nothing beside remains. Round the decay
> Of that colossal Wreck, boundless and bare
> The lone and level sands stretch far away.

The first foot of this passage I read as a trochee, followed by two feet of iambs. It's an odd line overall, marked by falling, trochaic rhythms in the first and fourth feet, and the hard, medial caesura that occurs after "remains." This falling rhythm might have been consciously chosen to rhythmically duplicate a statue crumbling to dust; whatever Shelley's reason for it, the line disrupts the regularity of his iambic rhythms, redirecting the reader's attention away from Ozymandias to the statue's surroundings. The poem's last sentence focuses entirely on the image of the "boundless and bare" sands that "stretch far away": an image of nothingness that speaks back to the statue's declaration of enduring power. In truth, there is no kingdom that survives in the poem, just as there is no complete representation of Ozymandias, just a "colossal Wreck" whose coherent shape can only be completed in the reader's imagination.

The sonnet's largely consistent iambic pentameter may suggest resolution, but Shelley everywhere creates fragmentation. Notice that he begins with an unnamed narrator recounting the story of yet *another* unnamed narrator: the sonnet is a frame text, in which stories become contained and absorbed within other stories, but without any conclusion. Ozymandias's own command—"Look on my Works, ye Mighty, and despair!"—is here related to the tourist via the sculptor's representation, which is then represented to the speaker of the sonnet. The sonnet becomes an artwork within a mesh of artworks—a series of interweaving representations matched by the sonnet's interweaving rhymes, all of which means I lose track of who finally speaks, who finally represents.

And this question of who represents is important because it's so closely related to politics. If Ozymandias makes his claim through an artist's representation of him, that claim—even in its ruined state—carries down through the centuries, even if its message is opposite to the one Ozymandias intended. So if political power cannot endure, does art carry more power than politics, since even fragments of it can survive to transmit meaning?

There's a judgment, too, about where this art is found. Notice the phrase "a traveller from an *antique* land" (italics mine), which underscores the pre-modernity of Egypt and thus, implicitly, its lack of global significance. Antiques are what you collect and display, much as you share stories. And here, the collector of all these stories is finally Shelley himself, an English poet, writing in a form long associated with Western Europe. Clearly, there's an implied Orientalist judgment here in that word "antique."

And yet the lesson suggested by this Egyptian ruler has political implications for Europe and, more specifically, Shelley and other Western poets as well, if the poem is about the relationship between art and power. It's not simply that art confers fame upon the artist that is greater than the fame of rulers: notice that *none* of the people relating this tale of Ozymandias has a name. I only assume the first speaker in this poem is Shelley, but it doesn't have to be. If Shelley's sonnet survives, then, it may be due less to his own reputation than the message his sonnet transmits. In that, the artist is less important than the art.

And yet art, too, doesn't overcome time and nature, as suggested by that final image of the desert sand, "boundless and bare" that "stretch[es] far away." You can see how Shelley matches his adjectives in their syntax and alliteration with those final two lines—"boundless and bare," "lone and level"—creating an equilibrium between the phrases that also highlights the desert's natural effects. Landscape, unlike art or politics, is the true leveler, one that stands outside of complete human perception and civilization, and which renders all things—rulers and artists, witnesses and creators—mortally equivalent.

Is the Ending Open or Closed?

Shelley's poem ends on an ambivalent note about those statuary remains. Is it their material composition that makes them fragile, considering Shelley's sonnet is constructed around the oral transmission of stories? Are specific artworks more or less likely to endure based on their relationship to the culture they interpret? Or are certain types of art in general, like certain types of empires, destined for extinction, while poetry alone—and maybe Western culture—survives?

Shelley's poem doesn't provide any final answers to these questions, and I suspect it's because Shelley himself was ambiv-

alent about his own interpretation of—or even connection to—
Ozymandias. Part of the poem's ambiguity is achieved by the
fact that this sonnet is more narrative than lyric, since it relates a
story told to the poem's speaker. By doing this, Shelley presents
us with an anecdote within an anecdote, not a lyric meditation
divided into specific units of thought organized by rhyme. All
attention is focused instead outward on descriptions of the statue,
rather than inward on the poet's self-conscious deliberation. The
poem ends when the traveler stops speaking, trailing off more
than it concludes, something the Petrarchan rhymes reflect in the
ending sestet.

You might find the lingering mysteries of "Ozymandias"
annoying; for me, they are what draw me back to the poem, since
the questions "Ozymandias" raises are ones I personally share
about art, artistry, and politics, too. Shelley moved beyond what
sonnets have trained me to expect: he not only absorbed the rules
of the form but found some measure—of thought and of narrative framing—that made the sonnet open up rather than shut
down. And no matter what form a poet chooses to write in, the
fundamental problem of structure always returns to a question of
closure. When a poem ends, does it allow for *more* interpretation
and readerly engagement, or does it close these options off? With
a free-verse form, closure comes when the poet has in some way
exhausted her subject matter. With a constrained one, the poet
anticipates where subject matter must be abandoned, if it cannot
be finished: the end is always foreseen. This doesn't mean that
free verse achieves resolution in ways that formal poems can't,
nor does it mean that closure itself is to be longed for, something that the poet Lyn Hejinian reminds us of in her essay "The
Rejection of Closure":

> Form does not necessarily achieve closure, nor does raw
> materiality provide openness. Indeed, the conjunction of *form*
> with radical *openness* may be what can offer a version of the

"paradise" for which writing often yearns—a flowering focus on a distinct infinity.*

Closed forms of poetry, Hejinian argued, are ones in which meaning is constrained, every part of the work driving toward a single reading that controls how we should feel about the poem overall. Open poems, by contrast, allow all parts of the poem to be "maximally excited . . . because ideas and things exceed (without deserting) argument that they have taken into the dimension of the work." It's not unlike Keats's argument about negative capability. Open poems allow for multiple interpretations and, in that, give up some of their agency to the reader. You might see the difference between open and closed effects in poems that strain toward epiphanies that readers already generally agree upon, or which they can too easily interpret. When, for example, Joyce Kilmer writes in her poem "Trees," "Poems were made by fools like me,/ But only God can make a tree," I have no question as to how to interpret her feelings about poetry and trees. The poem is trite, saccharine; it expresses a thesis, it doesn't allow me to experience for myself any wonder for the trees that moved Kilmer. This, of course, is an extreme example of a closed poem, but versions of closed endings exist everywhere, occasionally even in the work of very good poets, who look at the ending of a poem as an opportunity to restate their poem's intentions.

The challenge to writing formal poems is understanding that they do not require achieving every demand of the form, only that we use these demands as opportunities to expand more aspects of the poem as a whole: not just its subject matter, but whatever psychological or even canonical expectations we hold about the form itself. If I love "Ozymandias," it is in part *because*

---

* Lyn Hejinian, "The Rejection of Closure," The Poetry Foundation, Accessed April 14, 2024, https://www.poetryfoundation.org/articles/69401/.

of its swerving away from sonnet closure and sonnet thinking. And even as Bishop's "Sestina" and "One Art" perfectly achieve their formal requirements, I find something realistically regressive about both poems as well, the sense that the child will never stop drawing the grandmother's "inscrutable house," that the speaker of "One Art" will return again and again to the memory of her beloved. Like "Ozymandias," these poems, too, are about the limits of representation. And of course, all representations have an inbuilt limit to them, since an image can never replace or completely duplicate the original. We understand this in our own lives, so when it comes to the question of organic form in poetry, we are asking, ultimately, what structure best allows us to feel, not just represent an experience.

There is, of course, no one answer to this. There are free-verse poems that achieve this organic unpacking of experience, just as there are concrete and experimental and also baroquely patterned verse poems that can do it. Oulipo, a group of writers organized by the French writer Raymond Queneau and the mathematician François Le Lionnais, saw formal play as inherent to writing itself, their mission to mine radical constraints in order to create what they called "potential literature" or works "seeking . . . new structures and patterns which may be used by writers in any way they enjoy." An Oulipian work might be a novel written without the letter *e*, for example, or a poem that uses the $n+7$ formula, in which all the nouns in a line or sentence get exchanged with the seventh noun entry that follows that specific word in the dictionary. They produce books like Christian Bök's *Eunoia*, in which each short chapter is composed of words containing one of English's five vowel sounds, or something like "Ballad in A" by Cathy Park Hong, in which every word must include only the *a* vowel.

Some readers might treat Oulipian works as less meaningful than culturally received forms like sonnets because their formal decisions are arbitrary and self-selected, whereas the bal-

lad stanza or the villanelle arise from complex cultural histories. But all formal rules are, at root, arbitrary. The constraint
a poet like Bök or Hong places on their poem isn't parodying
or denying the importance of formal verse traditions so much
as pointing out the myriad constraints we *already* place on writing, whether that writing is culturally received or institutionally
enforced. For Oulipian writing, the point is process, not necessarily result. These results may be at times amusing or satiric,
but the inspiration is also serious if we are at all serious about
reinventing literature.

When poets choose to write in culturally received forms, the
question of what is or is not an organic choice for the subject
matter leads ineluctably to the poem's possible ending: what resolution does this form offer that a particular subject itself might
strain toward or resist? In many ways, if writing in form is the
most arbitrary of challenges, conscious showmanship and control are required for the undertaking. Writing a sonnet sequence,
no matter how natural a choice it may initially seem, is a poet
peacocking. Personally, I love how formal poems give both the
writer and reader pleasure to see two games played at once:
the formal game whose rules the audience knows, and the personal game of self-discovery whose revelations, ideally, no poet
or reader can anticipate. To play these games well, you have to
ask yourself questions similar to the ones I ask my writing students about their lineation: What desire or anxiety is this poem,
at heart, expressing? And what form—or, more important, what
alterations you have made to that form—best reflect these desires
and anxieties?

Writing in form allows us to experience the playful tension
that exists between creativity and restriction, to feel how constraint fires the imagination. That's something one of my first
poetry teachers, Richard Kenney, taught me in an independent study course I took from him in college. "I'm leaving the
room," he told me gravely one day. "While I'm gone, write me

a great poem. Either that, or just something in which every line starts with a letter of the alphabet." He walked off to get coffee. I picked up my pen, wrote down exactly three words of my "great poem," then gave up and wrote an abecedarian. You get the point: when you occupy one part of your brain with the rules of a game, it frees up the rest to actually play it. "Form is not a fixture," Hejinian wrote, "it is an activity," and I think this is why writing poetry becomes addictive to poets, and why I can only discover what I think or feel about a subject after I write about it. The poem is, as Hejinian reminds me, the mind itself, and like human consciousness, poems move between pattern and surprise, subversion and capitulation. When I read a great poem, I feel some part of that toggling occur within me as I follow its patterns of thought. Form helps me track the poet at that moment, just as, when I write, form helps me organize my own emotions and language. I become, as I work through form, subject and author, clown and audience, lion and ringmaster at once. Writing in form allows me to move fluidly through self-knowledge within closed systems of sense perception. And the more familiar the form is to me, the more intimate my engagement with its patterns and possibilities becomes. Form frees me up to reveal more of myself, letting me feel my way into a performance for which I've long ago learned the lines.

EXPERIMENTS

- Choose a poem from the list below and consider how it might exemplify and also expand your expectations of its verse form. What does this poem preserve of its formal requirements? What changes does it make to these requirements that for you correspond meaningfully with its particular speaker, subject matter, and theme?

- Choose a sonnet from below. In what ways might it resist the closure of its form?
- Write a sestina in which you focus on a character from a novel, movie, or short story. What six words best encapsulate the story of that character and the themes s/he represents? For an example, see Evie Shockley's "Clare's Song," which responds to Nella Larsen's *Passing*.
- Write a poem in which every word must contain the same vowel. For an example, see Cathy Park Hong's "Ballad in A."
- Take a family saying, cultural aphorism, or a line from a song that's always haunted you but that you've resisted in some way. Write a villanelle in which you use it as one of your refrain lines.

SUGGESTED WORKS TO CONSIDER

Rudyard Kipling, "Sestina of the Tramp-Royal"
Terrance Hayes, "Liner Notes to an Imaginary Playlist"
Katharine Coles, "Sestina in Prose"
Evie Shockley, "clare's song"
Cathy Park Hong, "Ballad in A"
Rupert Brooke, "Sonnet Reversed"
George Barker, "To My Mother"
Lady Mary Wroth, "from Pamphilia to Amphilanthus: 17"
Oliver de la Paz, "Diaspora Sonnet 25"
Elizabeth Barrett Browning, "Sonnets from the
    Portuguese 14"
Ben Jonson, "On My First Son"
W. B. Yeats, "Leda and the Swan"

Dylan Thomas, "Do Not Go Gentle into That
   Good Night"
Rita Dove, "Parsley"
Alberto Ríos, "Nani"

All poems can be found either at the Poetry Foundation or the
Academy of American Poets websites.

CHAPTER TEN

What Is the Poem's Mode?

When I consider how meaning is created in poems, I'm not just thinking about line and rhythm, sound or syntax, but also **mode**, a general term referring to a poem's mood, style, or subject. There are many poetic modes, such as satiric poems, which are characterized by parody, or didactic poems, which are characterized by their instructive purpose. Modes often have their roots in ancient literatures in which they were also accompanied by specific verse forms, but form and mode are different, and they increasingly divide the closer we get to today. Some of our most popular modes—like the ode and elegy—have changed significantly because the very concept of who or what deserves to be celebrated or mourned has itself fundamentally altered. So, too, has the pastoral mode of poetry evolved away from poems centered on idealized natural spaces to become more realistic depictions of humans and their environment. In this chapter, I want to consider these three popular modes to give you a general context for how they have been shaped, and to provide some new approaches for how poems in these modes might be constructed.

Writing with Attention: Conventions of the Ode

The **ode** is a celebratory poem meant for a public occasion. Odes in their earliest forms relied upon an elaborate and elevated diction and tone, often choosing a revered subject for their focus. The ode derives its name from the Greek *aeidein*, meaning "to sing" or "to chant," a word that in Greek became essentially synonymous with the lyric, as the ode was meant to be sung. Odes could either be monodies, meaning a poem sung by a single person, or a chorus. The Greek poet Pindar was a master of the choral ode, whose complex, tripartite poems were metrically irregular and long—around 300 lines or more—and, because they were meant to be accompanied by dance, tended toward the religious or ecstatic. Horace, master of the Latin ode, toned down these features, altering Pindar's complex structures with more symmetrical rhythmic patterns to conform to Latin. He also made the ode less about public celebration than private meditation. Horace's influence on the ode is, in that sense, more long-lasting than Pindar's, since the ode has ceased to be a formal structure in English poetry and has become instead a style we recognize based on its heightened diction.

Odes were usually recited on state occasions, and so the ode's address is public, though as the form has evolved, so, too, has our sense of what private interests can be praised. In part, the contemporary ode features common subjects to deflate our expectations, or to treat praise itself playfully, which you can see in this poem by Charles Simic.

MIRACLE GLASS, CO.

Heavy mirror carried
Across the street,

I bow to you
And to everything that appears in you,
Momentarily
And never again the same way:

This street with its pink sky,
Row of gray tenements,
A lone dog,
Children on rollerskates,
Woman buying flowers,
Someone looking lost.

In you, mirror framed in gold
And carried across the street
By someone I can't even see,
To whom, too, I bow.

Simic's poem is deliberately understated, which only high-lights the otherworldly qualities of the mirror he describes. Huge and "framed in gold," it not only reflects the physical world but its temporality, since everything reflected in the mirror appears once, and "never again the same way." The mirror itself is carried across the street by someone the speaker can't see, which makes it appear both self-animated and divine, leading the speaker to address the mirror directly by declaring, "I bow to you/ [a]nd to everything that appears in you." Everything that appears in the mirror is, on its own, unremarkable: a street with tenement housing, children skating, a random dog. And yet the parallelism of the mirror's spiritual qualities with this urban scene elevates the otherwise nondescript environment, making each action and object the mirror reflects feel similarly miraculous.

To underscore his point, Simic has even titled the poem "Miracle Glass, Co.," and ends it with the narrator making another bow, this time to the person carrying the mirror, "some-one [he] can't even see." I personally read this as a sly reference to a divinity holding up this mirror to us, his creations, so that we might witness the marvelousness of the world he reflects. At the same time, I can't help seeing Simic referencing himself at the end of that second stanza: he, too, is the "someone looking lost" in the mirror floating past.

Simic has upended the ode's conventions not just by prais-ing what we might see as unworthy but by celebrating what a mirror does—reflecting whatever passes in front of it. The poem's real subject, then, is the transience of ordinary life, here imbued with a mystery that approaches the sacred, though I also think Simic is making a point about the ode and class. Notice, in "Miracle Glass, Co.," that the street is populated by a "row of gray tenements." It's not an upper-class region of the city, and so if Simic's ode elevates all the mirror reflects, it height-ens my respect for the working-class environment the mirror frames, transforming it from a colorless street to a place where miracles might occur. I think this is another reason why the poem carries with it a Christian undertone, even though the poem overall isn't explicitly Christian. Still, Simic's poem calls back to the mode's religious origins through its use of an object that's linked with otherworldly powers, allowing the speaker and the other things in the poem to absorb these supernatural qualities themselves.

It's important that these objects and people are, and also feel, real. Not all odes achieve this. Certain eighteenth-century poets wrote odes for objects so encoded with baroque imagery and argument that the object itself ceased to be important; indeed, the object may not even have existed. You can see this in the English poet William Collins's poem "An Ode on the Popular Superstitions of the Highlands of Scotland, Considered as the Subject of Poetry." The title alone might explain why Collins's poem was doomed to vanish, though in general the ode's heightened diction and tone means that odes were and still remain the mode most likely to be burlesqued. That's what makes odes like Simic's so delightful: they poke fun at the mode even as they take some measure of its origins seriously.

What Does the Ode Celebrate?

Though the roots of the ode may be religious, the modern and contemporary ode is more often shaped by the poet's close attention to a thing or person: so close it elevates the poet's private encounter to a public event. I think about this with poems like Marianne Moore's "The Paper Nautilus," a poem as much about art as about the octopus it describes.

THE PAPER NAUTILUS

For authorities whose hopes
are shaped by mercenaries?
   Writers entrapped by
   teatime fame and by
commuters' comforts? Not for these
   the paper nautilus
   constructs her thin glass shell.

   Giving her perishable
souvenir of hope, a dull
   white outside and smooth-
   edged inner surface
glossy as the sea, the watchful
   maker of it guards it
   day and night; she scarcely

eats until the eggs are hatched.
Buried eight-fold in her eight
     arms, for she is in
     a sense a devil-
fish, her glass ram'shorn-cradled freight
     is hid but is not crushed;
     as Hercules, bitten

by a crab loyal to the hydra,
was hindered to succeed,
     the intensively
     watched eggs coming from
the shell free it when they are freed,—
     leaving its wasp-nest flaws
     of white on white, and close-

laid Ionic chiton-folds
like the lines in the mane of
     a Parthenon horse,
     round which the arms had
wound themselves as if they knew love
     is the only fortress
     strong enough to trust to.

A paper nautilus is a type of octopus whose females make a paperlike shell in which they incubate their eggs. Moore's syllabic ode to the nautilus largely focuses on its maternal aspects, though the octopus proves to be a complex mother, to say the least. "She is in/ a sense a devil-/ fish," Moore writes, one who "buries" her eggs in her eight arms. She's intensely protective of her offspring, which appear to entrap her just as much as they are trapped by her egg sac, since they "free [her] when they are freed." What they leave behind is the symbol of their origin: the shell itself, which Moore describes as like a Greek statue, its "white on white" folds "like the lines in the mane of/ a Parthenon horse." It's a way of representing the shell while also reminding me how organic natural forms might mimic elaborate and highly inorganic human art. Everywhere Moore has drawn my attention to *how* we look at the paper nautilus—whether through the lens of "authorities and mercenary teas," through the lens of mothering, or through the lens of Greek mythology and statuary. Ultimately all these things are acts of art-making: as the paper nautilus "constructs" her "thin glass shell," so, too, do we construct art, in order to represent the world. The paper nautilus is a human fantasy even as it stands apart from our projections. Notice how Moore starts her poem by reminding us that the paper nautilus makes her shell *not* for fame or reputation but out of a powerful, almost crushing maternal instinct. Her art, then, serves a different function, even as it produces something equally beautiful to Greek sculpture and, finally, just as empty of real life once the eggs have hatched. I think that's the power of the poem's ending, the way in which Moore inserts "as if" into the final lines describing how the octopus clutches her shell:

> round which the arms had
> wound themselves as if they knew love
>   is the only fortress
>   strong enough to trust to.

If the shell isn't only, or really, art, so her maternal instinct, too, isn't exactly love. Both shell and maternal protection are *like* things that humans make and experience, but they stand outside them too. We come as close as we can to understanding, but the wonder of Moore's ode is that, finally, we cannot truly represent what the paper nautilus has created, nor what she really feels.

Writing Out of Grief: Conventions of the Elegy

If the ode is a poem of joyful celebration, it would seem to be the opposite of the **elegy**, a poem of mourning. But both modes are forms of exquisite attention cloaked in public address, what Robert Hass, in *A Little Book on Form*, called a kind of desire. "Desire" is an important concept to both ode and elegy since, if the ode inspires desire in the reader to draw closer to the thing being described, the elegy has found some of its own deepest roots in erotic longing for the subject. We might even think about mourning itself as a kind of desire, whether that be the social desire to recapture the virtues of the lost beloved, or the personal desire to reinstate life itself.

In ancient Greek, elegies had metrical requirements, as they referred only to poems written in **elegiac couplets**—that is, a couplet in which the first line is written in dactylic hexameter, followed by one in pentameter. In terms of subject matter, however, elegies weren't relegated to mourning. Elegiac poems could take on a range of subjects, from meditations on war to erotic love to epitaphs. Our first elegies in Latin, in fact, were lovers' complaints. Ovid excelled at them, as did Propertius and Tibullus, just as Renaissance poets saw the elegiac mode as characterized by a sense of absence and sexual frustration; the term "elegiac" starts becoming solely linked with mourning only by the eighteenth century.

We may write elegies now for parents, friends, or even pets, but that is historically an evolution. The first funerary elegies were for public figures, often chosen as appropriate subjects because they reflected the virtues of the society that mourned them. One of the earliest public prose elegies is Pericles's funeral oration for the Athenian soldiers slaughtered during the Peloponnesian War, in which he links the value of these soldiers'

lives with the political power of Athens itself. Over time, however, the elegy became private, poems more likely to mourn the
unknown individual, such as Milton's "Lycidas," written for his
dead friend Edward King, or to anticipate the death of the poem's
author, as in Keats's "Ode to a Nightingale." Elegies might even
address the loss of whole groups or communities, as you can see
in Simon J. Ortiz's collection, *From Sand Creek*, which mourns the
Cheyenne and Arapaho women and children slaughtered by U.S.
soldiers at Sand Creek. As the elegy turns away from mourning
public figures to mourning individuals or the self, it becomes a
"form of poetry natural to the reflective mind," as Samuel Taylor
Coleridge argued: a mode that considers the brevity of human
life itself, which you see in Thomas Gray's "Elegy Written in a
Country Churchyard."

The biggest change in the elegy, however, occurred in the
emotions we expect the elegy to perform and, perhaps, heal. In
this, modern warfare might have made the greatest impact on the
elegy. Jahan Ramazani, in his book *The Poetry of Mourning*, argued
that the work of the contemporary elegist "tends not to achieve
but to resist consolation . . . not to heal but to reopen the wounds
of loss." This resistance is partly a result of the First and Second World Wars, which inspired both the need for more utilitar-
ian funerals and public anger around the mourning of millions
of dead. Due to these wars' impact, Ramazani notes, we might
see the evolution of modern poetry itself as intertwined with the
evolution of the elegy. Whereas Victorian elegies were meant to
be emotionally releasing, the modern elegy depends upon the
poet's unvarnished, perpetual mourning being seen as "realistic."

Regardless of its relationship to war, however, the question of
how readers react to the elegy is an ancient one. How does a private poem of loss move readers who have no personal knowledge
of the person being mourned? I remember watching *Four Weddings
and a Funeral* in school, crying when one of the characters mourns

his lover's death by reciting W. H. Auden's "Funeral Blues." But why should watching an actor cry over a fictional death trigger my own tears? And how does any representation of death create a community of mourning? Transmitting grief is complex because elegies have to align a reader's emotions with that of the poet, even as our experiences are different. This is, of course, the problem of any poem, but it places a particular burden on elegies whose very function depends on emotional release, and whose losses may resonate differently with us depending on when they occur in time. A poem to a soldier dead in battle over three hundred years ago doesn't move me as much as one written to a soldier *about to go* into battle—whether or not that war was in reality fought yesterday or a century before. Likewise, a poem whose title is a date stamp, such as "September 1, 1939," or "Photograph from September 11," suggests that the elegy speaks not just to its own moment of time but the larger sweep of history that contextualizes it and is encapsulated by it. It's the anticipation and continuation of loss that gives the elegy its piquancy, its implied connection to our own moment that gives it staying power.

I was thinking this especially with Anne Bradstreet's "Before the Birth of One of Her Children," a highly unusual lyric from an American Puritan that contains within it Bradstreet's understanding of the brevity of both marital and mortal time.

BEFORE THE BIRTH OF ONE OF HER CHILDREN

All things within this fading world hath end,
Adversity doth still our joyes attend;
No ties so strong, no friends so dear and sweet,
But with death's parting blow is sure to meet.
The sentence past is most irrevocable,
A common thing, yet oh inevitable.
How soon, my Dear, death may my steps attend,

How soon't may be thy Lot to lose thy friend,
We are both ignorant, yet love bids me
These farewell lines to recommend to thee,
That when that knot's untied that made us one,
I may seem thine, who in effect am none.
And if I see not half my dayes that's due,
What nature would, God grant to yours and you;
The many faults that well you know I have
Let be interr'd in my oblivious grave;
If any worth or virtue were in me,
Let that live freshly in thy memory
And when thou feel'st no grief, as I no harms,
Yet love thy dead, who long lay in thine arms.
And when thy loss shall be repaid with gains
Look to my little babes, my dear remains.
And if thou love thyself, or loved'st me,
These o protect from step Dames injury.
And if chance to thine eyes shall bring this verse,
With some sad sighs honour my absent Herse;
And kiss this paper for thy loves dear sake,
Who with salt tears this last Farewel did take.

Bradstreet's self-elegy is obviously a love poem to her husband, one that doesn't just worry about how he will remember
Bradstreet should she die in childbirth but demands that he protect her children from their future stepmother. Even in these dec-
orous heroic couplets, it's a remarkably frank poem that toggles
between accepted pieties about mortality and Bradstreet's more
realistic fears of birth. Dying in childbirth was not an abstract
possibility to any woman in the seventeenth century, though it
was a subject rarely addressed in poetry. Notice how Bradstreet
opens her poem by acknowledging that, though everyone dies,
some deaths may be more swift and assured than others. "How

soon, my dear, Death may my steps attend," she writes, "How soon't be thy Lot to lose thy friend," a warning for her husband to anticipate both her loss and his resulting grief, making her poem evoke both present and possible future fears.

This duality of time has echoes, too, in Bradstreet's reckoning with her faith. Throughout the poem, I feel two powerful chronologies at work: religious time, which speaks in platitudes about the brevity of all human life; and marital time, which speaks to her love for her husband and what her death will mean for their marriage. Religious time offers up human truths we might all accept, but the language feels a little too expected to me, abstract and bloodless:

> All things within this fading world hath end,
> Adversity doth still our joyes attend;
> No ties so strong, no friends so dear and sweet,
> But with death's parting blow is sure to meet.

It may be because these lines are end-stopped, their iambic pentameter so perfectly regular that they sound flat. You can sense how startling in comparison the following lines feel with their directness and intimacy:

> How soon, my Dear, death may my steps attend,
> How soon't may be thy Lot to lose thy friend,
> We are both ignorant, yet love bids me
> These farewell lines to recommend to thee,
> That when that knot's untied that made us one,
> I may seem thine, who in effect am none.

Bradstreet repeats her spondaic **"hów sóon"** twice in this complex sentence that unfurls over six lines to emphasize the suddenness of her loss. The lines feature some moments of metrical counterpoint—you could, for instance, read "We are both ignorant" as a hemistich of perfect iambic pentameter, though I hear its stresses as "Wĕ áre | bóth íg|nŏránt"—which serves to roughen up the rhythm at just the moment Bradstreet reminds her husband how swiftly their marriage could end. I'm struck, too, by the fact that Bradstreet calls herself her husband's "friend" in these lines, which suggests that what her husband will finally lose is a deeply trusted companion: a reading enhanced by the image of that marriage knot that's fused two individuals into a single person. This is, of course, the reason why Bradstreet writes at all, since in death, her poem will take her place in that marital vow, making her "seem" like she still belongs to her husband, even though she will now be no one's. Theirs isn't merely an erotic bond but a deeper, more spiritual one she hopes to extend through the act of writing, just as she would—if she could—extend her husband's life by granting him all the days allotted her that her own early death forfeited.

If religious time offers up abstract conceptions of death, marital time shows us the cost of mortality itself. Bradstreet's fear extends beyond the terror of childbirth and into a fantasy of her husband's future, in which she threatens to be further erased once he stops grieving. This is why she urges him to let her virtues "live freshly in thy memory," and to continue to love her "who long lay in thine arms." Death may put her outside of time and "harm" itself, but time also threatens to weaken her husband's feelings, especially if and when he remarries. For me, part of the pain that Bradstreet so beautifully encapsulates is the awareness that marital time for her freezes while, for her husband, it continues on, even as it changes to include someone else.

I think this is the reason the poem's opening falls tonally flat for me: religious time speaks to immaterial truths, while Bradstreet recognizes that our deepest feelings are pinned to physical bodies. It's likely why Bradstreet names the two most material things she leaves behind—her children and this poem—as "dear remains." It's not the first time Bradstreet compares writing with children; in her poem "The Author to Her Book," she calls her poetry collection an "ill-form'd offspring," and her "rambling brat." Here, however, the poem is depicted as *herself*. In that, she becomes metonymically attached to the poem she produces. Writing is the body her husband can kiss; her poem the living hearse that conveys her memory:

> And if chance to thine eyes shall bring this verse,
> With some sad sighs honour my absent Herse;
> And kiss this paper for thy loves dear sake,
> Who with salt tears this last Farewel did take.

The poem begins with Bradstreet's self-written epitaph and ends on her tearfully writing a self-elegy; in that, I thematically cycle back to the start of the poem. But Bradstreet's overall sense of time is radial—time for her stops and cycles back, while for others it fissures out in directions she can't anticipate. Only writing stops time long enough to refresh Bradstreet's memory and some shadow of her husband's love. While the elegy offers no consolation for *her*, Bradstreet seems aware that, practically, no elegy could; her elegy is for others, even as she mourns herself.

Of course, who else would the elegy be for? The dead, so far as I know, don't read. Like all poems, elegies and odes are written for a living audience, thus their authors try to create the *impression* of being overheard by someone else in the distant future. I recognize that many of the poems I've discussed here make writing itself some part of their subject, and this I think speaks to the anxieties undergirding the mode overall: When it comes to the dead, who am *I* to grieve, who am *I* to speak for those rendered eternally voiceless? Commemoration may stem from private feelings, but elegies are burnished with a propagandistic sheen insofar as we have chosen to honor slain soldiers or state figures. Even writing about those outside the public eye carries with it a whiff of politics. Memorialization makes an argument that we *should* care about the dead, not just because of who they were but because of what they represent. And once we put our memorialization into art, we've manipulated a reader's response to treat those values as shared, even fundamental to our understanding of history.

Writing with a Sense of History

I think this particular distrust of memorialization informs Layli Long Soldier's poem "38," a long, communal elegy for the 38 Dakota Sioux whom President Abraham Lincoln sentenced to hang in reprisal for what historians call the Dakota Uprising. The uprising, in fact, was sparked by the refusal of Minnesota authorities to pay the Dakotas money they were owed by rights of a U.S. treaty, which local officials and traders violated. The result was that the Dakotas, unable to buy food, starved. Andrew Myrick, a white trader who refused to offer the Dakotas credit, famously declared that if the Dakotas were hungry, they could eat grass. Long Soldier's poem is an examination of "the sentence"—both the death sentence Lincoln ordered for the Dakota Sioux, and the treaty sentences violated by the government. But it's also an examination of the sentences we write in any document meant to commemorate tragedies like the execution of the Dakota warriors, which Long Soldier highlights by drawing our attention throughout the poem to specific words and phrases. As Long Soldier writes:

> During the 1800s, when the US expanded territory, they
>   "purchased" land from the Dakota people as well as the
>   other tribes.

But another way to understand that sort of "purchase" is:
Dakota leaders ceded land to the US government in
exchange for money or goods, but most importantly, the
safety of their people.

Some say that Dakota leaders did not understand the terms
they were entering, or they never would have agreed.

Even others call the entire negotiation "trickery."

Long Soldier here points out the way certain words euphe-
mistically stand in for other, starker truths we either haven't
been taught or choose not to hear. Treaties are, of course, written promises between different communities meant to function
as law and, because of this, we choose to believe in the language
of the treaty, or to at least treat its language as more objective
than the language of a poem. Poetry is designed to elicit human
feeling; few people are moved by the language of a treaty. But
of course, a treaty has devastating emotional effects on people,
as the U.S. government's breaking of its own treaty had on the
Dakotas. In that, the difference between poetic language and
legal language is razor-thin, perhaps even an arbitrary distinction. Nevertheless, it's one that Long Soldier wants to preserve,
though that distinction frays as her poem continues. "I do not
consider this a creative piece," Long Soldier declares, adding, "I
do not regard this as a poem of great imagination or a work of fiction," even as she goes on to describe the breaking and rewriting
of treaties themselves as "a muddy, switchback trail," and continually calls the reader's attention to the synonyms and roots of
words like "Minnesota" and "turbid." "Everything is in the language we use," she declares, meaning that to unearth the roots of
words is to mine how we understand history. Essentially, to read a
treaty, we have to take the same care with it as we would a poem.

Likewise, whereas the language of the treaty is based on ideas of "logical" progression, Long Soldier's piece swoops back and forth across time, lyrically veering off into asides and even revisions of the same sentence to make her point.

Long Soldier can't abandon aspects of poetry, then, even as she distrusts how figurative language sanitizes events or highlights coincidence for poetic effect. Sentences, according to Long Soldier, should be "conveyors of thought." And yet this doesn't stop her from ending the poem on an image that's both historically true *and* metaphorically rich: the image of the trader Andrew Myrick's mouth stuffed with grass, followed by her own breaking of the poem's sentences to visually recall the hanging of the 38 Dakotas:

> Things are circling back again.
>
> Sometimes, when in a circle, if I wish to exit, I must leap.
>
> And let the body   swing.
>
> From the platform.
>
>   Out
>
>   to the
>   grasses.

Like Bradstreet's poem, Long Soldier's elegy, too, imagines the speaker from a third-person perspective, here becoming "the body" that duplicates the swinging motion of the hanged men. Long Soldier's poem argues that meaningful commemoration is a creative act; she depicts the Dakotas' own memorialization of the execution as more palpable than poems because they are deeds that incur personal costs to the Dakota people, rather than words that can be manipulated. The Memorial Riders, as these Dakota mourners are called, ride each year around the date of the execution on horseback from Lower Brule, South Dakota, to Mankato, Minnesota. As Long Soldier describes it:

> The Memorial Riders travel 325 miles on horseback for
> eighteen days, sometimes through subzero blizzards . . .

> The memorial for the Dakota 38 is not an object inscribed
> with words, but an *act*.

Acts are, according to Long Soldier, where "real" poems are to be found, though of course, even physical actions have poetic significance, which Long Soldier acknowledges in her description of the murdered Indian Agent's body:

> When Myrick's body was found,
>
>   his mouth was stuffed with grass.

> I am inclined to call this act by the Dakota warriors a poem.

> There's irony in their poem.

> There was no text.

> *"Real" poems do not "really" require words.*

Reading "38," I am returned to the relationship between mode and mourning that moves through the history of the elegy. Long Soldier's poem asks me hard questions about its mode: When it comes to truly expressing grief, are poetic devices, at heart, too limited? In order to mourn the full cost of our dead, might we abandon all conventional rules of writing, lift off the page, and into history itself?

Writing with Attention to Place:
Conventions of the Pastoral

Odes and elegies obviously share some commitment to memorialization, since both modes ask us to care about people or events that have larger resonance. In that sense, the pastoral mode might not seem to have much in common with them, even as odes and elegies have often relied upon pastoral tropes. But as the **pastoral** has evolved away from poems located in idealized landscapes to those shaped by ecological concerns, mourning has inevitably suffused our sense of the pastoral. This, too, has its earliest roots in the classical elegy, which weaves natural or pastoral motifs into poems of mourning, often combining some representation of nature with the elegiac lament. Historically, the pastoral elegy was the invention of three Sicilian poets who wrote in Greek during the third and second centuries BCE—Theocritus, Moschus, and Bion—and which included certain ritualized aspects that later English poets imported into their work, such as an invocation to the muse and extended descriptions of nature itself. Shelley's long poem "Lycidas," his elegy for Keats, is an example of a pastoral elegy, while elements of the pastoral feature strongly in Tennyson's *In Memoriam.*

The pastoral is one of the trickiest modes to define, in part because of the diverse ways poets have represented nature but also because the pastoral has been at once a mode, a form, *and* a subject for poetry. All poems, of course, rely on a sense of place to provide the poem's psychological and physical landscape, but our earliest pastoral poems gave landscape symbolic, not just situational, importance. Like odes and elegies, ancient pastoral poems were first identified by their formal verse structures.

They were poems written in hexameter, generally of 150 lines, focusing less on the development of character and narrative than on lyric songs sung by a shepherd living in an idealized, rural location. By the time of the Romantics, however, pastoral poems had shucked off their metrical conventions, becoming recognizable instead for their rural figures, whose own values stand in stark contrast to the cosmopolitan—and often artificial—values of town and court.

Ironically, though both the protagonist and environment of pastoral poems are rural, pastoral poems became aristocratic attractions due to their performed values. By juxtaposing an arcadian environment against an urban one, the natural world became a space in which the shepherd could rehearse larger conversations about friendship, love, virtue, and being in harmony with nature. But through all of it, the pastoral is marked by the lyric voice of the shepherd, who performs these virtues through first-person song, as in this famous poem by Christopher Marlowe:

THE PASSIONATE SHEPHERD TO HIS LOVE

Come live with me and be my love,
And we will all the pleasures prove,
That Valleys, groves, hills, and fields,
Woods, or steepy mountain yields.

And we will sit upon the Rocks,
Seeing the Shepherds feed their flocks,
By shallow Rivers to whose falls
Melodious birds sing Madrigals.

And I will make thee beds of Roses
And a thousand fragrant posies,
A cap of flowers, and a kirtle
Embroidered all with leaves of Myrtle;

A gown made of the finest wool
Which from our pretty Lambs we pull;
Fair lined slippers for the cold,
With buckles of the purest gold;

A belt of straw and Ivy buds,
With Coral clasps and Amber studs:
And if these pleasures may thee move,
Come live with me, and be my love.

The Shepherds' Swains shall dance and sing
For thy delight each May-morning:
If these delights thy mind may move,
Then live with me, and be my love.

As you can see here, early pastoral poetry was highly styl-
ized and romantic. Unsurprisingly, this trend starts to fade out
around the time of the Industrial Revolution, when public attention turned to urbanization and technology. It certainly stands in
stark relief to **eco-poetry** or **environmental poetry**, a modern
mode that became prominent around the 1960s and treats nature
neither as a peaceful nor idealized space but one inhabited, and
altered, by humans.

Eco-poetry has its earliest roots in ancient poems we now call
georgics, in homage to the Latin poet Virgil's book *The Georgics*. A georgic is any type of pastoral poem that includes lists
and instructions for how to care for farmland, intermixed with
digressions on philosophy, astronomy, meteorology, or even military history. Interestingly, Virgil places a Latin pun at the center of *The Georgics*: *vertere*, which means "to turn," and "versus,"
which refers to a line of verse, thus pairing the turns in plow-
ing a field with the act of writing poetry. In many ways, georgics
meld the work of tending land with the work of artmaking, functioning as much as an ars poetica as a genre of poetry invested

in nature. The georgic held sway most powerfully in the eighteenth century but influenced later Romantic writers such as Coleridge and Wordsworth. In America, you can see its impact in the poetry of Walt Whitman, Robert Frost, Lorine Niedecker, and Maurice Manning.

In both pastoral and eco-poems, however, nature still becomes the space to work out human conflicts, whether these tensions are philosophical, as in early pastoral poems, or existential, as nature is threatened by climate change. Because of this, both modes question the role that nature is meant to play: Is it an imaginative space that reflects the best of human psychology, or is it a real place that humans inhabit and destroy?

To a certain extent, contemporary pastoral poems toggle back and forth between these positions, sometimes combining them, while calling back to the pastoral's roots. The poem "Mock Orange," by Louise Glück, for instance, references the classical tradition of the pastoral, as its natural symbols reveal the speaker's disappointment with heterosexual intimacy.

MOCK ORANGE

It is not the moon, I tell you.
It is these flowers
lighting the yard.

I hate them.
I hate them as I hate sex,
the man's mouth
sealing my mouth, the man's
paralyzing body—

and the cry that always escapes,
the low, humiliating
premise of union—

In my mind tonight
I hear the question and pursuing answer
fused in one sound
that mounts and mounts and then
is split into the old selves,
the tired antagonisms. Do you see?
We were made fools of.
And the scent of mock orange
drifts through the window.

How can I rest?
How can I be content
when there is still
that odor in the world?

Glück's lyric poem is an anti-love song, in which the female speaker startlingly declares that she "hate[s] sex," just as she hates the flowers "lighting the yard." "Mock Orange" is a cascade of negative yet parallel assertions: it is not the moon but mock orange blooms that cast a pale light over the speaker's yard, just as the speaker hates the flowers in the same way she detests sex. Even the mock orange tree itself is not a true orange, though it gives off its scent. The mock orange becomes a symbol for the false intimacy that sex suggests between the man and woman in the poem: a union that only leads to more division, even oppression, as the man's mouth "seal[s]" the speaker's mouth, his body "paralyzing" the speaker's own. Even as the unnamed question "and pursuing answer/ fus[e] in one sound"—an image that suggests both orgasm and the desire for human connection—that moment of completion quickly "splits into the old selves,/ the tired antagonisms." The woman's cry of orgasm becomes something shameful that "escapes" the speaker, a "low, humiliating/ premise of union."

"Mock Orange" is both brutally realistic *and* symbolic, as the landscape reflects the speaker's internal state. Orange blossoms, interestingly, were the Roman wedding flowers of choice, and so Glück's reference to them carries with it an ironic classical allusion, even though the speaker's voice itself is direct and contemporary. Notice, too, that instead of a fragrance or perfume, the flowers carry with them an "odor," a word redolent with postcoital suggestiveness. Even as the mock orange and the romantic love it suggests "mak[es] fools" of the lovers in this poem, the fantasy of it persists in its scent. In her desire to dismantle the pastoral and classical references to idealized love, Glück's speaker cannot abandon all desire for the ideal: it drives her on, even as it leads to perpetual discontentment.

Compare Glück's symbolic landscape in "Mock Orange," however, with Camille Dungy's poem "Trophic Cascade," and you see a very different interaction emerge between speaker and environment.

TROPHIC CASCADE

> After the reintroduction of gray wolves
> to Yellowstone and, as anticipated, their culling
> of deer, trees grew beyond the deer stunt
> of the mid century. In their up reach
> songbirds nested, who scattered
> seed for underbrush, and in that cover
> warrened snowshoe hare. Weasel and water shrew
> returned, also vole, and came soon hawk
> and falcon, bald eagle, kestrel, and with them
> hawk shadow, falcon shadow. Eagle shade
> and kestrel shade haunted newly-berried
> runnels where deer no longer rummaged, cautious
> as they were, now, of being surprised by wolves. Berries

brought bear, while undergrowth and willows, growing
   now right down to the river, brought beavers,
 who dam. Muskrats came to the dams, and tadpoles.
      Came, too, the night song of the fathers
      of tadpoles. With water striders, the dark
      gray American dipper bobbed in fresh pools
 of the river, and fish stayed, and the bear, who
fished, also culled deer fawns and to their kill scraps
came vulture and coyote, long gone in the region
until now, and their scat scattered seed, and more
trees, brush, and berries grew up along the river
that had run straight and so flooded but thus dammed,
compelled to meander, is less prone to overrun. Don't
 you tell me this is not the same as my story. All this
      life born from one hungry animal, this whole,
      new landscape, the course of the river changed,
 I know this. I reintroduced myself to myself, this time
   a mother. After which, nothing was ever the same.

   Dungy's poem is about a real and not symbolic Yellowstone,
changed granularly by the reintroduction of wolves to the park.
But while the facts of the landscape's reinvention are scientific,
the poem retains its tone of high lyricism on account of its diction
and occasional syntactic subversion, as you see in Dungy's reversal of verb and subject in lines like, "And in that cover/ warrened
snowshoe hare," or "Came, too, the night song of the fathers/
of tadpoles." The poem feels at times Anglo-Saxon in its use of
poetic epithets, such as "eagle shade" and "kestrel shade," as well
as the fact it avoids definite and indefinite articles to focus our
attention on nouns and verbs, animals and actions. In that, "Trophic Cascade" creates a sense of wonder about the natural that
feels both ancient and scientific. And yet the poem's landscape

still retains symbolic meaning for the speaker, who reveals the
impact her pregnancy had on her own psychological landscape:

> Don't
> you tell me this is not the same as my story. All this
> life born from one hungry animal, this whole,
> new landscape, the course of the river changed,
> I know this. I reintroduced myself to myself, this time
> a mother. After which, nothing was ever the same.

If the natural images in "Mock Orange" function to reflect
the speaker's psychic distress, the natural world in "Trophic Cascade" also moves between the symbolic and the real. It's not that
the speaker's self and Yellowstone are separate, or that the park's
environment *only* reflects the personal experience Dungy relates:
the changed environment of the park becomes analogous to the
speaker's pregnancy. Both reflect each other, even though the trophic cascade kicked off by these wolves is indisputably its own
series of events. It's the poem's tone in which these facts are listed
that, for me, best reflects Dungy's argument and allows for that
connection Dungy makes in the poem's final lines. I'm particularly struck by the sharpness to her warning, "Don't/ you tell me
this is not the same as my story," as if Dungy anticipates an eco-
critical response that the personal comparison she makes to Yellowstone is pathetic fallacy. It's certainly a risk the poem takes,
and Dungy—an esteemed poet and nature writer—here wants
to circumvent that criticism, and perhaps suggest, through the
lushness of her writing, that not to make such a comparison *at all*
would devalue the importance of both the wolves' reintroduction
and the speaker's pregnancy. Both are stories about the sudden
flourishing of life, and if we culturally value one trophic cascade,
we certainly should respect the other.

In that, "Trophic Cascade" raises serious questions about our contemporary imagination of the natural world. Once we write a poem about a landscape, whether in scientific earnestness or out of an interest in reviving pastoral tropes, does that environment always and only become figurative? Do we harm ecological causes if we personalize them? Do we do them a *worse* disservice if we don't? Is there a way in which we can depict nature as its own material reality separate from the human consciousness that represents it?

The Canadian poet Karen Solie attempts to answer this with her poem "Wild Horses," a poem that's both ode and elegy to the wild horses of the North American plains, and which attempts to reclaim their natural splendor separate from their domesticated uses for humans.

WILD HORSES

The Iberian head, roman-nosed. Black,
bay, chestnut, dun, some buckskins, palominos,
roans, a few paints, stouthearted, with primitive
dorsal stripe, *equus callabus* returned
to the New World in the sixteenth century
as Spanish Andaluz mustangs, blessed with speed,
a good fear, their ears' ten muscles. Only a dog's
nose is keener. Escapees of expansion
from Mexico, their descendants travelled north along
the Rockies, millions to the coast to the Great Plains
restored to the authority of the herd, its shelter,
its law, knowing from birth which rivers
they can cross, where sweet water lies,
and the saltgrass. In wolf scent, winter hunger,
deerflies, rear blindspot. Points of balance triangulate
from the skull, behind the shoulders. Jaws
can snap a coyote's spine, hooves halve rattlers.

Before the twentieth-century machinery they fell
ahead of ranchers and oilmen, cleared
from coalfields staked at Bighorn, the survey's
immovable starting point in rocks above the falls.
From ridges traveled summer and winter,
they were driven into passes and corralled.
A few hundred remain on grizzly lands below
hanging glaciers, among Engelmann spruce, fir,
lodgepole pine, foothills of aspen and balsam poplar
in the Siffleur, White Goat and Peace Wilderness
where they're shot for sport, caught for rodeo stock,
sold for dog food at four hundred a head. Sixteen
left to rot in the forest northwest of Jasper,
two foals dumped at a gas well site by the only
animal who kills from a distance, noise for a voice
and noise for a home, for whom all places are alike.

Like "Trophic Cascade," "Wild Horses" is a series of natural
facts that unspool over the course of a poem. Solie, a former student
of zoology, clearly wants her readers to see these horses *as* horses,
and so fills her poem with evocative details about the mustang's
sense of smell, its instinctual ability to find new grazing territory,
its powerful jaw and hooves. And yet it's impossible not to sense
another human story behind this, one of slaughter and colonialism.
"Escapees of expansion," Solie calls these horses, then adds:

Before the twentieth-century machinery they fell
ahead of ranchers and oilmen, cleared
from coalfields staked at Bighorn, the survey's
immovable starting point in rocks above the falls.
From ridges traveled summer and winter,
they were driven into passes and corralled.

Like Indigenous people, these horses, too, have been driven from their home, corralled into designated areas that allow for "ranchers and oilmen" to stake their claims. But while the reader can sense the connection Solie wants to draw, her poem does it with a light touch: horses and Native people might share a similar history, even as that history must be supplied by the reader, since Solie's choice of phrases—even as they suggestively apply to Indigenous people—are finally and fundamentally about mustangs. That said, Solie's poem often uses human social terms to describe the mustangs' herd structure, since these horses are "restored to the authority of the herd, its shelter/its law," while the poem ends on a direct comparison between horses and humans as a whole: "the only/ animal who kills from a distance," Solie calls us, for whom—unlike horses—"all places are alike."

In contrast, mustangs are marked by individuation, as Solie opens her poem with a list of different coat types and colors, marveling at these horses' ability to navigate so many specific ecologies, even as they are hunted "for sport, caught for rodeo stock, / sold for dog food." Value is the true subject of this poem in which wild horses are esteemed not for their history, speed, looks, or resilience, but for their use to humans. Of course, that's the human value of land, too, as Solie's poem devolves from lush descriptions of "hanging glaciers, foothills of aspen and balsam poplar" to the gas-well sites at which two foals' bodies are dumped.

If the contemporary eco-poem asks whether we can depict nature as its own material reality outside of human culture, Solie's poem suggests that these horses, even as they're instinctually driven, can't be imagined as separate creatures due to our interference. Not only did the Spanish breed Spanish and New World horses to produce the mustang, human and animal worlds inevitably collide; to call one environment "wild" and another "civilized" is to ignore the permeability of both territories and terms. Humans are themselves animals; to write about wild horses, then, is implicitly to write about *human* wildness. In that, if you consider Dungy's poem too humanly focused or hopeful, Solie's is certainly more pessimistic. Hers is not a sentimental comparison but a critical one, a dual portrait of horses and humans alike in which the humans, both morally and ecologically, are the worse off.

Modes as Returns and Revisions

If we consider "Wild Horses" a revision of the pastoral, you can see that its natural world is not some arcadian, untouched space. That said, it certainly offers readers a space from which to critique "urban" values. I doubt Solie would classify this work as pastoral herself, and it may be that ecologically minded poets would prefer to shuck off the pastoral's trappings entirely, since you could argue that it's these very tropes that promote anthropocentric principles. Who cares about human friendship or love when we so casually slaughter whole species? That said, how do we value natural diversity without giving it *some* human characteristics or relationship to us, as Dungy's poem suggests?

Studying how modes change is one way of understanding how certain traditions—even as they arise from different origins—intertwine and deviate. Frankly, most poems combine modes and forms because abstract concepts require diverse scenarios that help us feel our way through thinking, such as the desire for human intimacy through a moment's erotic revulsion, or a personal awakening to wonder through a recitation of scientific facts. I think this is one reason why certain love poems locate the beloved against the poet's awareness of death and nature itself, something that marks this haunting meditation, "You, Therefore" by Reginald Shepherd:

YOU, THEREFORE

For Robert Philen

You are like me, you will die too, but not today:
you, incommensurate, therefore the hours shine:
if I say to you "To you I say," you have not been
set to music, or broadcast live on the ghost
radio, may never be an oil painting or
Old Master's charcoal sketch: you are
a concordance of person, number, voice,
and place, strawberries spread through your name
as if it were budding shrubs, how you remind me
of some spring, the waters as cool and clear
(late rain clings to your leaves, shaken by light wind),
which is where you occur in grassy moonlight:
and you are a lily, an aster, white trillium
or viburnum, by all rights mine, white star
in the meadow sky, the snow still arriving
from its earthwards journeys, here where there is
no snow (I dreamed the snow was you,
when there was snow), you are my right,
have come to be my night (your body takes on
the dimensions of sleep, the shape of sleep
becomes you): and you fall from the sky
with several flowers, words spill from your mouth
in waves, your lips taste like the sea, salt-sweet (trees
and seas have flown away, I call it
loving you): home is nowhere, therefore you,
a kind of dwell and welcome, song after all,
and free of any eden we can name

Shepherd's poem casts its spell through delay and repetition,
hypotactic hierarchy and paratactic equivalence, direct statement and extended comparison. The poem is a single sentence

that constantly interrupts itself, revising and embroidering upon its thinking. At times, it eddies around rhymes like "right" and "night" and the repetition of "sleep." At times, it culminates in a jumble of parenthetical phrases. It even contains two moments of **antimetabole** or near-antimetabole, as you can see in the lines: "if I say to you 'To you I say,'" and also "(your body takes on/ the dimensions of sleep, the shape of sleep / becomes you)," which create pauses in this poem that otherwise speeds through its images. "You, Therefore" is a love poem that's also a double elegy for the anticipated loss of the beloved and for the fact all forms of love must die. As mortal beings, our love expires when our bodies do. I see this in the many references to night, to sleep, to the "earthwards journeys" undertaken by snow, even the future and putative disappearance of trees and sea. The human beloved even ceases to be human as the poem progresses. "[S]trawberries spread through your name," Shepherd writes, as slowly the beloved changes to something that "remind[s]" the speaker of spring and of a plant to which "late rain clings to [its] leaves."

Eros, ecosystem, and loss twine together in ways that recall the pastoral elegiac tropes found in the "carpe diem" odes written since Horace's time. Here, the beauty of the natural world is fundamentally attached to its temporality, whether seasonal or diurnal, which may be one reason Shepherd's syntax feels so baroque and fast-paced. We cannot stay with a single image or moment of time before Shepherd leaps to another, rushing on to the next thought as both an act of celebration and avoidance. In that, "You, Therefore" also toggles between elegy and ode, its elaborate syntax trying to forestall what the speaker recognizes as inevitable from the start: "You are like me, you will die too, but not today," Shepherd announces, and every clause and parenthetical that follows becomes an attempt to keep the beloved alive. This may be, I suspect, why the poem ends without a period, trailing off into white space, reflecting both the transitory fact of nature, and the enduring desire to desire itself.

Like many poems in this chapter, it's too simple to consign "You, Therefore" to a single mode. Perhaps, as I wrote before, all great poems blur categories; even, as in the case of "38," genres of writing. While "Trophic Cascade" stems from the pastoral tradition, it is also an ode to the wolf and to incipient motherhood. Likewise, the pastoral "Mock Orange" is a confessional poem, a feminist poem, a lyric cry and stringent critique. Recovery and mourning, love and grief are the Janus faces of poetry. When we turn our attention to a subject, when we engage all our senses and ways of looking, how can we not also engage the many shapes and forms our looking takes? When we talk about modes, then, we are talking about global issues in reading poetry; that is, the long conversation that constitutes literature, a dialogue any poem enters, consciously or not, as soon as it's written.

Mature poets understand what part of the conversation they've joined in order to speak back to the tropes that seem outmoded or conventional, playfully subverting our cultural expectations. As readers, we can track these subversions through an examination of the elements all poems include: sound and sentence, form and line, etymology and image, rhythm and rhyme. But though each provides us a way into the poem, they cannot stand alone. As they interact with and influence one another, they fuse into one unique structure we comprehend as a unit. In essence, the elements I have been forensically examining throughout this book become meaningful only when I see them work in concert or contention across all a poem's particulars, as it is through our close reading that we see these patterns coalesce.

And so this chapter ends where the book itself began: with a reminder that, as poems innovate their own rules, reading and writing poetry become processes of accrual. Poems are hybrids of public and private utterance, of individual and collective looking. That's what makes reading and writing poetry complex activities, even as it's intoxicating to discover how one aspect of a work opens up a new way of seeing the work as a whole. We are, as I said before, in a long and ever-evolving conversation with thousands of other poems, poems that have also absorbed the thinking of myriad poets. Reading and writing poetry is the slow excavation of these dialogues, as much as it is an entry into them. Your reading illuminates the poem, which in turn illuminates you. The better you get at understanding poetry, the more facets of language you can experience, which in turn allows you to reread the same poems over time, to refract the beauty—in them, and in you—you'd never before seen.

EXPERIMENTS

- Select an elegy from the list below. What historical conventions of the elegy does the poet preserve and what, to you, does the poet change? What images, social virtues, or symbols get attached to the person or thing being mourned? How does this elegy imagine the time of the mourning process itself?
- Select an ode from the list below. What historical conventions of the ode does the poet preserve and change? What makes this person—or thing—worthy of celebration for the poet? What kinds of personal connection might the poet be drawing between herself and who or what she celebrates?
- Choose at least two pastoral poems from the list below, ideally from different time periods. How do these pastoral poems imagine and depict nature? What do they share in common, if anything? What seems to be the speaker's relationship to the natural world in each of these poems?

- Write an elegy or an ode about someone—or something—we typically do not mourn or praise. What do you admire about this person—or thing—that others might overlook?
- Write a poem about a landscape, flower, or animal that you feel gets ignored or overlooked. How can you convince others to value its beauty? Alternative exercise: Write a poem in the voice of the animal, flower, or landscape that has been overlooked.
- Write a poem in which you create an extended comparison between yourself and an animal. What are the parallels between you?

SUGGESTED WORKS TO CONSIDER

Odes

Marcus Jackson, "Ode to Kool-Aid"
Percy Bysshe Shelley, "Ode to the West Wind"
Bernadette Mayer, "Homage to H & the Speedway Diner"
John Keats, "Ode on a Grecian Urn"
William Carlos Williams, "Proletarian Portrait"
Amit Majmudar, "Ode to a Drone"
Ben Jonson, "Ode to Himself"
C. Dale Young, "Ode to a Yellow Onion"
Mahmoud Darwish, "Your Night Is of Lilac"

Elegies

Wisława Szymborska, "Photograph from September 11"
Frank O'Hara, "The Day Lady Died"
Ross Gay, "A Small Needful Fact"
Miller Oberman, "Taharah"
Gjertrud Schnackenberg, "Supernatural Love"
Garrett Hongo, "The Legend"

Allen Ginsberg, "Kaddish"
John Milton, "Sonnet 23: Methought I saw my late
    espoused saint"
Larry Levis, "Winter Stars"
Yusef Komunyakaa, "Facing It"

Pastoral

d. g. nanouk okpik, "If Oil Is Drilled in Bristol Bay"
Andrew Marvell, "The Garden"
Aimee Nezhukumatathil, "Hummingbird Abecedarian"
Mark Doty, "A Display of Mackerel"
Sir Walter Raleigh, "The Nymph's Reply to
    the Shepherd"
Jennifer Chang, "Pastoral"
Jorie Graham, "Reading Plato"
George Oppen, "Psalm"
Brigit Pegeen Kelly, "Song"
Seamus Heaney, "The Glanmore Sonnets"

All poems can be found either at the Poetry Foundation or the
Academy of American Poets websites.

Putting It All Together

I f reading a poem depends on seeing the interplay between all the different questions this book raises, I want to conclude by looking at one final poem, Robert Hayden's "Those Winter Sundays," to study the poem from the ground up, from its images to its sentences and lines, to its etymologies, sounds and rhythms, and finally to its form and mode to see how all these critical perspectives together produce a comprehensive forensic reading.

THOSE WINTER SUNDAYS

Sundays too my father got up early
and put his clothes on in the blueblack cold,
then with cracked hands that ached
from labor in the weekday weather made
banked fires blaze. No one ever thanked him.

I'd wake and hear the cold splintering, breaking.
When the rooms were warm, he'd call,
and slowly I would rise and dress,
fearing the chronic angers of that house,

Speaking indifferently to him,
who had driven out the cold
and polished my good shoes as well.
What did I know, what did I know
of love's austere and lonely offices?

Robert Hayden's sonnet "Those Winter Sundays" reflects upon the difficult, at times potentially explosive relationship the speaker had with his father, a man whose care for family is demonstrated not by effusive gestures but routine acts of self-sacrifice; something the reader can sense from the poem's very first line of the poem, as Hayden notes that "Sundays *too* [his] father got up early" (emphasis mine).

Hayden's poem focuses on one specific moment of paternal care: the father building a fire to warm the house for his waking family during wintertime, an activity that reveals not only the frigidity of the speaker's house but the toll of hard labor on the father himself, who

... put his clothes on in the blueblack cold,
then with cracked hands that ached
from labor in the weekday weather made
banked fires blaze. No one ever thanked him.

Hayden's first stanza is replete with consonance and alliteration: in the second line, "clothes," blueblack," and "cold" pick up on each other's harsh *c* consonants, cracking sounds that extend into the next line with the phrase "cracked hands that ached." The repetition of the hard *a* and *ah* sounds cascading through the stanza in phrases such as "weekday" made" and "banked fires blaze" and "thanked him" similarly extend the sense of the poem's physical ache, reinforcing the connection between the father's labor and pain itself, as well as suggesting the popping and cracking of wood logs burning in a fire. Hayden's sonic repetitions are also reinforced by the poem's occasional and slant end rhymes: "ached/made."

Hayden's first stanza is composed of only two sentences: the first one extends over five lines, during which Hayden breaks up the single action of the father's fire-building into clauses that reinforce different activities, different senses of time, and also specific aspects of the father's body and labor. The father builds this fire on "Sundays too," as Hayden notes, "*and* puts his clothes on. . . . *Then* [builds the fire] with cracked hands *that* ached/ from weekday labor' (emphasis mine). Notice here that Hayden's syntax inverts how we might normally describe this activity, by placing the modifying phrase—"with cracked hands that ached from weekday weather"—before the main verb and action of the sentence itself: "made banked fires blaze." By doing this, Hayden delays my expectation of how the sentence itself is supposed to conclude to linger instead on the father's hands and the "weekday weather" and labor that roughened them. Here Hayden uses synecdoche so that I understand the whole of the father through this single image of his painfully cracked hands, just as I can also see, in this daily act of building a fire, the father's larger devotion to his family.

Hayden's complex, extended syntax in the first sentence makes the second, simple sentence that ends the first stanza pop: "No one ever thanked him." This sentence feels abrupt, almost curt in its frankness. Its sonic connection with the previous sentence through its rhyming of "thanked" with "banked" gives the stanza a strong feeling of finality, since the stanza's last line contains within it a rhyming couplet. It's here, too, that the poem switches its focus from the father to the speaker himself. If the first stanza starts with a long complex sentence and ends on a short one, the second stanza reverses that pattern. As the speaker announces, "I'd wake and hear the cold splintering, breaking." From there,

Hayden's syntax wends over six lines and two stanzas, reverting my attention to both the house and the father, again laddering clauses in such a manner that I sympathize less with the speaker's "indifferent" reactions to his father and more with the father's sacrifices for his son. Notice that though the speaker admits that he "feared" the "chronic angers of that house," he also

> [s]peak[s] indifferently to him,
> Who had driven out the cold
> And polished [his] good shoes as well.

By ending the sentence on descriptions of the father's labor, Hayden critiques and diminishes the speaker's childish reactions. I can recognize the effect the father's anger had on the speaker, of course, but here it has been so contextualized and syntactically reinforced through Hayden's stacking of clauses that whatever fear or rudeness the speaker admits to pales beside the simple, routine, and thankless tasks his father undergoes.

Throughout the poem, the home's frigid temperature takes on physical dimensions as it "splinter[s]" and "break[s]," just as it also takes on psychological and human characteristics in its "chronic angers" the speaker fears rousing. If the father's simmering anger is the poem's tenor, the vehicle becomes the house itself snapping to life from the growing fire. But cold, too, is a vehicle, as it recalls not only the father's temper but possibly his race. Hayden, a Black poet and professor, uses the phrase "blueblack" to describe the cold, suggesting both early dawn and possibly the father's skin color.

Hayden's poem is littered with Anglo-Saxon and Germanic root words: "splintering," "breaking," "cracked," "ached," "banked," "weekday" and "cold," all of which emphasize the poem's sonic richness along with the physicality of the father's labor and body. But it also makes that turn to the poem's final two lines the more startling, as the language here moves from the Anglo-Saxon to the Latinate registers:

> What did I know, what did I know
> Of love's austere and lonely offices?

"Austere" and "offices" come to English via Latin, meaning alternately "severe" and "performance of a duty." In medieval Latin, "officium" also referred to a religious service. Both words perfectly encapsulate not only the father's character and labor but the father's sense of family duty and how it isolated him. If the bulk of the first stanza feels earthy and physical—the world and memory of a child—the poem's increasing use of more Greek and Latinate words, including "chronic" and "indifferently," makes the last third of the poem feel increasingly adult and reflective. And yet the two worlds remain profoundly connected, as the speaker's memories of the past turn inevitably toward his more mature understanding of his father in the present. Essentially, Hayden grounds what might otherwise be a rhetorical question about love and duty in details of the father's physical world in which this question was rooted.

Hayden's final couplet repeats the phrase "What did I know" twice, likely recalling the father's own rageful declaration to the younger speaker. It's certainly a phrase I can imagine any father saying to a child he perceives to be ungrateful, but here it's repeated by the speaker to himself in a moment of rueful, adult self-reflection. Tonally, it's a complicated moment in the poem, as the repetition recalls both the father's frustration with his son and the speaker's pained admission of his own failings to be sympathetic to his father. At the same time, of course, its accusatory tone reminds me *why* a young boy might have felt more fear than empathy, as it also carries within it an echo of the father's fury.

If the father in "Those Winter Sundays" sees labor as an act of love, Hayden's poem is a loving ode and elegy in turn for a father that the speaker could not perfectly communicate with. Hayden's poem is a sonnet, a poem whose form is rhetorically structured and, like the father's life, highly constrained. While Hayden eschews any strict iambic pentameter or rhyme scheme, his fourteen-line poem is highly rhythmic in its stack of mono-syllabic and strong-stress Germanic words; in its use of allit-eration, assonance, and consonance; and of course in its move between complex and simple sentences. If I focus specifically on nouns and verbs as receiving sonic attention or "stress" in each line, I notice that each line generally sticks to around four or five strong beats.

While Hayden's sonnet isn't rhetorically organized around changing rhymes in the ways we might expect from Shake-spearean or Petrarchan models, it does break down into three stanzas that telegraph three different thought-movements. The first stanza focuses on the father's labor and the family's indif-ferent response to it. The second focuses on the speaker's reac-tion to his father's labor and his fear of his father's anger. The third and final stanza, however, combines the perspective of both father and son into one, returning to more images of the father's labor, but also to the father's language, ending the sonnet on a couplet that transforms the father's repeated accusation of his son's ingratitude into a son's self-lacerating lament. In its volta and concluding couplet, Hayden's poem retains the ghost of the Shakespearean sonnet, which Hayden makes newly his own. It is this volta that turns the speaker's long-held resentments into adult regret, childhood fear into love. If we treat this sonnet as both a depiction of parental labor and a consideration of the tra-ditions we inherit and chafe against, Hayden's formal choice here speaks volumes about the tender, and complicated, esteem in which this young man finally holds his father.

EXPERIMENT

- Find a poem that fascinates you and read it, step by step, through as many of the forensic lenses as you can. What new aspects of the poem do you notice? What alternative meanings arise for you from these different critical perspectives when they are applied together?

ACKNOWLEDGMENTS

This book could not have been written without the attention, care, and support of Jill Bialosky, my editor, and Melanie Rae Thon, one of my dearest friends. There is no one word or role for Melanie in my life, as she has been my mentor, my reader, and my walking companion, ever a sympathetic ear and a spiritual guide. I have not written a book of any worth without her eyes first upon its pages, without her gentle questions and revisions. She is one of the best *thinkers* about writing I know because she is herself an excellent writer; she is and remains my gold standard for teaching.

I'd also like to thank my husband, Sean Myles, both for ferociously supporting my poetry and for being wise enough never to read it. (Seriously: sometimes it's better not to know.) Thank you for protecting my writing time as much as I do.

Finally, I would like to thank my many students for (patiently) teaching me how to become a better teacher over the years. My experience teaching classes in college, in prisons, and in K-12 classrooms across Utah opened my eyes to how people encounter poetry, and why they reach for it in times of joy and crisis. These students taught me how to read poetry, and why. This book is for them.

GLOSSARY

Accent: The syllable or syllables in a word naturally emphasized in speech. Accent determines **stress** in **metrical scansion**.

Accentual verse: The oldest form of meter in English, which comes from Anglo Saxon poetry. A rhythm in which only stresses are counted in a line regardless of the number of syllables. In accentual meter, poetic lines are not broken up into feet, though **accents/stresses** and **caesuras** are marked. See also **meter**.

Accentual-syllabic verse: Verse written in a metrical rhythm in which every syllable and stress is counted. Every syllable in a line of accentual-syllabic verse is marked with either a strong stress mark (′) or an unstressed mark (˘). **Iambs, trochees, anapests, dactyls**, and **spondees** are the most common feet in accentual-syllabic verse. See also **meter** and **foot**.

Allegory: When an entire work of art takes second place to its meaning, or when abstract concepts in an artwork are themselves personified.

Alliteration: A form of rhyme that depends on the repetition of initial vowels or consonants in nearby words rather than the exact duplication of sounds.

Allusion: When one work of art briefly makes either direct or indirect reference to another, whether through symbolism or naming.

Anaphora: The repetition of a particular word or phrase either at the beginning or the end of every sentence throughout an entire poem or a part of a poem.

Antimetabole: The repetition of a phrase in reversed order.

Aphorisms: Concise, generally revealing declarations about human truths.

Apostrophe: A speech or address to an individual who is absent, or to a personified object. Also a cry of delight or grief. See also **lyric apostrophe**.

Archetypal symbols: Culturally received images in a poem that are recognizable from other works of art. See also **symbolism**.

Assonance: A form of rhyme in which the repetition of the same or similar vowel sounds occur within a sentence, line, or passage.

Autonomous line: A line in a poem that completes a thought.

Ballad: A four-line stanzaic poem, usually in iambic tetrameter. Ballads are popular verse songs that are highly narrative, and deal either with tragic or comic love, death, disaster, the supernatural, and the political. See also **meter** and **quatrains**.

Blank verse: Unrhymed iambic pentameter containing any number of lines.

Blason: A descriptive poem in praise or blame of a person or object, which generally relies upon hyperbole.

Burden: Repetition of an entire stanza as a poetic refrain. See also **refrain**.

Caesura: A strong rhetorical or rhythmic pause within a line, often signaled by punctuation or a visual break. A caesura can occur just after or inside of a metrical **foot**, and in **metrical scansion** is graphically represented by ($||$). See also **meter**.

Conceit: An elaborate metaphor or simile that spins out over the course of a stanza or the entire poem.

Consonance: A form of rhyme in which the repetition of the same or similar consonants occurs within a sentence, line, or passage.

Conventional symbols: Symbols whose meanings are specific to communities, such as national flags, religious signs, or military insignia. See also **symbolism**.

Couplet: Two lines rhyming together. A single couplet considered in isolation is sometimes called a **distich**.

Closed couplet (also, **heroic couplet**): Two lines rhyming together in which a complete thought is expressed and also ended with a terminal mark of punctuation. Called **heroic couplets** from their popularity in the heroic tragedies and poems of the seventeenth century.

Counterpoint: Assigning a metrical value to a foot or set of syllables according to the metrical expectations of the verse, as opposed to how it would naturally be stressed in speech. See also **meter** and **substitution.**

Deixis: A rhetorical term referring to any words that determine a sense of speaker, addressee, time, and location.

Distich: A single couplet considered in isolation. See also **couplet**.

Dramatic monologue: A poem spoken by an imagined speaker specifically addressing someone else.

Eco-poetry or **environmental poetry**: A poetic mode that treats nature neither as a peaceful nor idealized space but a realistic one altered by humans. See also **pastoral**.

Ekphrasis: A poem that responds to a piece of visual art, music, or dance.

Elegiac couplets: A Greek or Latin couplet in which the first line is written in dactylic hexameter, followed by one in dactylic pentameter. See also **elegy**.

Elegy: A poem of mourning.

End-stopped lines: Verse in which every line ends with a strong mark of punctuation, such as a period, a question mark, or a semicolon.

Enjambment: When the meaning of a sentence carries over from one line to the next, or to a series of lines.

Envelope rhymes: Quatrains in which the first and fourth rhyming lines enclose the second and third rhyming lines, in an ABBA pattern. See also **quatrain**.

Envoi: A three-line stanza that ends a poem. See also **sestina**.

Epanalepsis: The repetition of a word or phrase from the beginning of the sentence at the end of it.

Epigrams: Witty, often satiric statements commenting on human behavior.

Epistle: A poem written as a letter, addressed either to a public or private person.

Feminine ending: A single extra unstressed syllable found at the end of a line of metrical verse. See **meter** and **masculine ending**.

Foot: A metrical unit that is repeated to give a regular rhythm to a poem, graphically represented in **metrical scansion** by |. See also **meter**. In English, it usually consists of accented and unaccented syllables in one of these basic patterns:

Iambs, which consist of an unstressed followed by a stressed syllable, as in *repeat* or *indulge*. In scansion, an iamb is written: (˘´).

Trochees, which consist of a stressed syllable followed by an unstressed syllable, as in *triad* or *moment*. In scansion, a trochee is written: (´˘).

Anapests, which consist of two unstressed syllables followed by a stressed syllable, as in *in the night*. In scansion, an anapest is written: (˘˘´).

Dactyls, which consist of a stressed syllable followed by two unstressed syllables, as in *Washington*. In scansion, a dactyl is written: (´˘˘).

Spondees, which consist of two successive stressed syllables, as in *heartbreak* or *headline*. In scansion, a spondee is written: (´´).

Pyrrhic, which consist of two successive unstressed or lightly stressed syllables, as in *in the*. In scansion, the pyrrhic is written: (˘˘).

Free verse: Poetry characterized by a lack of predetermined metrical or stanzaic patterns.

Georgic: Any type of pastoral poem that includes lists and instructions for how to care for farmland, intermixed with digressions on philosophy, astronomy, meteorology, or even military history. See also **pastoral**.

Ground: In figurative language, all the aspects and items that are similar between the two things being compared. See also **tension**.

Haiku: A short poem totaling seventeen syllables broken down into three single-line units of five, seven, and five syllables each.

Hemistich: From Greek, meaning "half row" or "half line," it is half a line of verse that is seen most commonly in Anglo-Saxon verse.

Heterometric: Lines of different metrical, rhythmic, or visual length. See also **isometric**.

Hypotaxis: A grammatical device that relies on a pileup of subordinating clauses, distinguished by subordinating conjunctions such as "although," "since," "before," "once," "while," or "because."

Imagery: Figurative language that approximates what we can smell, hear, see, taste, and touch.

Isometric: Lines of equal rhythmic units and length. See also **heterometric**.

Line: A unit of meaning, a measure of attention. An **autonomous line** in a poem completes a thought and is also **end-stopped** with punctuation, even if the sentence itself is a fragment or grammatically incomplete.

Lyric: A meditative or song-like poem whose movement is defined by chronological departure from narrative to focus instead on a speaker's private feelings, mood, or sense of crisis. In ancient Greece, lyric poems were meant to be accompanied by a lyre.

Lyric apostrophe: A commonly used form of address in which the poet appears to address the reader directly. See also **apostrophe**.

Masculine ending: A single extra stressed syllable found at the end of a line of metrical verse. See also **feminine ending**.

Metaphor: Figurative language that makes a direct comparison between two different things.

Meter: Poetic rhythm structured into a recurrence of regular units. There are four metrical systems in English: **accentual**, **accentual-syllabic**, **syllabic**, and **quantitative**. Of these, the most common in English is accentual-syllabic meter, in which every syllable (stressed and unstressed) is organized into feet based on the regular placement of **stress**. The feet may be either **iambic, dactylic, trochaic, anapestic,** or **spondaic** or a combination of these. See also **foot**.

Metonymy: A figure of speech that substitutes one thing for another based on a close material, conceptual, or causal relationship.

Metrical scansion: How changes of sound are graphically represented in a line of metrical verse by marking particular syllables as stressed and others as unstressed. See also **foot** and **meter**.

Mode: A general term referring to a poem's mood, style, or subject.

Monostich: A one-line poem.

Narrative: A poem of any length that tells a story.

Near-nonsense: Poems that occasionally include invented or nonsense words whose meanings the reader can guess or imagine based on context.

Nonce form: Verse forms created by poets for specific, one-time use.

Octave: The first eight rhyming lines of a **Petrarchan sonnet**.

Ode: A celebratory poem meant for a public occasion.

Parallelism: A structural pattern in which phrases, clauses or even whole sentences are repeated in a passage of verse.

Parataxis: Simple, declarative sentences that combine actions through the use of coordinating conjunctions like "and," "for," "but," "or," or "nor."

Pastoral: A poem centered on an idealized natural space in which the landscape has symbolic, not just situational, importance. In its earliest tradition, poems recognizable for rural figures whose values stand in stark contrast to the cosmopolitan—and often artificial—values of town and court. See also **eco-poetry** or **environmental poetry**.

Persona: A character or mask; a **persona poem** is a poem purportedly written from the perspective of a specific person other than the poet.

Private symbols: Symbols unique to individual authors whose meaning we construct by how they appear over the course of a specific text. See also **symbolism**.

Prosody: The study of poetic meter and form.

Quantitative meter: Poetry in which each syllable is assigned a value sometimes dependent upon stress or "quantity" of sound, sometimes dependent on its proximity to a diphthong, consonant, or other vowel. See also **meter**.

Quatrain: A stanza of four lines, rhymed or unrhymed. It is the most common of all English stanzaic forms. Rhymed quatrains generally follow one of these patterns:

    Interlaced or **alternate rhymes** (ABAB)

    Envelope rhymes (ABBA)

Double-couplet rhymes (AABB)

Unbounded or **ballad rhymes** (ABAC or ABCB)

Refrains: Lines, parts of lines, or even groups of lines that repeat in a poem, usually at the end of stanzas. Whole repeated stanzas are called **burdens**, while fragments of repeated lines, including individual words or inexact repetitions, are called **repetends**.

Repetends: Individual words or inexact repetitions of a single line. See also **refrain**.

Rhyme: A repetition of accented sounds in words, usually those falling at the end of verse lines. There are a variety of rhymes; below are a brief list of the most common or popular.

> **Full** or **end rhymes**: Rhymes in which the stressed vowels and all subsequent consonants rhyme exactly. Example: *cat/hat*.
>
> **Internal rhyme**: Rhymes occurring within a single line. Example: "Mary, Mary, quite contrary."
>
> **Slant rhyme**: Words that rhyme inexactly, but whose syllables recall each other. Examples: *back/buck*; *years/yours*; *tigress/progress*.
>
> **Eye rhymes**: Words used as rhymes that look alike but are pronounced differently. Examples: *alone/done*; *remove/love*.
>
> **Vowel rhyme**: Rhymes that have only their vowel sound in common. Examples: *boughs/towns*; *green/leaves*; *starry/barley*; *climb/eyes/light*.
>
> **Rime riche** or **identical rhyme**: Rhymes of two or more syllables where matching consonants appear before the last accented vowel (*compare/despair*), or of homographs (*cleave/cleave*), or of homophones (*pair/pear*).

Masculine rhymes: Rhyme words of different syllables rhyming on the final syllable (*abound/round*).

Feminine rhymes: Words of different syllables rhyming on the initial syllable (*soreness/doorless*).

Rhyming action: Repeating images and actions that link disparate stories or periods of time, creating narrative unity out of lyric fragmentation.

Sestet: A stanza or poem of six lines; also, the final six rhyming lines ending the Petrarchan **sonnet**.

Sestina: A poem of six stanzas of six lines each, which repeats six end words in a specific pattern, ending with a three-line stanza, or **envoi**.

Shaped poems: Poems written so as to visually resemble the object or idea they are describing.

Simile: Figurative language that uses "like" or "as" to compare different things or states of being.

Speaker: The narrator, point of view, or voice in a poem. The speaker of a poem is not necessarily the poet, as the speaker may also be a specifically invented or imagined historical character. See also **persona**.

Sonnet: From Italian, *sonnetto*, a little sound or song. A fourteen-line poem normally in iambic pentameter in English. The rhyme scheme has varied widely in practice; still, there are three most widely recognized versions of the sonnet with their traditional rhyme schemes:

> **The Italian or Petrarchan sonnet** (octave: ABBAABBA, sestet: CDECDE or CDCDCD or a similar combination that avoids the closing couplet)

> **The Spenserian sonnet** (ABAB BCBC CDCD EE)

> **The Shakespearean sonnet** (ABAB CDCD EFEF GG)

Stanza: A recurring unit of a poem consisting of a number of verse lines.

Stichic: A poem that is made up of one long stanza. Also, the term for a line of verse. A single-line poem is called a **monostich**, a couplet a **distich**, and a half line a **hemistich**.

Stress: The syllable (or syllables) in a polysyllabic word naturally emphasized in speech. See also **accent**.

Strophe: A structural division of a poem containing stanzas of varying line length, especially odes. It is also occasionally applied to units of free verse and verse paragraphs. In poems divided into identical or similar units (such as long narrative or epic poems or ballads), the term "strophic" is synonymous with "stanzaic."

Substitution: The substitution of a foot (or feet) in meter different from what characterizes the regular meter of a particular line of verse. See also **meter**.

Syllabic verse: A poem in which every syllable is counted to determine line length while the stresses are ignored. See also **meter**.

Symbolism: The use of images, objects, or actions to figuratively represent specific ideas or meanings. There are three types of symbols: **archetypal symbols**, which are culturally received images recognized from other works of art; **conventional symbols**, whose meanings are specific to communities, such as national flags, religious signs, or military insignia; and **private symbols**, which are unique to individual authors whose meaning we construct by how they appear over the course of a specific text.

Syncope: The omission of a syllable or sound from the middle of a word. Examples: "prob'ly," "ev'ry."

Synaeresis: The drawing together of two contiguous vowels within a word for metrical purposes. Example: "disobedience" pronounced "disobed-yence."

Synesthesia: The blending of different senses in one image, or of describing one sense in terms of another.

Synecdoche: A figure of speech in which a part of something is used to represent the whole.

Tenor: The object, person, or idea being described in a metaphor. See also **vehicle** and **metaphor**.

Tension: In figurative language, all the aspects and items that are dissimilar between the two compared things. See also **ground**.

Tercet: A stanza of three lines, sometimes linked with a single rhyme.

Terza rima: From Italian, meaning "three rhymes." A poem of linked tercets in which the second line of each stanza rhymes with the first and third lines of the next.

Trope: A repeated phrase, image, or word that connects a figure of thought with figures of speech. A commonly used device, storytelling convention, or motif.

Vehicle: The image that describes the object, person, or idea being described in a metaphor. See also **tenor** and **metaphor**.

Villanelle: A nineteen-line poem of five tercets, a quatrain and two repeating rhymes, in which the rhyming first and third lines from the opening tercet recur as alternating refrains across the following stanzas, becoming the ending couplet of the final quatrain.

Voice: The combination of poetic elements—including syntax, diction, rhythm, repetition, tone, and even form and meter—that taken together comprise the style of a poem's speaker.

Volta: A rhetorical or metrical turn in the poem that also marks a change in argument or thought. See also **sonnet**.

Zuihitsu: A poem of fragmentary personal observations that combines poetry with prose.

ADDITIONAL READING

Addonizio, Kim, and Dorianne Laux. *The Poet's Companion: A Guide to the Pleasures of Writing Poetry.* New York: W. W. Norton, 1997.

Bloom, Harold. *The Art of Reading Poetry.* New York: HarperCollins, 2004.

Boland, Eavan, and Mark Strand. *The Making of a Poem: A Norton Anthology of Poetic Form.* New York: W. W. Norton, 2001.

Burt, Stephanie. *Don't Read Poetry: A Book About How to Read Poems.* Cambridge: Harvard University Press, 2023.

Dobyns, Stephen. *Best Words, Best Order: Essays on Poetry.* New York: Palgrave MacMillan, 1996.

Doty, Mark. *The Art of Description: World into Word.* Minneapolis: Graywolf Press, 2010.

Eagleton, Terry. *How to Read a Poem.* Oxford: Blackwell Publishing, 2007.

Fussell, Paul. *Poetic Meter & Poetic Form.* New York: McGraw-Hill, 1979.

Hass, Robert. *A Little Book on Form: An Exploration into the Formal Imagination of Poetry.* New York: Ecco, 2017.

Hirsch, Ed. *How to Read a Poem and Fall in Love with Poetry.* New York: Mariner, 1999.

Hoagland, Tony. *The Art of Voice: Poetic Principles and Practice.* New York: W. W. Norton, 2019.

Hollander, John. *Rhyme's Reason: A Guide to English Verse.* New Haven: Yale University Press, 2014.

Longenbach, James. *The Art of the Poetic Line.* Minneapolis: Graywolf Press, 2007.

Oliver, Mary. *Rules for the Dance: A Handbook for Writing and Reading Metrical Verse.* New York: Ecco, 1998.

Pinsky, Robert. *The Sounds of Poetry: A Brief Guide.* New York: Farrar, Straus and Giroux, 1999.

Turco, Lewis Putnam. *The Book of Forms: A Handbook of Poetic Forms, Including Odd and Invented Forms.* Hanover: Dartmouth College Press, 2011.

Voigt, Ellen Bryan. *The Art of Syntax: Rhythm of Thought, Rhythm of Song.* Minneapolis: Graywolf Press, 2009.

Zapruder, Matthew. *Why Poetry?* New York: Ecco, 2018.

CREDITS

A. R. Ammons, "Calling" from *The Really Short Poems by A. R. Ammons* by A. R. Ammons. Copyright © 1990 by A. R. Ammons. Used by permission of W. W. Norton & Company, Inc.

Russell Atkins, "Trainyard by Night" from *World'd Too Much: The Selected Poetry of Russell Atkins*, edited by Kevin Prufer and Robert E. McDonough. Copyright © 1962, 2019 by Russell Atkins. Reprinted with the permission of The Permissions Company, LLC on behalf of the Cleveland State University Poetry Center, csupoetrycenter.com.

W. H. Auden, "Musée des Beaux Arts" from *Collected Poems by W. H. Auden*, edited by Edward Mendelson. Copyright 1940 and © renewed 1968 by W. H. Auden. Used by permission of Random House, an imprint and division of Penguin Random House LLC. All rights reserved. "Musee de Beaux Arts," W. H. Auden. Copyright © 1939 by the Estate of W. H. Auden. Reprinted by permission of Curtis Brown, Ltd. All rights reserved.

Matsuo Bashō, "[year after year]," translated by Jane Hirshfield and Mariko Aratani, from *Ten Windows: How Great Poems Transform the World* by Jane Hirshfield. Copyright © 2015 by Jane Hirshfield. Used by permission of Alfred A. Knopf, an imprint of the Knopf Doubleday Publishing Group, a division of Penguin Random House LLC. All rights reserved.

Elizabeth Bishop, "The Fish," "One Art," and"Sestina" from *Poems* by Elizabeth Bishop. Copyright © 2011 by the Alice H. Methfessel Trust. Publisher's Note and compilation copyright © 2011 by Farrar, Straus and Giroux. Reprinted by permission of Farrar, Straus and Giroux and The Random House Group Limited. All rights reserved.

Louise Bogan, "Solitary Observation Brought Back from a Sojourn in Hell" from *The Blue Estuaries* by Louise Bogan. Copyright © 1968 by Louise Bogan. Copyright renewed 1996 by Ruth Limmer. Reprinted by permission of Farrar, Straus and Giroux. All rights reserved

Gwendolyn Brooks, "Sadie and Maud," reprinted by consent of Brooks Permissions.

Jericho Brown, "The Tradition" from *The Tradition*. Copyright © 2019 by Jericho Brown. Reprinted with the permission of The Permissions Company, LLC on behalf of Copper Canyon Press, coppercanyonpress.org. From *The Tradition* first published in 2019 by Picador, an imprint of Pan Macmillan. Reproduced by permission of Macmillan Publishers International Limited, Copyright © Jericho Brown 2019.

Paul Celan, "Death Fugue," translated by Michael Hamburger, from *Poems of Paul Celan*. Copyright © 1972, 1980, 1988, 1995 by Michael Hamburger. Reprinted with the permission of the publishers, Persea Books, Inc (New York), www.perseabooks.com. All rights reserved.

Lucille Clifton, "cutting greens" from *How to Carry Water: Selected Poems* by Lucille Clifton. Copyright © 1974, 1987 by Lucille Clifton. Reprinted with the permission of The Permissions Company, LLC on behalf of BOA Editions, Ltd., boaeditions.org.

Keith Douglas, "Vergissmeinnicht," from *The Complete Poems of Keith Douglas*, reprinted with permission of Faber and Faber Ltd. "Vergissmeinnicht"

Seamus Heaney, "St Kevin and the Blackbird" from *The Spirit Level*, reprinted with permission of Faber and Faber Ltd. "St Kevin and the Blackbird" from *Opened Ground: Selected Poems 1966–1996* by Seamus Heaney. Copyright © 1998 by Seamus Heaney. Reprinted by permission of Farrar, Straus and Giroux. All rights reserved.

Susan Howe, "Thorow" from *Singularities* © 1990 by Susan Howe. Published by Wesleyan University Press, Middletown, CT. Used by permission.

Langston Hughes, "Letter" from *The Collected Poems of Langston Hughes* by Langston Hughes, edited by Arnold Rampersad with David Roessel, associate editor. Copyright © 1994 by the Estate of Langston Hughes. Used by permission of Alfred A. Knopf, an imprint of the Knopf Doubleday Publishing Group, a division of Penguin Random House LLC. All rights reserved. Used by Permission of Harold Ober Associates and International Literary Properties LLC.

Randall Jarrell, "The Death of the Ball Turret Gunner," from *The Complete Poems of Randall Jarrell*, reprinted with permission of Faber and Faber Ltd. "The Death of the Ball Turret Gunner" from *The Complete Poems* by Randall Jarrell. Copyright © 1969, renewed 1997 by Mary von S. Jarrell. Reprinted by permission of Farrar, Straus and Giroux. All rights eserved.

June Jordan, "Letter to the Local Police" from *Directed by Desire: The Complete Poems of June Jordan*, Copper Canyon Press. Copyright © 2007 by Christopher D. Meyer. Reprinted by permission of the Frances Goldin Literary Agency.

W. S. Merwin, "Elegy," currently collected in *The Second Four Books of Poems* by W. S. Merwin. Copyright © 1960, 1961, 1962, 1963, 1964, 1965, 1966, 1967, 1968, 1969, 1970, 1971, 1972, 1973, 1993 by W. S. Merwin, and two poems currently collected in *East Window: The Asian Translations* by W. S. Merwin. Copyright © 1998 by W. S. Merwin, used by permission of The Wylie Agency LLC.

INDEX

Page numbers in **bold** refer to glossary definitions.